BACK FROM THE
BRINK

**LESSONS FROM THE CANADIAN
ASSET-BACKED COMMERCIAL PAPER CRISIS**

PAUL HALPERN
CAROLINE CAKEBREAD
CHRISTOPHER C. NICHOLLS
POONAM PURI

BACK FROM THE BRINK

LESSONS FROM THE CANADIAN ASSET-BACKED COMMERCIAL PAPER CRISIS

UNIVERSITY OF TORONTO PRESS
Toronto Buffalo London

ISBN 978-1-4426-4192-1

∞ Printed on acid-free, 100% post-consumer recycled paper with
vegetable-based inks.

Library and Archives Canada Cataloguing in Publication

Halpern, Paul, author
Back from the brink : lessons from the Canadian asset-backed commercial
paper crisis / Paul Halpern, Caroline Cakebread, Christopher C. Nicholls,
Poonam Puri.

Includes bibliographical references and index.
ISBN 978-1-4426-4192-1 (cloth)

1. Asset-backed financing – Canada. 2. Banks and banking – Canada.
3. Negotiable instruments – Canada. 4. Capital market – Canada.
5. Investments – Canada. 6. Financial crises – Canada. 7. Global Financial
Crisis, 2008–2009. I. Cakebread, Caroline, author II. Nicholls,
Christopher C., author III. Puri, Poonam, author IV. Title.

HG4028.A84H34 2016   658.15′224   C2016-900030-3

University of Toronto Press acknowledges the financial assistance to its
publishing program of the Canada Council for the Arts and the Ontario
Arts Council, an agency of the Government of Ontario.

Canada Council Conseil des Arts
for the Arts du Canada

ONTARIO ARTS COUNCIL
CONSEIL DES ARTS DE L'ONTARIO
an Ontario government agency
un organisme du gouvernement de l'Ontario

Funded by the   Financé par le
Government   gouvernement
of Canada   du Canada

This book is dedicated to a handful of important people who supported the authors through this process. It took years to complete and we experienced illness, death, and the birth of a new baby in the process. This book is dedicated to:

Purdy Crawford, the catalyst for the book and our biggest champion.

Irene Devine, who provided us with crucial support during the ups and downs of writing this book. We wish she were here to see the final result.

James Mitchell, champion and supporter of this book who held down the fort and acted as a single Dad during many weekend hours.

This book is also dedicated to Andrea Nicholls, Jaiden, Amaris, and Shiloh.

Contents

PART FOUR: Conclusions

Preface

In a way, the restructuring story and the writing of this book faced similar existential threats. The ABCP restructuring negotiations were impacted throughout by serious outside events that delayed and almost derailed its conclusion. Similarly, the manuscript preparation was delayed by illness, childbirth, pressures from our real-life occupations, and one death. Just as in the actual restructuring, we persevered, and although somewhat late, the story is here to read.

While the book is arriving about the same time as the maturity of the final underlying transactions in the ABCP, there are many reasons why it remains timely, useful, interesting, and – hopefully – a good read. First, the restructuring negotiations are an interesting blend of financial and political theatre in which small retail investors held the power in the outcome of the restructuring. While the large investors negotiated, the small investors organized and, using social media, exerted an important influence on the outcome.

Second, the restructuring used existing insolvency legislation in an innovative way. The *Companies' Creditors Arrangement Act* (CCAA) was intended to facilitate the restructuring of a company; here it was applied to an entire market. This fact led to a lot of legal wrangling. The CCAA decision also led to legal challenges.

Third, by design – and, in fact, fiat – the solution to the crisis was a private one, unlike the public resolutions found in other countries. However, the federal government was crucial in the ultimate resolution of the crisis and ended up making money on the deal.

Fourth, the resolution required the creation and implementation of a new set of financial securities, which would ultimately trade in a liquid market. More interesting is the private sector solution to introducing liquidity to this market after the restructuring.

Fifth, there are interesting regulatory aspects associated with the crisis and lessons to be learned.

Our goal and purpose has been to produce a book that will interest general readers who are prepared to read some charts and tables. In addition, the book will provide some interesting introductions to issues for business and law school students as well as the risk management committees of major financial institutions.

We hope you enjoy the book.

Acknowledgments

Many people shared their memories, data, and insights into the ABCP Crisis. We would not have been able to write this book without their help.

A significant supporter of this book was Purdy Crawford, who generously encouraged us in the writing of the manuscript and provided us with initial access to data and resources that were instrumental in the final product. Without him, this book would not have been written.

In addition to Purdy, others stepped forward to provide us with their views and perspectives on the crisis – some for the first time ever. Henri-Paul Rousseau and Claude Bergeron both gave us many hours of their time through interviews, manuscript reviews and help with checking data and facts. Louis Vachon, David Dodge, Brian Hunter, Richard Guay, Darryl Ching, Huston Loke, Paul Potvin, Marlene Puffer, and Richard Pascoe were also key resources for us during this process.

Additional insights came from Stephen Halperin, Ken Kivenko, Diane Urquart, Mike and Wynne Miles, Tiff Macklem, Mark Carney, David Dodge, Brian Davis, Leon Dadoun, Hy Bloom, Brad Ballard, Bill Fedyna, Arthur Jacques, David Allan, Brendan Calder, Geoff Cornish, Mark Maybank, Doug Steiner, Jonathan Polak, Hal Jackman, Greg Foss, David Patterson, and Barry Denis.

We would also like to acknowledge the input of Justice Colin Campbell, Kent Thompson, and Sean Campbell (Davies, Ward, Phillips & Vineberg); and Monique Jileson & Tom Curry (Lenzner, Slaight).

We would also like to thank Brooke Smith who copyedited our manuscript and of course our stalwart and patient editor at University of Toronto Press, Jennifer DiDomenico. We are also grateful for the comments, experience, and balanced perspective provided by our legal counsel, Brian Rogers.

In addition to these names, we would also like to acknowledge the time and insights provided by many who were not able to allow us to use their names for various reasons.

Thanks to all of you.

Introduction

On 31 January 2009, at 9 a.m., Purdy Crawford, the chair of the Pan-Canadian Investors Committee (PCIC), announced to a conference organized by the Capital Markets Institute at the University of Toronto that the third-party asset-backed commercial paper (ABCP) restructuring deal had just closed. While the details of the deal were impenetrable to many Canadians, that deal was hard won. It had taken eighteen months of negotiations and wrangling over details to reach a successful conclusion, which had been pulled together by sheer will, a few moments of brinkmanship, and workarounds for the many setbacks encountered along the way.

Those on the dais, including Crawford, the PCIC financial adviser, Andrew Kresse, and two members of the legal team, Stephen Halperin and Gale Rubenstein, had represented the major investors during the ABCP negotiations. Against huge odds, this group had been instrumental in negotiating with both foreign and Canadian banks – along with the very firms that had manufactured and sold the paper – for a full-scale restructuring of the $32 billion Canadian third-party ABCP market. Investors caught in the ABCP crisis included many of Canada's top institutional investors and pension funds. When the market froze, they found themselves holding paper (often in alarmingly large amounts) that they could not sell. Along with the biggest investors, there was a group of retail investors – a small but vocal group of individuals who had been unwittingly caught holding this complex product and who fought their own battle to have their own losses recognized and recover their funds. Some would even find themselves on the brink of financial ruin, depending on acts of decency from individuals involved in the restructuring. And, of course, losses were also shared across much of corporate Canada as many of the country's biggest companies found themselves embroiled in the ABCP mess.

One important and largely untold story behind the ABCP crisis is how the solution was reached. What went on behind the scenes and what brought players on all sides together to eventually broker a solution during one of the largest Canadian financial crises in history? While other global markets fell during the 2008 financial crisis, the non-bank ABCP market in Canada miraculously survived, albeit with a different face: through the sheer will of the groups at the negotiating table, the market narrowly managed to pull back from a significant cliff – one that could have seen the $32 billion frozen non-bank ABCP market tip Canadian and foreign credit default swap markets into chaos.

The absence of these stories, and of details about the intricacies of the actual restructuring, troubled Purdy Crawford, the Canadian lawyer and businessman who had been brought in to orchestrate the deal. Late in 2009, he approached us to talk about the possibility of a book that would provide a unique perspective on what had gone on at the highest levels of the negotiations. Newspapers and media outlets have covered the plight of retail investors unjustly sucked into the crisis through bad advice or poor disclosure, but many other important stories and details remain untold and largely unshared. This book is an attempt to find out what happened behind the scenes during this ambitious market restructuring and to understand and provide context for how and why decisions were made that led us to where we are today.

The journey would see an innovative use of an important element of Canadian insolvency law, the *Companies' Creditors Arrangement Act* (the CCAA), as well as the creation of a new market for restructured ABCP notes. This market – to the surprise of many – has performed quite well since it was launched. Along the way, the deal was jeopardized by market gyrations, tense emotions, the failure of Lehman Brothers, and the building anger of retail investors who, when pushed to the wall, went to extraordinary lengths to pit themselves against Canada's biggest and most sophisticated financial players.

That is the story we aim to pull together in this book. In addition to that, we address some of the larger questions raised by the crisis that have to this day not been adequately resolved. What exactly caused the ABCP crisis? And how could so many sophisticated investors from mid-size to large pension funds end up holding so much of the paper? How could one investor alone – the Caisse de dépôt et placement du Québec (Caisse) – end up with $13.2 billion of these instruments?

And how could the investment dealers who should have known better have recommended ABCP to retail investors?

The ABCP crisis has had a lasting impact on the market for complex investments. Investors who bought ABCP with little understanding of its complicated and convoluted underlying structure were ultimately surprised by what happened. Were the assets underlying this paper in fact "toxic," as has been suggested by many commentators? And how exposed were Canadian ABCP assets to the US subprime market? What was the role of the niche investment banking firm Coventree Inc., and should it have borne the brunt of the punishment for the ABCP crisis that unfolded? What was the role of the Dominion Bond Rating Service (DBRS) in the crisis? And were regulators asleep at the switch? Finally, what, if anything, are the lasting implications of the restructuring for Canadian capital markets?

The restructuring has not been without its detractors. It was very expensive. The only unambiguous winners were the financial and legal advisers. Some investors received what may prove to be far less than the face value of their investment in the restructuring, and the ultimate payoff would depend on the uncertainties of a newly established market to provide liquidity. The restructuring also offered broad legal releases from liability to all participants in the deal and to some who were not in the deal, from dealers to sponsors of the conduits, to DBRS, the credit rating agency that rated them, to Canadian and foreign banks, among others. And although Coventree was ultimately fined by the Ontario Securities Commission (OSC), it was punished not for its structuring activities but for its failure to disclose information to its own shareholders.

Many commentators viewing the restructuring noted that it was "a uniquely Canadian solution to a uniquely Canadian problem." This is an excellent summary of the problem and its resolution. As those involved knew well, Purdy Crawford was a significant part of that very Canadian solution. It wasn't a perfect solution, he told us, but then again, as he also pointed out, a perfect solution to any problem is next to impossible to find. Instead, as Crawford explained, the final deal had to be the best possible – not the best imaginable. As he put it, the ABCP restructuring was all about "the art of the possible." A solution would be possible only if the individuals at the table were willing to accept it – to make it real. And while no one emerged from the ABCP crisis completely unscathed, the deal managed to bring everyone together under a single agreement. And that is the story that unfolds in this book.

PART ONE

The ABCs of a Crisis

CHAPTER ONE

The Day Montreal Stood Still

They should have known better. That was the conclusion of nearly all the individuals we spoke to about the $32 billion third-party ABCP market that froze in August 2007. "They" refers to the network of institutional investors on both the buy and sell sides and the advisers who had helped grow the market and put ABCP in portfolios, large and small, across Canada. One of our most surprising findings is how little some of Canada's largest investors – including pension funds, banks, and big corporations – knew about the risks in the underlying assets of ABCP. Those investors had accepted without question the highest commercial paper rating, "R-1-High," from Canada's Dominion Bond Rating Service (DBRS), and had failed to look beneath the complex surface of those products. Even some of Canada's most sophisticated investors, who routinely assess and conduct due diligence on a host of complicated and opaque investment vehicles, were lulled into a false sense of confidence by that R-1 label.

Not all ABCP was as problematic. What made third-party ABCP different was that it was not sponsored by a major bank. Rather, third-party or "non-bank" ABCP was provided by third-party suppliers such as Coventree Inc., which packaged and sold it while offering higher rates of return than traditional bank-sponsored paper. But as investors would soon find out, the third-party brand of ABCP was a lot harder to understand – and it contained assets very few knew were in there.

"No one had a clue of the complex structure of underlying assets," says Claude Bergeron, when asked how so many investors ended up holding such large quantities of ABCP. As vice-president, legal affairs, at one of Canada's largest pension funds, Caisse de dépôt et placement du Québec (Caisse), during the crisis and negotiations, Bergeron had a window on how hard and how fast a once busy, liquid market could come to a halt. He had witnessed the devastating effects of the freeze-up on a multitude of investors, including his own pension fund.

In the weeks leading up to 13 August 2007 – the day the market ultimately collapsed – the Caisse, National Bank, and other major play-ers in Montreal scrambled to avert a complete market disaster. The Caisse held the largest exposure to third-party ABCP of any investor in Canada – a $13.2 billion share of the total $32 billion market. Rum-blings of trouble had started on 24 July 2007, when a primary source of the paper, Toronto-based Coventree, sent a memo to investors about the subprime[1] exposure in US mortgages in some of the Coventree-sponsored trusts that were issuers of ABCP. Like many investors, Bergeron and Caisse CEO Henri-Paul Rousseau spent a frantic few weeks trying to learn more about the asset class and how so much of it had made its way onto the pension fund's balance sheet.

Surprisingly, Bergeron admits the Caisse didn't know how much ABCP it held in total. It made its first investment in 1997 in line with the fund's investment policy and diversification requirements, and in 2004, the Caisse increased its ABCP exposure as part of a strategy to use available liquid assets. By the time of the collapse, its holdings were spread across forty-four separate issues in twenty-two different trusts, making it especially hard for the pension fund to unravel its own ABCP holdings and determine where specific problems were waiting.

Alban D'Amours, president and CEO of Desjardins and head of the Caisse's risk management committee at the time, acknowledged that even the committee did not know exactly how much ABCP the Caisse had bought. D'Amours would remain head of the Caisse's risk manage-ment committee until March 2008 – right into the thick of the crisis.

As Caisse management worked to come to grips with its ABCP hold-ings during those August days leading to the market freeze-up, down the street Desjardins Group was gathering information. It had a $2.5 billion non-bank ABCP portfolio representing not only customer cash investments but also "a substantial portion of the liquid assets support-ing its capital guarantee note structure."[2] This concentration was likely due to the perceived low risk and to the slightly higher yield on ABCP relative to investments considered of equivalent risk. This was a com-mon theme among financial institutions that were heavily invested in non-bank ABCP.

That August, Montreal became the epicentre of the ABCP crisis, and the city would eventually lend its name to the final agreement reached by investors seeking an alternative to a crashing market. Montreal-based investors and dealers at Desjardins, National Bank, PSP, and the Caisse were at the heart of much of the ABCP market. How did this happen? And how could so many sophisticated investors come to decide that ABCP was a safe investment when, as we now know, it was highly risky? Part of the story lies in the history of ABCP in Canada, which started as a simple form of commercial paper and, through the power of financial engineering, was transformed into something highly complicated, with a new set of embedded risks that investors failed to fully comprehend due to the structure's limited transparency.

ABCP is short-term debt supported by a range of financial instruments. The assets, such as mortgage or consumer loans, or exposure to risk such as credit default swaps, are acquired by a conduit by means of various types of transactions, including the purchase of financial assets and derivatives. ABCP is generally issued for a term of 30, 60 or 90 days ... The financial assets for a conduit that issued ABCP generally have maturities that are longer than the maturity of the ABCP issued.

Caisse de dépôt et placement du Québec Annual Report, 2008

ABCP: It's Complicated

On the surface at least, ABCP resembled its more established predecessor, commercial paper, a well-known investment staple for some of the world's most risk-averse investors: corporations looking to manage cash flow or park money after selling assets, retail investors looking for a safe place to park their retirement money, and pension funds managing their own cash positions. Many of the largest investors in third-party ABCP fit this description: Canada Mortgage and Housing Corporation (CMHC; invested $257 million), NAV Canada pension fund (held $368 million), Ontario Financing Authority ($700 million), Alberta Treasury Board ($945 million), CP Rail ($144 million), Domtar Inc. ($420 million), the Public Service Pension Plan (PSP) ($1.97 billion), Jean Coutu ($35.9 million), and Transat A.T., Inc. ($143.5 million). A long list of risk-averse retail and small corporate investors also turned to ABCP as a temporary place to park funds from sales of assets such as a home or a family business.

In its simplest form, traditional commercial paper (the most sterling financial predecessor of third-party ABCP) makes sense for short-term investors. It consists of unsecured promissory notes issued by large blue-chip companies looking to raise short-term capital. Such debt can be issued and sold through an investment bank with maturities of 30 to 60 days; the company can then use those funds for working capital or seasonal inventory needs or to bridge financing until a larger debt issue can be made. Just how risky a particular issue is can be determined with relative ease by looking at the issuing company's reputation in the marketplace and examining easy-to-find information on the financial position of the issuing company. Credit ratings also serve an important role in the traditional commercial paper market; however, because investors can easily conduct basic due diligence on the basis of readily available public financial information about commercial paper issuers, they need not lean heavily on external credit ratings. Any liquidity or redemption risks for traditional commercial paper are simply covered by the issuing company's bank line of credit or through its own cash reserves.

Relatively straightforward to understand, commercial paper is a simple and early example of the so-called "disintermediation" process that has so many global regulators concerned: instead of borrowing money from a bank or other financial intermediary, a company can issue the paper directly to investors on its own or with the help of an investment bank. As part of the emerging "shadow banking system," investment banks take this kind of financing even further, applying the science (and even art) of financial engineering in an effort to find new and bolder ways to help companies raise capital.

ABCP is a product of such financial engineering. It is a distant cousin of commercial paper but also a much more complex beast: an asset-backed security made possible by the growing practice of securitization. Securitization is the technique used by financial engineers to pool together different kinds of contractual debt (i.e., residential and commercial mortgages, car loans, and credit card debt) in order to sell investors bonds based on claims to the pool's cash flow. By securitizing loans to create asset-backed securities, companies can remove from their balance sheets the default risk of the underlying assets and obtain cash. Unlike traditional commercial paper – an instrument issued by a single blue-chip company in return for short-term financing – ABCP can be backed by multiple pools of assets with different risks tied to potential differentials in the maturity of the paper (issued for 30 to 60 days) relative to the underlying assets, which often have different and longer maturity dates (e.g., car loans versus mortgages).

Instead of being issued by an industrial corporation or a bank, ABCP is issued by a "conduit" – a separate, special-purpose entity (usually a trust) that is "bankruptcy remote" (in other words, bankruptcy of the sponsor or originator of the assets does not affect the conduits). This means that assets and liabilities in the ABCP won't show up on the sponsoring company's financial statements.

In Canada, the first ABCP was issued in 1997 by CIBC, which established the RAC Trust, a conduit created by the bank to securitize receivables (i.e., loan payments) on behalf of different companies. Throughout the 2000s, securitization in the form of ABCP became a popular way for companies to shed their receivables: they would sell them to a conduit, which would then structure and sell debt backed by those receivables to investors in the form of short-term notes. The proceeds could be used to finance other activities. Without big pools of risky loans on its balance sheet, a company could suddenly look much more attractive to investors.

Herein lies an important distinction: companies that shift their receivables into a special-purpose vehicle don't have to have the same blue-chip pedigree as traditional issuers of commercial paper. Instead, the value of ABCP lies in the rating given to the pool of receivables – in other words, in the reliability of the cash flow provided by those credit card receivables, mortgages (prime at first – later, subprime and other riskier kinds of loans). So while the risk of traditional commercial paper was tied directly to the fortunes of the companies that issued it, ABCP risk was tied to the strength of the pool of underlying assets (various loans and receivables). Those assets came directly from the asset providers who were central to the ABCP market, including Canadian Schedule 1 banks such as CIBC and Royal Bank as well as big foreign banks like Deutsche Bank, Bank of America, Citigroup, HSBC, and UBS.

In 1997, when the RAC Trust was established, the total amount of ABCP issued in Canada stood at $10 billion. By 2007, the point at which the market collapsed, it had grown to $115 billion. This market included both bank-sponsored paper (the biggest share of the market) and third-party- (non-bank-) sponsored ABCP. For investors in Canada, ABCP offered a place to park money at a time when Treasury bills were under severe pressure: in 2000, federal budget surpluses had driven the Government of Canada to reduce its bond and T-bill issuance. With less government supply and limited growth in the issuance of corporate commercial paper and banker's acceptances (BAs or short-term debt instruments issued by firms and guaranteed by a bank), some of Canada's largest and most sophisticated investors turned elsewhere to fill the void in their short-term fixed income portfolios. ABCP fit the bill.[3] And why not? Investors buy products such as ABCP and other higher-yielding kinds of fixed income securities because of compelling credit spreads – that is, the difference between what the paper is yielding and the yield on government bonds. In the case of ABCP, the spread is related to the Canadian Dealer Offered Rate (CDOR), the benchmark index for BAs with terms to maturity of one year or less. In the ABCP market, CDOR maturity is 30 days. CDOR, Canada's homegrown version of LIBOR (London Interbank Offered Rate), is determined through a daily survey of eight participants and publicly disseminated by Reuters.[4]

Spreads between a product such as ABCP and the CDOR rate typically reflect investors' views on how much extra risk they may be taking on – the greater the perceived risk, the wider the spreads. Of course, spreads can also widen when there is an imbalance between demand and supply of the paper. The spread is measured in basis points (bps). One per cent is equivalent to 100 basis points.

Years before the 2007 debacle, however, ABCP investors had experienced problems with widening spreads, reflecting increased risk. In the fall of 1992, when property developer Olympia and York defaulted, spreads widened by 50 bps for twelve days. In 1995, spreads widened by 40 bps over two days during the 1995 Quebec sovereignty referendum campaign. Events like those didn't last long, but in some situations they did have a longer-term impact on investors, usually because of an associated event. During the 1998 Russian ruble crisis, for example, the Canadian ABCP market took a huge and immediate hit – and the timing couldn't have been worse. As the 1998 crisis hit and investors fled to safety in the form of T-bills, ABCP issuers were coming to the market with a new supply of paper. With no one to soak up the excess supply, spreads ballooned to 35 to 40 bps above CDOR. The market recovered, however, and by 2000, spreads were back to normal levels of around 0 to 2 bps above CDOR.

But none of these events led to defaults or to any type of disruption in the market. In those early days, underlying assets in the ABCP conduits were traditional in nature – loans and other receivables with cash flows that buoyed investors' confidence when market conditions were tough.

However, things were changing. As the market grew, the composition of ABCP was undergoing a dramatic shift, and, by 2007, it had become heavily exposed to collateralized debt obligations (CDOs) and credit default swaps (CDSs), as well as residential and commercial mortgage-backed securities, which together made up more than 50% of the underlying assets. The already complex world of ABCP had become even more convoluted and opaque. Yet many investors of all levels of sophistication continued to pour into that asset class.

The Rise of CDOs

CDOs were first used at Michael Milken's firm, Drexel Burnham Lambert, in the 1980s to allow issuers to take a pool of assets and create securities with different levels of risk, known as tranches. They are created by banks seeking to pool together and then sell debt instruments (e.g., bonds and mortgages). By packaging and subsequently selling them to investors in the form of CDOs, banks not only reaped big profits but also were able to remove the obligations from the balance sheet and use the funds released for other bank-related activities.

The main difference between CDOs and more traditional asset-backed securities was that the pool of underlying CDO assets was a basket of debt products, each of which could have different risk profiles. By pooling the assets, creators of CDOs believed they could reduce the overall risk through diversification. Cash flows from the assets were divided into tranches, which were then sold to investors. Each tranche (which could be thought of as a slice of the overall risk and, hence, cash flow return) had risks tied directly to the level of priority of its claim to the underlying cash flows and, on the flipside, to any losses that would be suffered in the event of default. Because entitlement to payment was determined by the priority of each tranche, available cash from the underlying assets metaphorically flowed or poured first to the highest-ranking tranches, and then, in turn, to the lower-ranking tranches. That was why the CDO tiered payment priority scheme was often referred to as the waterfall.

Figure 1.1 shows the assets involved in the CDO and how a waterfall works. The waterfall determines how much investors in each tranche get paid depending on their position in the payment stream. At the highest point, investors in the senior tranche are the first to receive interest and, at maturity, principal payments. What is left

Figure 1.1. CDOs and waterfalls

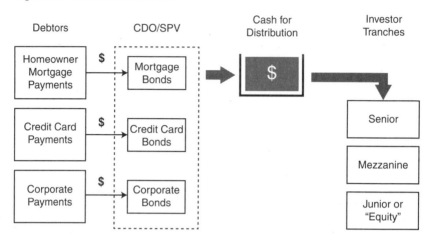

after they've been paid in full trickles down to the mezzanine tranche, and, finally, if there is any money left, down to what is referred to as the equity (highest-risk) tranche.

Returns trickle down the waterfall, but the losses move in the opposite direction. The lowest-ranking tranches absorb losses first and often most severely. Once the losses take up the amount invested in the equity tranche, they move up to the mezzanine tranche. Then when losses exceed the investment of the lower tranches, the senior tranche is at risk. However, the senior tranche has, in theory, very little risk given the underlying risk of the pool and the existence of the lower tranches.

The amount of loss in the tranches is specified by the CDO structure. In exchange for taking on more risk, investors at the bottom part of the waterfall have access to potentially better yield. Each tranche has a yield based on its risk – the senior tranche has the lowest yield and the equity tranche, the highest.

The overall risk of the pool is based on the quality of the underlying assets. Even though the number and type of assets in the pool should provide diversification benefits, those benefits are ultimately related to the degree of correlation among the assets in the pool. For example, if a pool includes assets from different parts of the country and different mortgage originators, some risks can be diversified away. But the risk of the pool is crucial: if the correlations turn.out to be greater than expected – in other words, if the assets all suffer losses at the same time – the overall risk of the pool and the risks of the tranches can be greater than expected.

Of course, dividing up risk by issuing multiple tranches doesn't mean that the overall risk of the underlying portfolio is reduced – only that the tranches have different risk levels and will appeal to investors who are prepared to accept it in exchange for the yield offered on the securities. Financial engineers are able to structure the tranches so that the risk preferences of investors are met, typically by working with a credit rating agency to obtain the needed credit ratings for the non-equity tranches. But the combined risk of the tranches, must, of course, equal the overall risk of the pool.

The entity that structures the CDO will generate profits after expenses based on the structuring. These profits reflect the return from constructing the tranches. In some cases, whoever structured the CDO will retain some of the equity tranches, and each tranche will sell for a price (and have a yield) that reflects the risk of the tranche. However, yields paid to investors could be lower and not reflect the true risk of the securities they hold, because of an incorrect, low assessment of tranche risk by investors, as a result of a deliberate strategy on the part of the people who structured the CDO or just poor due diligence on the part of the investor. Or, lower yields could be due to an increased demand for the securities. If yields are lower than the risk of the portfolio, the entity that structured the CDO will earn above-normal profits. Thus, when the tranche risk is incorrectly assessed as too low, the investor loses since the yield is too low, while the party that structured the transaction gains.

CDOs generated huge profits for the banking industry. They also fuelled growth in another business sector: credit rating agencies. From 2000 on, structured finance, including CDOs, accounted for a growing percentage of credit rating agency revenues. In the case of Moody's, for example, profits from rating securitized products drove up the price of its shares. The rating agency's stock price as of 2001 was about $20 per share; in early February 2007, it peaked at approximately $75, spurred by growth in new ABCP issues. But by March 2009, following the subprime crisis in the United States, its share price had fallen precipitously to a low of about $16.04 (Source: Google Finance). Credit rating agencies assigned ratings to each tranche, with AAA ratings supporting the senior tranches at the top, making them enticing to investors.

The Rise of CDSs

As the market for Milken's CDOs boomed, the Wall Street firm J.P. Morgan took them to the next level by creating credit default swaps (CDSs) in the late 1990s. CDSs act like term insurance: the insured, the credit protection buyer, makes an annual insurance payment in exchange for a promised payoff by the credit protection seller in the event of default on a reference bond or other obligation (the equivalent of death in a common term life insurance policy). The cost of the insurance is the spread in the CDS market.

A CDS provides insurance on a specific debt instrument for up to five years[5] and pays out based on triggering events such as the bankruptcy of the referenced entity or the failure to pay principal or interest (default) as specified in the contract.

CDSs are found in both the corporate and sovereign debt markets and took off in the 2000s, swelling to more than $62 trillion at the end of 2007 from just $900 billion in 2000. The insurance coverage was usually in the $10 to $20 million face value (called notional) range. CDSs were traded in the over-the-counter market and in general were liquid. The cost of this kind of insurance reflects the default risk in the same way that people with health risks – like smokers – pay higher life insurance premiums. That can create big problems for products based on CDS instruments.

The ups and downs of the Greek economy during the financial crisis provide a great example of how the product works. As investors worried about a massive default of Greek sovereign debt, the five-year CDS spread on Greek bonds was huge, and understandably so. Using the insurance analogy, Greece was so unwell that it was nearly uninsurable. On 3 January, the CDS spread was 1,000 bps, or 10% (Figure 1.2).

This spread amount meant that an investor holding outstanding Greek debt and wanting to buy insurance on $10 million of that debt would face an annual payment of $1 million (0.1000 x $10 million) to the credit protection seller. Who would want to buy this insurance? The most likely buyers would be large institutions and banks already holding Greek debt that wanted to remove the risk of default. The sellers could be investors who believed that the market's assessment of the risk of default was exaggerated such that the insurance premium they received more than compensated for the actual default risk they believed they were accepting.

Figure 1.2. CDS for Greek government debt

Source: Markit Financial Information services

Sick as Greece was, however, it did begin to get better – at least in the eyes of investors. As time passed, the cost of Greek sovereign CDSs fell: in late January and early February of 2011, the spread retreated to 800 bps as investors breathed a sigh of relief about the increasingly unlikely prospect of a default in Greece. This meant that the cost to purchase new credit protection on that same $10 million of Greek debt had fallen to $800,000 – a drop that benefited credit protection sellers under existing contracts, who continued to receive $1,000,000 annual payments for insurance that had been sold when risk was higher. However, the buyer of insurance, locked into the older, higher-priced contract, lost. In a secondary market, the insurance seller could monetize this gain by selling the CDS contract; the gain would be related to the difference in payments it received under the 1,000 bps contract compared to the new contract at 800 bps – the reduction in the spread of 200 bps.

Fast-forward to 2 May, and the opposite had happened. Greece had relapsed, and the cost of insurance for its bonds had spiked even higher, to almost 1,350 bps. The annual insurance fee for a new contract based on the new CDS spread was now $1.35 million. Here, an existing buyer of insurance at 1,000 bps would enjoy a gain, since it was receiving insurance for a $1 million payment that would now cost $1.35 million. The seller of insurance was worse off since the risk of default had increased, but its compensation reflected a lower default risk.

It Gets More Complicated

Greece is just one example of CDSs in action. However, financial engineers recognized that you could put CDSs into the CDO structure. This led to the second generation of CDSs, referred to as synthetic CDOs. Here, the protection seller "insures" the buyer against losses on a reference *portfolio* of corporate debt issues and not a specific debt instrument. Again, no funds change hands when the deal is first set up, since there is no actual purchase. Instead, collateral must be provided and held by the protection seller in case of negative events affecting the CDS value. It means the protection buyer has assurance that the protection seller will be able to honour its commitments if called upon to do so. But there is a major difference between synthetic CDOs and conventional CDSs: instead of insuring against all losses in the event of default, in the CDO structure the insurance is only provided for a portion of the losses. Through sophisticated financial engineering, the protection seller identifies the level of losses, and hence risk, for which it wants to be responsible by insuring a tranche of the CDO for an agreed fee.

Synthetic CDOs became very popular in the non-bank ABCP market. Of the $32 billion of ABCP that was restructured in the Montreal Accord, about $21 billion was backed by synthetic CDOs. Underpinning a synthetic CDO is either a reference portfolio of debt of companies that have been chosen by the protection seller to meet its specific need or a CDS index composed of a pre-specified portfolio of companies. The former CDO is called a "bespoke" transaction, and the entity on the other side of the transaction is usually a financial institution that arranges the portfolio.

The second type of synthetic CDO is based on a benchmark index composed of a predetermined set of corporate debt obligations – for example, 125 names, and specific contract terms. This synthetic CDO is an insurance policy on the CDS index, and there are now several widely accepted CDS indices with market makers providing liquidity. Market makers are prepared to buy and sell the CDS for their own account and to fill orders from inventory.

The indices reference geographic regions, and high yield and investment grade debt, and have different maturity choices (e.g., 5 or 10 years). For example, the iTraxx index is composed of 125 high-grade European corporations, and the CDX IG is an investment grade index of 125 North American companies. These indices have standardized tranches that reference different segments of the loss distribution and maturities. These can be observed in the typical "stack" or waterfall discussed below based on Table 1.1.

For example, 0% to 3% is the equity tranche: holders of this tranche must absorb the first 3% of the default losses. This tranche, accordingly, has the greatest risk for investors. The equity tranche would not be rated and could be held by the asset provider. If the reference index sustained a 3% loss, the investor in the equity tranche would be wiped out; this point is called the *detachment* point. If the detachment point is reached before all the default losses are covered, the remaining losses are then covered by the next tranche. In this example, this is the 3% to 7% tranche, for which the 3% level is called the *attachment* point. The risk of any losses in excess of this 3% attachment point would now attach to this tranche. This second tranche is less risky than the equity tranche and could be rated C grade. At a 10% attachment point (i.e., for any default losses exceeding 10%), the AAA senior tranche would be affected. The super senior tranche absorbs default losses in excess of 15% (the attachment point) to 30% (the detachment point). Above 30% is called the *tower*. The higher the attachment point for any tranche, the lower the risk that holders of that tranche will have to absorb a default loss. The risk that sellers will be asked to fund a default loss becomes lower the higher the attachment point. Because the super senior tranche has a very high attachment point (15%), the likelihood that the super senior tranche will have to make payments is sufficiently remote. As credit deteriorates in general with an increased probability of default,

Table 1.1. Waterfall in super senior structure

Tranche	Detachment point (%)
Tower	Above 30
Super senior	30
Senior	15
Mezzanine	10
Class C subordinated notes	7
Equity	3

the spread attached to the overall index or the tranches within the index will increase. Also, spreads reflect changes in probability of default for companies within the index.

These synthetic CDOs provided yet another layer of complexity – one that would play a big, and often poorly understood, role in the ABCP crisis. However, the ABCP market became more problematic and confusing when the CDSs were leveraged such that a protection seller could provide credit protection on (and so receive premiums for) underlying amounts well in excess of the funds placed in collateral. This ability of ABCP conduits to provide credit protection for amounts much larger than the value of the ABCP they had sold was what constituted the essence of leverage in the CDS market. Since no investment in the underlying securities (e.g., the "insured" bonds) was actually made, the leverage did not require borrowing. This process increased the amount of insurance premiums received by the insurance seller, but at a cost – added risk. For example, the conduit could issue securities (ABCP) for $100 million, which was placed in a collateral account, and then leverage that amount 10 times so as to have insurance exposure of $1 billion and, therefore, receive insurance premiums to provide credit protection on a $1 billion portfolio, rather than merely a $100 million portfolio. Contracts providing for this 10 times level of leverage were the most popular of the leveraged CDS contracts. It was these leveraged super senior (LSS) tranches that ultimately were the major problem in the ABCP crisis. We provide more detail on LSSs later on when we discuss the impact of leverage on collateral calls.

An example of a CDS structure and of the use of leverage is the Barclays LSS first transaction shown in Table 1.2.[6] It was structured with an attachment point of 15% and a detachment point of 62.5%. The principal value was $6.316 billion. Investors would be responsible for losses in excess of $947,000,000 (0.15 x $6.316 billion), and their exposure would cease at $3.947 billion (the detachment point). Thus, the principal (also called notional) amount in the tranche was $3 billion ($3.947 – $947 million). With 10 times leverage, the collateral amount was $300 million. The insurance fee that was paid was 0.061% or 6.1 bps. A small number times a large base of $3 billion generates substantial cash flow to the investor – $1.8 million.

Even though there are a number of tranches in the stack, since this is a synthetic CDO not all of the tranches will necessarily be used. There may be quotes for specific tranches and for the whole tranche – 0% to 100%.

Table 1.2. Barclay's CDS structure

Barclays transaction portfolio of 131 equally weighted names	Tranches, %	
	Tower	Over 65
	Super senior	15–65
Bespoke synthetic CDS	Senior	7–15
	Mezzanine	3–7
	Equity	0–3

By 2007, the largest asset provider for ABCP in the synthetic CDO market was Deutsche Bank. As of August 2007, Deutsche Bank had entered into agreements to provide liquidity (discussed below) for 59% of the affected third-party ABCP in Canada, or $9.2 billion. That blurry line between asset provider and liquidity provider in trusts in which there were LSS trades would become a huge bone of contention once the market was in jeopardy. And among the pioneers in the LSS space were the financial engineers at Toronto-based Coventree.

The Rise of Coventree

The first issuer of third-party ABCP in Canada was Coventree Inc. Its founders – former IBM treasurer Dean Tai and Bay Street lawyers David Ellins and Geoffrey Cornish – were well versed in the widening world of credit derivatives by the time they founded the firm in 2000. Tai had already established himself as a pioneer in the growing CDS market, a global market with a notional value of US$20 trillion by 2006. CDSs allowed non–bank-sponsored ABCP to thrive in the Canadian marketplace and allowed Coventree to make its mark in an expanding space dominated by the big banks. Daryl Ching, who worked at Coventree before the ABCP crisis, recalls the entrepreneurial spirit at his former firm. Ideas for new products were welcome, and staffers were able to cut their teeth on new and innovative approaches to investing. Within that culture, third-party ABCP took shape, and synthetic CDOs based on CDSs quickly became a prominent underlying asset in the ABCP produced by Coventree. By 2007, about $21 billion of the $32 billion of non-bank ABCP restructured in the Montreal Accord was backed by synthetic CDOs.

Coventree also changed how ABCP was bought and sold, creating a new avenue for providers outside of the major banks to create and sell the paper. Tai and Cornish developed an "acquire to distribute" business that would break away from the lenders' "originate to hold" model, where the originator (e.g., a major bank) finances the securitized asset (e.g., the mortgage or the loan receivable) and continues to bear the credit risk. Sponsors of the first third-party ABCP didn't originate the assets held by their conduits in the way that CIBC had done with the RAC trust, for example. Instead, they acquired assets for the conduits from others, placing an additional distance between investors and the loan originators.[7]

Coventree was the first to bring the "acquire-to-distribute" model to Canada, and for the most part, it was a positive addition to what was a fairly narrow financing field. Tai and Cornish spotted third-party ABCP as an opportunity to help smaller companies raise capital for all kinds of businesses and sectors of the economy. Such companies had trouble getting financing through bank-sponsored securitization, so Coventree's third-party acquire-to-distribute model opened a door to a whole new segment of the Canadian economy.

Other firms soon followed Coventree into the third-party space, including established players such as National Bank Financial and Dundee Securities.

Third-party ABCP was a boon to smaller Canadian companies looking to grow. As an early example of what could be done, Cornish notes that Coventree's first deal saw the team securitize equipment leases for a medium-size company in Quebec, a firm that was jointly owned by the Caisse and National Bank. It was Coventree's first big deal; it was also its first encounter with the giant Quebec pension fund. From that point on, the Caisse would keep in close contact with Coventree, doing numerous deals in different areas of the fund and eventually taking a 30% stake in the new Canadian finance firm.

It was Coventree's decision to introduce LSS tranches into the marketplace that, at least in part, contributed to the ABCP market's undoing. The super senior tranche in the ABCP market was proving to be unprofitable. The super senior notes had the smallest exposure to default loss and the highest ratings, but with the high demand for low-risk paper, the yields were very small, just six to eight bps; with this yield and the costs associated with structuring and distributing the paper, the conduit was unable to make a profit. LSS tranches were the answer to this low-yield problem. Coventree and other LSS issuers could use this structure to generate profits that were not available under the standard unleveraged super senior. For example, a $100 million investment in a CDS transaction could be leveraged 10 times (10:1) – in some cases, as high as 40 times (40:1). The leverage would permit exposure to super senior notes of $1 billion or $4 billion, respectively. The latter values were called the notional amount, since no real assets were being purchased (the contracts were "synthetic"). The conduit's ability to obtain cash flow through the use of leverage now made the structure profitable. The original $100 million raised was used as the collateral (margin) for the transaction. Unlike with equities, where buying on margin requires borrowing and paying interest costs, since no funds were transferred the collateral was necessary to protect the asset provider in the event that prices of the CDS contract fell and an unmet collateral call made an unwind – sale – of the trade necessary. The collateral provided a buffer so that the asset provider would reduce its risk of not obtaining its initial investment in the event of an unwind.

An appropriate credit rating had to be obtained both for the ABCP trust and for the underlying assets, including LSS tranches. However, the leverage introduced funding risk to the conduit. Although we present a more detailed discussion of this risk later, suffice it to say at this point that the leverage introduced the possibility that an increase in CDS spreads could lead to a collateral call by the asset provider. In other words, a call for more cash in the collateral account. An unmet collateral call would mean that the asset provider could unwind the transaction and use the existing collateral to meet any shortfall. With 10 times leverage, a 5% loss in the value of the CDS swap results in a 50% loss to the conduit, since the collateral will be reduced by one-half. If the leverage were 40 times, a 5% loss would wipe out the collateral entirely, and the conduit could be required to make additional payments to keep the asset provider whole.

Figure 1.3 shows the LSS structure and related cash flows. The spreads, quoted in bps, are based on discussions with practitioners and are illustrative of those used in the structures. The process begins with the conduit structuring the ABCP. Let's assume that the ABCP is based solely on the LSS transaction. With this structure, the paper is sold to investors. On the right-hand side, investors provide $500 million to the conduit for a return on the ABCP of Canadian Bankers Acceptance (BA) plus 4 bps. This amount of money is not used to buy any assets but rather to provide collateral, which is invested in eligible collateral securities that earn a return and can be used as cash flows in the structure. The eligible assets are generally low-risk and short maturities.

The example shows a return on collateral of BA plus 9 bps to the conduit. The conduit sells protection on a CDS investment grade index

Figure 1.3. Leveraged Super Senior Structure – How Leverage Makes It Profitable

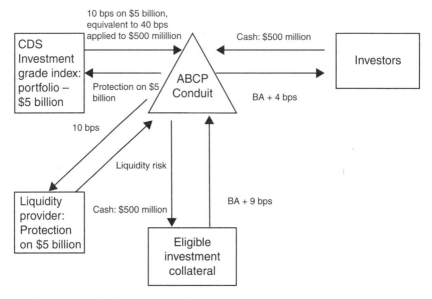

Notional Amount: $5 billion, leverage 10 times

portfolio for a payment of, say, 40 bps on the $500 million amount invested in the ABCP. In fact, it is only because the investment is leveraged 10 times that the fees are this high. The buyer is actually buying protection on $5 billion worth of debt, at a cost of 4 bps per dollar of debt. This amount is the actual cost to insure the CDS. But of course, a 4 bps payment on $5 billion is equal to 40 bps on $500 million. So the fees received by the conduit for providing this credit protection are 10 times higher than they would be if there were no leverage and the conduit was only providing credit protection for a portfolio equal in value to the $500 million amount invested in the conduit – the benefit of leverage.

The liquidity provider, which is generally also the asset provider, is paid from the insurance proceeds to take care of liquidity risk (the risk that the conduit is unable to refinance maturing ABCP) – the cost is, say, 10 bps and is shown on the left-hand side of the figure. There are distribution costs for the conduit, including a dealer spread to sell the paper of about 2 bps, that have to be recovered as well. These are not shown in the figure.

Table 1.3. Flows to conduit

Inflows			Outflows		
CDS premium	40 bps	$2,000,000	Payment to ABCP investor	BA + 4 bps	$5,200,000
Collateral interest	BA + 9 bps	$5,450,000	Liquidity protection cost	10 bps	$500,000
			Distribution cost	6 bps	$300,000
Total	BA + 49 bps	$7,450,000	Total	BA + 20 bps	$6,000,000
		Net to conduit: 29 bps: $1,450,000			

It is always helpful to follow the money to see who gains in this transaction, and we do so in Table 1.3. Note that the base for all of the cash flows is $500 million, the amount actually provided by investors.

Looking first at the inflows, the premium obtained on the swap is 40 bps, or $2 million (i.e., 0.4% of $500 million). The next cash inflow reflects the amount provided by the investor, which is used as collateral and earns BA + 9 bps. Assuming a BA rate of 1%, the collateral dollar return amount is therefore 1.09% of $500 million, or $5.45 million. The total inflow to the conduit is simply the sum of these first two amounts: BA + 49 bps (i.e., 1.49% of $500 million) or $7.45 million.

On the outflow side, there is payment to the investors on their $500 million investment, which is a spread of 4 bps over the BA rate – in other words, with a BA rate of 1% it is 1.04% of $500 million, or $5.2 million. There are also liquidity protection and distribution costs that are incurred by the conduit of 16 bps, resulting in total outflows of BA + 20 bps (i.e., 1.2% of $500 million, or $6 million). The net amount accruing to the conduit is 29 bps – an amount equal to $1.45 million (i.e., 0.29% of the $500 million invested).

The cash flow example shows that the leveraged super senior structure is certainly profitable to the conduits and the asset provider. Without the leverage, the CDS premium would have been only 4 bps (one-tenth of the leveraged premium of 40 bps) applied to $500 million, and the structure would have generated a net flow to the conduit of –7 bps (i.e., –0.07% of $500 million), or a loss of $350,000 on the transaction. For a profitable transaction to the conduit on an unleveraged basis, the investor in ABCP would have to accept a smaller spread over the BA rate – which is not a saleable proposition, since the ABCP spread is market determined.

In fact, the conduit could not find a way to make this a profitable transaction without leverage.

With bond yields at all-time lows, the market for LSS took off. By 2007, it accounted for $17 billion of the $21 billion in synthetic CDOs at the time of the crisis. While this increased the size and expected profits of the LSS transaction, it also increased the risk. Indeed, leveraged super seniors had many in the industry concerned. In a May 2007 letter to clients, two months before the crisis began to unfold, Ed Devlin, senior vice-president of Newport-based bond giant PIMCO, issued a White Paper on Canadian credit markets that contained an early warning on third-party ABCP. "Changing on the Fly: Canadian Credit Markets," which was sent to PIMCO clients, characterized ABCP as an asset class that benefits issuers and dealers rather than investors. Devlin called the creation of LSS notes of synthetic CDOs "leverage in the extreme": "simply put, for every $100 invested by the conduit, [investors] were exposed to $1,000 of credit risk. You don't have to be a financial engineer to understand that, by definition, these are risky investments ... The leveraged tranches of CDOs are not necessarily bad in and of themselves. It is when they are held in conduits with poor disclosure and leveraged by another 100% by the issuance of ABCP that one starts to worry about the prudence of such an arrangement." While PIMCO's letter did call out ABCP for its use of leverage, it did not specifically refer to the subprime crisis in the United States, which would soon become ABCP's undoing.

In fact, many in the investment industry were critical of the LSS market, suggesting that the paper should never have been sold to investors.

Liquidity: ABCP's Achilles Heel

ABCP wasn't sold to investors directly by conduits: it was sold by investment dealers, mainly on the strength of its credit rating. With a minimum approved rating of R1, it could be sold without a prospectus. For ABCP to get the required credit rating and thereby become more palatable to investors, it had to have credit and liquidity enhancements. Credit enhancements protected against the lack of cash flows that could arise due to problems in the underlying assets. Liquidity enhancements, on the other hand, could mitigate the risk of a market freeze-up or liquidity crunch where the existing securities could not be refinanced in the market. In this situation the underlying securities did not have cash flow problems. Overcollateralization is one form of credit enhancement in the ABCP space, whereby conduits ensure there are more assets in the pool than are required to pay off investors in full. How large a collateral cushion was required was determined by the default assumptions: How much cash would be needed in the event of a major default? Another form of credit enhancement used in the ABCP market was a reserve account to cover excess losses. During the summer of the ABCP market crisis, investors began to get nervous that credit enhancements for some of the trusts wouldn't be enough to cover potential losses. That fear would ultimately prevent investors from rolling (refinancing) their paper.

Liquidity enhancements were another and crucial part of the ABCP puzzle – these were meant to ensure that paper kept rolling in the event there were no buyers for ABCP. Since the maturity of the assets underlying ABCP was longer than the maturity of the ABCP itself, it was necessary to issue ABCP regularly to replace holders who did not want to continue their investment when their paper matured. If rolling the paper in this way became impossible, then there had to be a provision that would provide needed liquidity; this provision was the liquidity enhancement. Conduits used different forms of enhancements; these included extendible notes (i.e., if the paper failed to roll, the maturity of the paper would be automatically extended for a prescribed period of time at an enhanced yield) and liquidity loan facilities, where a loan could be drawn to finance the assets or assets could be purchased out of the conduit by the liquidity provider. The liquidity arrangements were akin to insurance policies, provided at a cost, and would be triggered under defined events. These liquidity agreements were another key element in the downfall of ABCP in Canada, due, in particular, to definitions of the events that could require a liquidity provider to step in and provide cash to the conduit to purchase the outstanding paper or to purchase the ABCP directly. In addition, investors were unable to obtain, and perhaps were not even interested in obtaining, the specifics of the liquidity arrangements.

ABCP came with a gold-plated rating from one of Canada's most reputable credit rating agencies: DBRS. Without an R1 rating from DBRS, and the resulting prospectus exemption, the ABCP market would not have grown as quickly as it did. It certainly would not have turned up in the portfolios of large institutional investors or vulnerable retail investors unable to bear much risk. This rating was crucial to the growth of the ABCP market and conduit sponsors, and originators worked with the rating agencies in order to obtain the required rating to meet the exemption requirement and make the paper marketable. Factors included obtaining the appropriate rating for the underlying assets in the conduit and appropriate credit enhancements. The rating agencies used quantitative models to assess the risk and hence the rating for the paper.

In Canada, a rating from a single agency was enough to make ABCP saleable to investors and to obtain a prospectus exemption. In the United States, two ratings were required. DBRS was the only agency willing to rate the paper – others, such as Standard & Poor's and Moody's, refused to rate Canadian ABCP because of the inadequacy of the Canadian-style "general market disruption" liquidity provision, which placed some risk of liquidity problems on the investor. Indeed, in January 2007, DBRS itself stopped rating new ABCP trusts without global-style liquidity, which placed more of the liquidity risk on the asset provider. At that time, despite DBRS's move for new ABCP, existing ABCP with Canadian-style liquidity was not downgraded. This was a surprise, since the risk of the existing ABCP was recognized as higher due to the liquidity arrangement. DBRS most likely believed that the existing liquidity arrangements were still solid. Also, at that time the ABCP market was still considered "frothy." Finally, in May 2008, DBRS removed its non–bank-sponsored trust ratings altogether (at the request of the trusts themselves). However, given the state of the market at that time, this would have been a mere formality.

What were the characteristics of Canadian-style liquidity agreements that made them potentially problematic? Outside of Canada, ABCP issues were typically backed by global-style liquidity agreements: if, for any reason, the paper failed to roll, under a global-style liquidity arrangement, the liquidity provider would have to step in if a few basic conditions were met. Because of the possibility of having to take back the assets, asset providers (the banks) – which also provided the liquidity arrangements – couldn't remove the assets (and hence risk) from their balance sheets, since a successful liquidity call would shift the assets right back to them (one reason the LSS market failed to thrive in the United States).

Canadian-Style Liquidity Explained

The liquidity arrangement, found primarily in Canada, was Canadian-style liquidity or what became known as general market disruption (GMD) liquidity. This provision was based upon Guideline B5 issued by the Office of the Superintendent of Financial Institutions (OSFI), the primary regulator and supervisor of federally regulated deposit-taking institutions, insurance companies, and private pension plans. This guideline came from Basel Committee international standards as found in paragraph 580 of Basel II and was applied to entities under OSFI regulation. The original guideline was issued in 1994, with a revision in 2004. A GMD was defined in Section 2.3 of the 2004 revision as "a disruption in the Canadian commercial paper market resulting in the inability of Canadian commercial paper issuers, including the SPE, to issue any commercial paper, and where the inability does not result from a diminution in the creditworthiness of the SPE or any originator or from a deterioration in the performance of the assets of the SPE."

The guideline was directed at the capital charges that OSFI-regulated companies would have to incur for holding securitized products. While applicable to Canadian banks, the GMD provision was incorporated into the liquidity agreements for third-party ABCP.

Upon a market disruption event (MDE) as defined in the liquidity arrangement contract, the conduit sponsor was to provide the liquidity provider with a written request for a liquidity draw. The MDE was a GMD in which maturing ABCP could not be refinanced (rolled over). Upon receipt of the request, the liquidity provider would review the contract to determine whether the request was consistent with the GMD provisions in the contract. If the liquidity provider deemed it was not, it could choose *not* to meet the liquidity request; potentially leading to negotiations or litigation.

The definition of a GMD varied among the liquidity providers, though there were some common features. Generally, specific liquidity providers had their own contractual provisions for the GMD; those provisions, while including the GMD provision under Guideline B5, also incorporated a notwithstanding clause that identified the conditions for a GMD (e.g., Deutsche Bank and CIBC had their own GMD language).

An example of such language: In some liquidity agreements, all of the outstanding ABCP in the Canadian market – be it third-party or bank-sponsored – had to be unable to roll. Such an event was unlikely, since banks were very likely to purchase their maturing paper (and did), given reputation risk. An alternative formulation was one requiring that some proportion – say, 65% of the outstanding ABCP – was unable to roll; since bank-sponsored ABCP constituted significantly more than 50% of the total ABCP market, as long as the banks rolled their paper, the GMD could not be invoked. Finally, if there was a hard-nosed liquidity/asset provider and a willing rating agency, it was possible to structure language in liquidity contracts so that there would almost certainly never be a GMD event – for example, by providing that even if a small dollar amount of third-party-sponsored ABCP did roll, there was not a GMD and, therefore, no right to make a liquidity call.

In June 2006, DBRS changed its rating criteria to require more objective standards for defining an MDE in liquidity agreements. Following this change, only three swap dealers' liquidity arrangements were approved by DBRS: Barclays, ABN, and Merrill Lynch. The newer language provided much stricter terms and would be of no interest to asset providers that did not want to entertain the possibility of having to take the assets back onto their balance sheets.

Obtaining information on the specific content of liquidity agreements has been a difficult task. The definitions of an MDE in these agreements are not public, and individuals who might have detailed knowledge about the agreements are less than forthcoming about them, perhaps due to non-disclosure agreements. Thus, in reviewing the market freeze in August 2007, it is impossible to determine which liquidity providers if any did not follow the definition of a market disruption event in their particular agreements and so may have refused improperly to meet their liquidity calls.

However, in late 2011, information on certain liquidity arrangements became available due to a lawsuit between Barclays Bank PLC and Devonshire Trust. The transcript and associated exhibits provide information on one specific liquidity arrangement and the liquidity provider's intention to meet the liquidity request under an MDE as defined in that agreement. This case also demonstrates the importance asset providers placed on keeping the assets off their balance sheets in the event of a liquidity problem. It is important to remember, of course, that this example should not be generalized beyond this particular case, since we do not have the specifics of other liquidity arrangements. But it does provide food for thought.

The Barclays Case

Barclays Bank PLC came late to the ABCP party. In 2006, it sold two LSS swaps to Devonshire Trust. In the structure, Quanto was the financial services agent and Metcalfe & Mansfield Capital Corp., a wholly owned subsidiary of Quanto, was the administrative agent. Both

Devonshire and Quanto were considered important customers of Barclays. Each swap was for $300 million, and with 10 times leverage, the total notional amount of the two swaps was $6 billion. The major note holder at $385 million was the Caisse; by October 2008, the Caisse was the last large note holder.

As was the custom, Barclays not only supplied the assets to the structure but also provided the liquidity. By 2006, as discussed above, stricter rules for defining an MDE had been put into place by DBRS as a condition for receiving an appropriate DBRS rating, and the Devonshire trust liquidity arrangement reflected this change. Barclays provided liquidity support for $205 million of the total $600 million of ABCP that was sold by Devonshire to finance the purchase of the assets. Under the arrangement, in simple terms, an MDE event occurred if Devonshire and an unrelated ABCP trust could not roll maturing notes. As part of the liquidity arrangement, Barclays could not make a collateral call if there was an MDE. Finally, the deal was non-recourse – if the transaction had to be liquidated by Barclays following an unmet collateral call and the proceeds of the liquidation plus the collateral were less than the original value of the CDS, there was no recourse to Devonshire to make up the shortfall; Barclays would have to eat the loss. For example, if the CDS was $1,000, collateral was $100, and the swap was ultimately sold in the market by Barclays for $800 following an unmet collateral call, the $100 loss on this transaction by Barclays (i.e., the $200 loss on the sale of the swap at a value of $800, offset by the $100 in collateral) could not be recovered from Devonshire. An outcome like this was possible in turbulent markets because spreads could widen quickly between the time the liquidity provider (Barclays, in this example) made its collateral call and the time it was actually able to sell the underlying swap. Just as bond prices fall when market interest rates rise, CDS values – from the perspective of the protection seller – fall when spreads widen (increase). So, rapidly widening spreads mean rapidly tumbling CDS prices.

What is obvious from this structure is that risk could be shifted to Barclays from Devonshire if there was a collateral call or an MDE. These were risks to which Barclays did not want exposure. On 19 August 2006, Barclays, recognizing the liquidity risk, tried to sell it to a third party. It approached Aegon and PSP. No deal was made, and Barclays remained exposed to liquidity risk.[8]

In mid-July, Barclays purchased $10 million of ABCP from Storm King Trust, a conduit administered by RBC. What could be the purpose of such a small purchase of ABCP and its continued rolling of the paper even on 12, 14, and 15 August 2007, in the very eye of the storm? In a July 2008 memo the purposes came clear. One reason was to get "colour" on the market. The second and potentially more sinister reason was "to possibly show, if we decide to show (for the Devonshire trades), that there is no disruption in the CAD CP market since we are able to roll our position daily."[9] The latter rationale appeared to be an attempt to provide ammunition to reject a liquidity call on the basis that there was no MDE.

On 13 August 2007, Quanto issued a liquidity demand under the MDE provision. Barclays refused to fund, arguing that an MDE had not occurred. Barclays decided that it was not going to fund the liquidity requests from their trusts. Barclays decided that it did not want to be an outlier. In any event, bank ABCP continued to roll. During the period from 13 to 15 August, Devonshire was unable to roll all of its maturing notes, and Quanto's liquidity requests were again rejected. DBRS also noted in an 14 August 2007 memo that other ABCP issuers had claimed that an MDE had occurred. On 8:07 p.m., 14 August 2007, Quanto sent Barclays a default notice under the ABCP agreement. Under the default notice, Devonshire could reclaim its $600 million collateral unless the requested liquidity payments were made before a specified time and date. Barclays continued to claim that no MDE had occurred and that no liquidity payments were forthcoming. The decision in the Barclays/Devonshire story is presented in a subsequent discussion.

So why didn't ABCP investors – at least the large institutional investors – have a better grasp on the uncertain nature of market disruption triggers as defined under Canadian-style liquidity? Probably because the contracts were not available for review to investors wishing to purchase ABCP – yet another example of the lack of transparency surrounding the distribution and sale of this product.

The liquidity arrangements were available to DBRS, however.

With an airtight liquidity agreement, liquidity providers would be required to step in once clear liquidity triggers were breached in the market. Given the risks in ABCP, especially in LSSs, a solid liquidity agreement should have been paramount, especially given a very serious and poorly understood risk in the structures: a substantial mismatch between the maturity of the paper that was issued and the maturity of the underlying assets. Because they were short-term notes built on long-term underlying assets, the paper had to be rolled over many times during the life of those assets. Building short-term notes on long-term assets presents a rather jarring contrast in timing and a big risk for the conduit, which could potentially be unable to roll the paper and pay the investors. This left ample room for liquidity problems, as would be seen when the market unravelled in 2007.

A related question is why the rating agency did not appear to consider the possibility of a liquidity call and whether the liquidity arrangement could be relied on to solve the liquidity problem. Since they had access to the liquidity arrangements and the arrangements were sufficiently different to have a potential impact if there were a market disruption event, it seems reasonable to suggest that these differences might have been reflected in the ratings. While DBRS did consider the credit risk aspects of the underlying assets – the CDS products were rated AAA – the liquidity risk seems not to have been an important issue. If the underlying purpose of the rating was to reflect the probability that the investor would receive a return on capital, the liquidity arrangements were pertinent to a high credit rating for ABCP. Perhaps the buoyancy of the market prior to 2006 had instilled complacency in DBRS, which was corrected only later in the crisis.

Among the liquidity providers to third-party ABCP conduits in Canada were some of the asset providers (more tangles in the ABCP web). These institutions were household names and major players in global banking. Some even sponsored ABCP of their own: ABN AMBRO Bank N.V. Canada branch; Bank of America N.A. Canada branch; Canadian Imperial Bank of Commerce; Citibank Canada; Citibank N.A.; Dansk Bank; Deutsche Bank AG; HSBC Bank Canada; HSBC Bank USA; Merrill Lynch Capital Services Inc.; Merrill Lynch International; Royal Bank of Canada; Swiss Re Financial Products Corp.; Bank of Nova Scotia; Royal Bank of Scotland plc; and UBS AG.

The Trouble with Mark-to-Market Triggers

The mark-to-market trigger structure was a major issue in the market freeze and one that had to be addressed in the solution to the problem – the restructuring of ABCP. As can be seen in the ABCP structure shown in Figure 1.4, the underlying assets included traditional assets, CDOs (both cash and synthetic), and super seniors (both leveraged and unleveraged). Each of these assets involved different risks. Of course, by the time of the market freeze, the subprime assets were close to valueless: the risk of loss had been realized in spades.

For the unleveraged assets, there was limited risk. For example, although being left with a portfolio of automobile loans (or even longer-term BBB corporate bonds) was not a good news story, the loss from such a portfolio would most likely be less than 50%. With "hard assets" underlying the trust, it would be a reasonably straightforward process to convince investors to eschew the default process (where assets would be sold at fire sale prices) and instead enjoy a better financial outcome by holding the assets.

But once the underlying transactions had leverage, risk was magnified. In fact, the biggest risk facing the conduits was the threat of collateral calls in the LSS transactions. With any leveraged transaction where the investor intends to finance a major part of the cost with borrowing, collateral or margin is required. With a stock purchased on margin, if the value of the stock falls below a certain level – the mark-to-market trigger – the broker can require that more cash be advanced to meet the required margin. In an LSS transaction, no asset is purchased and therefore no money is required to enter it. Instead, the transaction involves synthetic assets in which the conduit issuing the ABCP does not own traditional financial assets but is the party to CDS contracts.

Collateral is required, however, to ensure that the provider of the super senior will have funds available in the event that the market value of the transaction falls and the swap is terminated. The collateral is equal to the aggregate value of the paper issued to individual investors, while the exposure of the transaction equals the leveraged value of the swaps – the notional value.

If the market value of the underlying transaction falls below a certain level (the mark-to-market trigger point), then a collateral call can be made requiring the investor (in the case of ABCP, the conduit) to contribute more capital. Note that the reduction in value of the swap is a gain to the protection buyer. If the conduit can't, or chooses not to, fund the added collateral request, the asset provider can unwind (sell) the swap and return unused collateral, if any, to the conduit. Of course, it is possible for the difference between the notional value of the swap and the proceeds from the sale to be greater than the collateral value, in which case the protection buyer incurs a loss. The risk of this outcome is referred to as "gap risk."

Since this concept is critical to the market's ultimate failure and subsequent restructuring, consider the following example: A conduit issues $1 million of ABCP (the original collateral level) and leverages the transaction 10 times to have a notional value of $10 million by entering into CDS (as the protection seller) for reference obligations with a notional value of $10 million. CDS spreads increase, and, as agreed to by the parties to the transaction, the asset provider calculates the current (market) value of the swap. Remember that if the market is illiquid, the asset provider typically will not be able to rely on market quotations and so will have to use a model to calculate the market value – a model based on a number of assumptions that, in times of market stress, may prove unreliable.

Suppose that spreads have increased such that the swap market value falls by 5% to $9.5 million. This 5% reduction in market value has been established as the trigger point for a collateral call. If the collateral call is not met, the swap can be unwound by the asset provider at that point and there will be a $500,000 loss on the swap. However, the insurance buyer (the party that is also, typically, the asset provider) can recover that amount from the collateral and be made whole, whereas the conduit will lose that amount and have left $500,000. Here a 5% loss in the notional value of the swap has led to a 50% loss in the collateral value. The leverage has magnified the risk to the trust by a factor of 10.[10]

But suppose the asset provider makes a successful collateral call, say, for an additional 2% of the original swap value – an additional amount of $200,000 – leading to a collateral pool of $1.2 million. The amount of the collateral call would be specified in the contract. If the swap is subsequently unwound following another unmet future collateral call after this increase in collateral, the asset provider will have an increased buffer of $1.2 million to cover CDS spread volatility.

Another way to look at the collateral issue and the mark-to-market trigger issue is to recognize that an increase in spreads leads to a gain in the protection buyer's LSS investment since it is receiving protection but paying less than the current higher price. The buyer wants to ensure that it receives the full value of the increase. To do that, collateral is necessary. Thus, in the example above, the reduction in market value of the swap of $500,000 is a gain to the protection buyer. The trigger point had been set to be activated when the LSS value to the protection buyer was 50% of the original collateral amount of $1 million;[11] then, a collateral call would be made. If the collateral call was unmet and the swap was unwound at this point, the buyer would take $500,000 of the collateral and return the remainder. If the swap market fell dramatically to, say, $8.5 million, the value of the protection buyer's LSS transaction would be $1.5 million. At this point, however, an unwind would provide only

$1 million – the original collateral value – and the buyer would be out by $500,000.

The collateral arrangement has risks for both parties to the swap. For the conduit, the trigger adds funding risk. If a collateral call is made, the conduit can address it in one of three ways: by selling additional ABCP; by negotiating with the asset provider for a revised margin framework; or by liquidating other assets of the conduit sponsor. The usual approach is to issue ABCP to fund the call. If attempts to meet the call are unsuccessful, the transaction is unwound; the underlying swap is sold. This sale occurs even though the underlying transaction (swap) is still of low risk and rated AAA. The 2007 market freeze was an example of a situation where all factors conspired against a simple resolution of collateral calls. None of the approaches to addressing the collateral call were possible since new paper could not be issued, assets could be sold only at fire sale prices, and CDS spreads were volatile, making liquidation of the underlying swaps a losing proposition.

Not all triggers were related purely to market value; one type (called spread-loss triggers) was based on a combination of a CDS spread level and the amount of actual cumulative losses in the underlying CDSs; another was based simply on actual cumulative losses. These triggers were more benign to investors. However, although other trigger structures were used, the problematic mark-to-market trigger was the most common in the LSS structure. About 92% of the transactions used mark-to-market triggers.

The collateral arrangement, surprisingly, was also risky for the asset provider. Once a collateral call was made, there would be a short interval during which the conduit decided whether to dispute the call or meet it by providing funding. If the CDS market was volatile, the spreads might increase enough during that short time to wipe out the benefit of the collateral and force the asset provider to eat a loss. For example, if the collateral call was made with a 5% trigger and the swap value fell to $8.5 million due to a sudden increase in spreads, the asset provider would have a net loss of $500,000 after applying the $1 million collateral. This arrangement is called a non-recourse transaction since the asset provider has no recourse to the conduit to make up the loss. This example reflects "gap risk" to the asset provider.[12] The structure, of course, could have been designed to provide full recourse, which would have reduced the risk for the asset provider (typically, a bank). However, a non-recourse transaction would most likely involve a lower

Figure 1.4. ABCP Structure

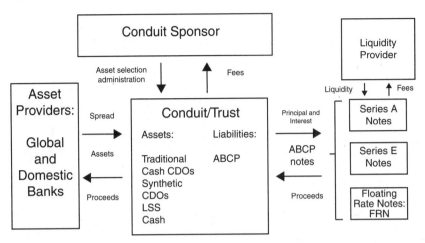

"insurance premium" paid by the credit protection buyer (i.e., the asset provider) to the protection seller (the ABCP-issuing conduit) as compensation to the asset provider for accepting this higher level of risk. Since most of the collateral arrangements in the Canadian market were non-recourse, the ABCP investors potentially had a strong bargaining chip in the restructuring negotiations with the asset providers if CDS spreads became volatile: the last thing the asset providers wanted was to be forced to seize the underlying assets then sell them at a loss.

There was another possible risk facing asset providers: clauses typically found in their agreements with the ABCP-issuing conduits that prohibited the asset providers from making collateral calls during a liquidity event. Such clauses were a potential problem for asset providers and are consistent with their position that the events were not a general market disruption.

Selling Third-Party ABCP

By 2007, when the market started to see signs of trouble, Coventree's ABCP was being sold to investors through a syndicate of investment dealers, including some of the biggest banks and dealers in Canada. These dealers included National Bank Financial, Scotia Capital Inc., CIBC, RBC, Deutsche Bank Securities, HSBC, Laurentian Bank, and

BNP Paribas. Coventree was directly sponsoring seven conduits – Apollo Trust, Aurora Trust, Comet Trust, Gemini Trust, Planet Trust, Rocket Trust, and Slate Trust – and, indirectly through Nereus, a partially owned subsidiary of Coventree, Structured Investment Trust III (SIT III) and Structured Asset Trust (SAT).

At the head of the distribution pack was National Bank, the lead dealer of Coventree's initial conduits. In this role, National Bank would allocate the paper to other dealers in the selling syndicate and would also set the interest rate or yield on the ABCP. In addition to its role as dealer, National Bank was a sponsor of three trusts (one of which had 100% subprime exposure). By 2007, Scotia Capital had become the lead dealer for Nereus.

As agents for Coventree-sponsored ABCP, dealers sold it to investors and were paid commissions by each conduit for those sales. The biggest dealers also had market-making lines that allowed them to purchase and hold unsold ABCP overnight and sell it to investors the following day. Since ABCP in Canada was traded in the over-the-counter market rather than through exchanges, dealers could sell the paper directly to investors on behalf of the conduits. When the ABCP matured, the dealer would try to resell the ABCP to the same investors for another term or find other investors to buy the paper. When a buyer couldn't be found, dealers could keep the paper rolling through their market-making lines, holding it in inventory and reselling it at a future date.

In 2007, the biggest purchasers of Coventree-sponsored ABCP were institutional investors – pension funds, insurance companies, financial institutions, and mutual funds. And Coventree's biggest ABCP customer by far was in fact the 30% owner, the Caisse. Since that first equipment financing transaction, the huge fund had maintained a relationship with Coventree; indeed, it had bought a large equity stake in the company before Coventree went public. The unique structure of the Caisse's investment in Coventree played an important role in the company's decision to go public in November 2006.

The Caisse held a put option in Coventree, which gave the pension fund an exit from its investment – a common feature in private equity deals, according to some. The option could be triggered in 2006 and would require Coventree to purchase back its shares from the Caisse – unless, of course, the company had gone public by that time. Coventree's Cornish says that without funds to buy back its shares from the pension fund, his firm was forced to go public in less-than-ideal conditions. He also insists that his staff tried to work with the Caisse to avert the share repurchase – something the Caisse denies. Coventree maintains that it wanted to renegotiate the put and did not want to undertake an initial public offering (IPO) in 2006, since it felt that, but for the contingent put liability, going public was not the best strategy for the company at that time. As a private company, Coventree would have had reduced reporting requirements, greater flexibility to manage its business, and no need to engage in costly shareholder relationship exercises. The Caisse, according to Coventree, was not prepared to extend the put, and Coventree had little time – just six to seven months – to look for alternatives.

As part of the process, the Caisse hired RBC Dominion Securities (RBC DS) to set a value for the Caisse's put option. The amount that RBC DS came up with would, according to Cornish, have nearly wiped out most of the cash and equity on Coventree's balance sheet. Since DBRS had introduced rules regarding equity levels required by conduit sponsors, this also would have put Coventree offside on its rating requirements. When push came to shove, Coventree decided that the IPO was the only option.

For its part, the Caisse has stated it was prepared to renegotiate and extend the period of the put. But its staff had the impression that Coventree wanted the pension fund out. The Caisse concluded that Coventree believed its growth would be stronger if the Caisse was not a major shareholder. In fact, pension fund staffers believe Coventree wanted to keep the profits for itself – a primary reason why it felt the Caisse representative on the Coventree board had been excluded from the discussions. The Caisse also contends that it would not have been a smart financial move on its part to push to exercise the put if it ended up destroying value for the pension fund.

Whatever transpired between Coventree and the Caisse, Coventree did complete an IPO of its common shares in November 2006. The IPO price ($10.75 per share) was in the lower range of RBC DS's valuation. And while the original private equity agreement entitled the Caisse to sell off only 50% of its holdings in a secondary offering qualified by the IPO prospectus, Coventree agreed to permit the Caisse to increase this number and sell off enough securities to bring the holding below 10% of the outstanding shares. This 10% threshold was important for the Caisse, since it reduced its regulatory reporting requirements in Coventree share transactions. No doubt, the negotiations and Coventree's perception of a forced IPO likely left a lingering bad taste for both participants going into the crisis.

The Subprime Mortgage Crisis

Coventree's 2006 IPO turned out to be very poorly timed. Deep troubles were brewing in the United States in the form of the subprime mortgage crisis. As early as 2002, the Mortgage Bankers Association of America had been reporting problems with the market for subprime mortgages – that is, with mortgage loans made to borrowers with poor credit histories who otherwise would not have qualified for a conventional mortgage loan. These mortgages, it was reported, had a delinquency rate five-and-a-half times higher than that of prime loans. US policymakers were well aware of the growing risks, yet these types of mortgages were proliferating, fuelled by low interest rates and huge gains in housing prices. The Federal Reserve Bank of St Louis, in a 2006 report, listed the probability of default in subprime loans as six times higher than for non-prime loans. By 2006, 25% of new mortgages in the US were subprime. As housing prices climbed higher and higher, the amount of subprime debt ballooned.

Unfortunately, the high likelihood of default did not bar subprime loans from being folded into the underlying assets that made up ABCP. Globally, the senior tranches of CDOs based on the subprime loans (subsequently referred to as toxic assets) were being sold with the high-yield risky tranches held by many originating banks and by hedge funds. It was only a matter of time before funds would bear the consequences of these investments, and that time came in 2007. Mortgage-backed securities are an asset-backed security staple for investors. But the market exploded as low interest rates and lax and "creative" lending standards enticed more and more Americans to buy homes with huge mortgages. And securitization allows financial institutions to move mortgage risk off their own balance sheets, reducing the incentive to review the creditworthiness of potential borrowers. This became another factor that drove up the probability of default in the underlying mortgages.

The implosion of the subprime market saw foreign banks as well as US financial institutions incur massive losses. Across the global market, subprime risk was leading to increased risk perception by investors and a consequent repricing of that risk. By one estimate, losses associated with subprime-related assets between 2007 and 2008 amounted to about $387 billion, $200 billion of which was incurred by European banks and the remainder of which was incurred by US financial institutions.[13]

By June 2007, the Power case ABCP market excluding Canada had seized completely. In July, Rhineland Funding, a wholly owned ABCP conduit of the German bank IKB, found itself with investors refusing to roll outstanding paper. Rhineland held about €20 billion in ABCP, with underlying assets that included subprime mortgages and CDOs based on residential mortgages. As the liquidity provider, IKB, a public company, was faced with a liquidity call in excess of its available cash and liquid assets – an extremely precarious position. The situation was defused by a credit facility provided by IKB's largest shareholder, a major state-owned bank. On 7 June, Bear Stearns announced that it was halting redemptions on two of its funds.

July 2007 turned out to be the most traumatic month in the crisis as Standard & Poor's held a conference in New York dedicated to ABCP. There, the rating agency made a surprise announcement: it was engaged in rating actions regarding subprime exposure in structured investment vehicles (SIVs), which are ABCP-like structures. "Rating action" is a euphemism for reviewing the rating provided on the underlying mortgages and the SIVs and is not good news. Any reduction in the rating for this paper issued by SIVs would be catastrophic for the market, since its value depended heavily on having the highest rating.

On 25 July 2007, the CEO of Countrywide, the largest mortgage lender in the United States, declared that only the Great Depression had had the same impact on housing markets. On 27 July 2007, Mark Zandi, chief economist at Moody's, stated that house prices in one year would be down 10% below their start-of-2006 values – a price decrease not seen since the Great Depression. He also noted that by the summer of 2008, about 3.6% of all mortgages would be in default, with second mortgages defaulting at an even greater rate. Finally, on 31 July 2007, two Bear Stearns funds collapsed. On 9 August 2007, French banking giant BNP Paribas froze three of its funds because of valuation difficulties resulting from the lack of transactions in the structured products market.

Canada was not immune to the issues affecting European and US ABCP. In mid-July, the Canadian ABCP market became more fragile. The Caisse's money market group tested the waters by not rolling some of its paper in order to see what kind of reaction it created. Bergeron says the Caisse was immediately met with a flurry of e-mails from other financial intermediaries asking why it wasn't rolling its ABCP. At that point, the Caisse's fears were confirmed: the giant pension fund was supporting the third-party ABCP market, and given the size of its holdings, its decision *not* to roll some or all of the paper was already creating serious problems for intermediaries. This concern continued through much of the summer. From mid-July to early August, the money market group at the Caisse supported the ABCP market, buying both bank and non-bank ABCP. As a result, ABCP continued to roll.

Coventree's Letter

Events in the United States were having a profound effect behind the scenes at Coventree. On 24 July 2007, a day before Countrywide's CEO made his dramatic announcement, the staff at Coventree released a letter to their dealer network (eight dealers) concerning subprime exposure in its conduits. Signed by Judi Dalton, a Coventree principal, the letter stated that Coventree had an overall exposure to subprime of approximately 4% across all conduits, with one conduit holding about 40%. Coventree's exposures were also to older subprime vintages, 2004 and 2005 – a small but important distinction because, in those years, lending practices hadn't deteriorated to the same extent as in later years.

Dalton's letter was forwarded by some of the dealers directly to clients. The letter was meant to quell the angst generated by global distress among investors in ABCP, but according to another Coventree staffer, Daryl Ching, it had the opposite effect. Investors began to panic and ask questions, suddenly concerned about the complexity and their lack of understanding of the underlying assets in their ABCP holdings. Even holding a small amount of subprime (and not even the poorest quality) in an ABCP issue was enough to spook the market.

As investors continued to worry, Coventree and the distributors of its ABCP held a telephone conference call on 30 July 2007. On the call were representatives from lead distributor National Bank and representatives from CIBC and Scotiabank. These banks also had ABCP that they structured and sold to clients. At the time of the call, the total ABCP market stood at about $120 billion, of which $34 billion was third-party, non–bank-related. On the call, CIBC executives expressed their concerns about dwindling liquidity in the market as cash disappeared for the non-bank ABCP. CIBC staff also informed participants on the call that the bank was being asked to bid on its own paper as panicked investors sought to cash out before maturity. The other banks, in turn, were purchasing their own ABCP and assuring investors they would stand behind their ABCP. It meant their paper was rolling. By now, the banks were already putting a lot of the ABCP back onto their balance sheets because there were no buyers.

Surprisingly, during that same call, no one expressed concern that non-bank third-party ABCP would not roll. Investors were expected to reinvest their funds back into new ABCP at maturity without blinking an eye.

At the time, many Canadian market participants were sanguine about the eventual outcome of the problem. There had been many crises in Canada and globally, and the ABCP market had withstood them: the Quebec referendum, the Long-Term Capital Management (LTCM) collapse, the Asian crisis, the Russian currency devaluation, and the 9/11 terrorist attacks. The strength of the ABCP market throughout these crises provided comfort to many in the industry. But that sense of comfort didn't last long. Those were different times, and the transactions underlying the ABCP this time were not the same.

Major Investors React

Early in August, the Caisse's money market group made the decision to reduce the pension fund's exposure to ABCP. At that time, the group lacked a clear picture of its overall exposure to ABCP, and it was unaware of the split between bank- and non-bank-sponsored ABCP in the holdings. Later, it discovered that it had sold off its bank-sponsored ABCP because banks were buying it back. However, it was unable to shed its third-party ABCP, leaving the group with a significant holding in non-bank paper.

From December 2002 to April 2007, the differential between bank- and non-bank-sponsored ABCP was, on average, 10 bps, as reported in a study into the causes and effects of the ABCP crisis conducted by the Investment Industry Regulatory Organization of Canada (IIROC).[14] This should have taken into consideration the differential in risk between bank- and non-bank-sponsored ABCP. If the differential was overly small due to a misunderstanding of the risk in third-party ABCP, the beneficiaries were the conduits, which did not have to pay investors the true risk adjusted spread over CDOR. Over the same period the spread over CDOR was on average 25 bps. For most of the period in late July and early August, however, the market did not make a distinction in yields between bank and non-bank ABCP.

It was the senior executives at National Bank Financial, the bank's investment banking subsidiary, who first started getting nervous in late July as they watched spreads widen in the ABCP market. A buying opportunity, perhaps? Perhaps the spreads had increased too much, driving down prices. If investors bought at the low, "bargain" price, they could sell for a profit when spreads returned to a lower level and prices increased. That was how two senior executives saw it. Louis Vachon, the president and CEO of National Bank, and Ricardo Pascoe, the co-president and co-CEO of National Bank Financial, had once watched the spreads on ABCP increase dramatically during the LTCM collapse in 1997–8; spreads on plain-vanilla ABCP had increased dramatically to 50 bps, and then, two days later, they had plunged. In retrospect, the two executives understood that this had been a missed buying opportunity. Were the rising spreads they were watching unfold in 2007 a similar sign? Could it be happening again? Grimly, as the situation evolved, Vachon and Pascoe came to realize that what they were in the midst of wasn't anything like the LTCM crisis – in fact, it had no precedent at all.

For National Bank, this crisis had particular importance since it was the lead dealer for Coventree, selling ABCP to retail and institutional customers and conduit sponsors. Also, and unhappily, it was soon to repurchase the ABCP of some of its retail investors in the paper. National Bank's concern was that major defaults on trusts would lead to a massive liquidation that would destroy the value of those trusts. On 8 August, still trying to get a handle on the scope of the problem, Pascoe called the Bank of Canada. Despite rumblings about subprime issues at international gatherings, Bank of Canada Governor David Dodge and his group were unaware of the current state of the market in Canada. In fact, Pascoe's call was the first sign Dodge had that there might be a serious problem.

As other financial institutions began to experience problems rolling their paper, investors finally began asking about liquidity arrangements: What were they, and when would those liquidity agreements kick in? Investors couldn't read the contracts on purchasing ABCP since they were not publicly available. They believed incorrectly that a market disruption event would simply lead to a successful liquidity call. Financial institutions such as National Bank had been involved with structured products such as ABCP for years, and market disruption calls had always been part of the contracts. The problem was that the contracts had changed over time. For example, in 1997 and 1998, National Bank Financial had held commercial paper, which included traditional assets such as car loans, commercial mortgages, and credit card receivables, in which market disruption liquidity arrangements were clearly stated.

But over time, the underlying assets had changed. The products had become more complex and exotic, and so had the language in the liquidity contracts. These liquidity contracts, especially those related to ABCP, weren't always reviewed in depth, and in the case of National Bank Financial, according to Vachon, changes in the assets underlying the ABCP had escaped the notice of the new products committee. Without question, there was "product (or risk) creep," in that the term "ABCP" did not truly distinguish among commercial paper that had very different risk exposure due to the nature of the underlying assets. Perhaps the product committees had been taking the easy route and not doing their due diligence, since this was short-term commercial paper and in spite of the changes, it continued to have a high rating. The impact on some financial institutions was devastating; it was an expensive and crucial lesson on the need for due diligence.

On 9 August 2007, Pascoe met with Richard Guay, the chief investment officer of the Caisse at the time, to find out why the fund was buying ABCP when it was clear that some investors were not rolling the paper. The pension fund had become the residual buyer, and as the buyer of last resort, it was increasing its holdings dramatically. In fact, the money market group at the Caisse had been acutely aware of impending problems with ABCP as it watched the market through July 2007. The Caisse's chief legal officer, Bergeron, based on an after-the-fact review, has said that the Caisse didn't have a handle on the extent of the paper's underlying exposure to subprime-related assets. This conclusion is a serious indictment of the money market desk and of the risk management practices of the Caisse.

The meeting between Pascoe and Guay was short, and the message was clear: something was going wrong in the ABCP market. Pascoe told Vachon that there was a problem in the money market and that Vachon should meet with Henri-Paul Rousseau, the CEO of the Caisse. Immediately after the meeting, Guay contacted Rousseau to tell him Vachon would be asking for a meeting to discuss a serious problem in the money markets.

On 10 August 2007, senior staff at the Caisse called a meeting to discuss the impending problem. Since transactions in the money market are concluded in the morning, by Friday at noon, the severity of the problem was clear. Chaired by Luc Verville, the head of money markets at the Caisse, the meeting brought together senior management from National Bank, Desjardins, the Public Sector Pension Plan (PSP), and Coventree along with the other players: BNS, CIBC, RBC,

Deutsche Bank, and ABN Amro. The Bank of Canada was not present, but it would be informed of the discussions at this meeting and of others held during the subsequent restructuring. The group tabled two different scenarios. According to Coventree's head of capital markets, David Allan, the group took only one of these seriously: the "soft landing scenario," which would see players slowly reduce the amount of outstanding ABCP by about $4 billion over a 60-day period by selling assets and retiring an equivalent amount of outstanding ABCP. At the end, those participating would see where the market stood and decide whether to reduce further the outstanding ABCP. As this retrenchment occurred, the liquidity in the market would be supported by the dealers.

For this to work, the Bank of Canada would have to allow third-party ABCP to be used as eligible collateral for the banks. The group was hopeful – the Bank of Canada had allowed bank-sponsored ABCP to be used as collateral in the past during the Y2K non-event and could introduce liquidity to the system in the fall of 2007 through the same mechanism. However, this problem was very different. At the time of the Y2K episode, the ABCP was bank-issued and was backed by traditional assets. Now the instruments were third-party ABCP, and the underlying assets included synthetic CDOs, instruments that were very hard to value. It is not a surprise that this ABCP was not permitted as collateral.

Despite pleas from the Caisse's Rousseau, who wanted government assistance, the Bank of Canada did not relent: it asserted that a solution would have to be found through the private markets. Rousseau, despite strong efforts, could not convince Dodge of the severity of the problem. The Bank of Canada's message to the market was clear: *you made the mess, now you can clean it up.*

An alternative was Plan B, the details of which seem to vary depending on whom you speak to. In the first scenario explained to us, the plan was to trigger the liquidity lines by not rolling the maturing paper. However, sources who attended the same meeting saw the solution differently: they hoped that if the paper didn't roll, the Bank of Canada would declare a market disruption, thereby opening up the liquidity lines. This was a faint hope, since it was unlikely that the Bank of Canada would interfere with contractual arrangements that were in place in order to declare a market disruption event. Either way, the proposed Plan B clearly underscored a possible lack of understanding of the shaky liquidity foundation on which third-party ABCP was built.

In the end, the group left the 10 August meeting in support of Plan A, the soft landing: participants agreed to roll their maturing paper and reduce the chance of liquidity calls. But this did not eliminate the possibility that other investors outside the group might want cash for their paper. After the meeting, Coventree's David Allan shared with the Caisse's Verville his concerns that the paper would not be rolled. He suggested that Verville obtain more specific commitments from the participants regarding what would happen on Monday when the market opened and investors rolled their paper.

After the meeting, Guay met with Verville for a debriefing. Guay reports that Verville said that all investors would have to roll to avoid a market collapse. Guay told Verville that on Monday, at the first chance to roll its maturing paper, the Caisse should not be the only investor rolling in a particular trust. If that happened, it would end up in a worse position than not rolling at all.

Late in the afternoon on Sunday, 12 August, Allan received a call from the Caisse asking what the Caisse's options would be if there were a failure to roll the paper. During this call, the Coventree executive realized that the market was in serious trouble.

In the meantime, Vachon, D'Amours, and Rousseau had kicked into gear over the weekend, spending time on the phone with other investors trying to understand what was happening. They still had little or no information on the extent of the ABCP problem; while investors thought they knew their own holdings, they had no idea how much other investors held.

They thought Plan A would buy them some time. But when Monday, 13 August, came, the paper failed to roll. By 9 a.m. that morning, the investors had to face the reality that a soft landing wasn't going to happen and that participants were going it alone. The Caisse's money market division, along with other investors, did not roll the paper. As institutions began to operate in their own interests instead of working towards a collective solution, a bigger problem emerged: although the amount of the paper that failed to roll on that Monday wasn't large, it sent a signal to the market that liquidity was no longer available. Liquidity is like the water that flows through the plumbing in your house, Rousseau would later tell us: it isn't important until it is *not* there. In the case of the unfolding ABCP crisis, liquidity had evaporated. It was time to cash in on the insurance: conduits made their liquidity calls. Unexpectedly, however, those calls were met with denials that the problem was a general market disruption; in some cases, collateral calls actually ensued.

The concern facing ABCP conduits over this period is dramatically displayed by the spreads on the 7-year CDX IG (On the run) Index in

Figure 1.5. CDX 7Y OTR index spread (bps)

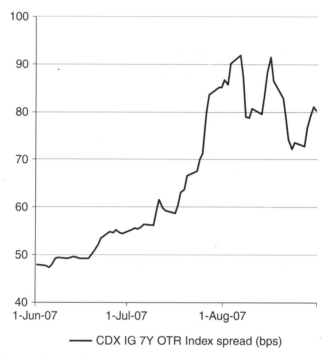

— CDX IG 7Y OTR Index spread (bps)

Source: Thomson Reuters Datastream

Figure 1.5 and the spreads on 7-year super seniors in Figure 1.6 for the period 1 June to 31 August 2007. Both show a frightening and similar picture. Starting on 1 June, the CDX index spreads increased dramatically, peaking on 8 August, falling, and then increasing to another peak on 16 August 2007, following the date when some of the ABCP did not roll, precipitating the crisis. In Figure 1.6, super senior spreads on 1 June 2007 were 3.43 bps, increasing dramatically to 27 bps on 30 July. The spreads fell, and on 15 August were 22.5 bps. The increased spreads in August reflect difficulties in the credit markets consistent with higher risks. With the increasing spreads and the widespread use of LSS structures, there was a spate of mark-to-market collateral calls. Also, given the state of the ABCP market, the normal ways of meeting these collateral calls – such as issuing more ABCP, negotiating with the

Figure 1.6. Super senior spreads: 7yr 30–100% tranche (bps)

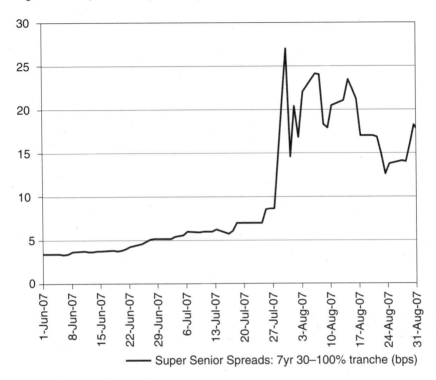

— Super Senior Spreads: 7yr 30–100% tranche (bps)

Source: Thomson Reuters Datastream

asset provider, or liquidating other assets of the conduit sponsor – were either problematic or simply not available. Of course, when a collateral call is not met, the assets can be sold by the asset provider. At this point, in the volatile market that existed, there was a good chance that the CDS would be sold in a fire sale.

What Happened?

Why, then, didn't the maturing paper roll, and who, if anyone, precipitated the crisis? There are many possible factors that could have caused the informal Plan A agreement to fall apart: one or all of these could have played a role. One story is outlined in the court case between Barclays and Devonshire Trust discussed above. The case was split into two halves, and the trial decision on the first half was rendered in September 2011. That trial decision was upheld by the Court of Appeal, and leave to appeal to the Supreme Court of Canada was dismissed. The dispute was ultimately settled in 2015, as discussed in chapter 10, so the second half of the trial never took place. Barclays was the asset and liquidity provider in transactions with Devonshire. Devonshire Trust was sponsored by Quanto Financial Corporation,[15] and its major investor was the Caisse, which ultimately wrote off its investment in the trust in 2009. Devonshire was not included in the restructuring negotiations when, in December 2007, Barclays decided to leave the restructuring process and negotiate directly with the main note holder in Devonshire Trust: the Caisse. The negotiations broke down, and the court case ensued. Devonshire had issued liquidity calls to Barclays, its liquidity provider. Barclays had responded by arguing that the liquidity freeze did not constitute a general market disruption.

Consequently, one issue that was expected to be litigated was whether the events from 13 to 16 August 2007 constituted a general market disruption. However, as discussed above, the trial was bifurcated and the market disruption issue was to have been determined at the second trial, a trial that never occurred once the matter was settled.

As expressed in Barclays' Reply and Defence to Counterclaim (paragraph 67),[16] their view of the failure to roll could have a sinister interpretation:[17]

On or about August 11 to 12, 2007 (the weekend prior to the market freeze on Monday, August 13, 2007 ...) certain other large ABCP investors ... and certain other 3rd party ABCP conduit sponsors ... wrongfully, and lacking bona fides, conspired and agreed together to attempt to artificially manufacture a "Market Disruption Event" by simultaneously issuing Market Disruption Notices on August 13, 2007 and thereafter (the attempted manipulation) ... [A certain] number of ABCP market participants ... in the course of the weekend prior to August 13, 2007, planned ... how to attempt to generate a Market disruption.

The Attempted Manipulation involved a coordinated agreement amongst the group including certain large 3rd party ABCP Noteholders to refuse to roll maturing 3rd party ABCP and to issue Liquidity Notices with respect thereto. The predominant purpose of the attempted manipulation was to cause injury to Barclays (and other Asset Providers) by forcing Barclays to provide liquidity to Devonshire in the absence of a Market Disruption Event.

As they awoke to the possibility of a real crisis in the ABCP market, investors belatedly began to delve into the actual meaning of the general market disruption clause in the liquidity agreements put in place to backstop payments to ABCP investors in certain circumstances. As the crisis unfolded, they learned a hard lesson in the importance of understanding the details of such terminology and of ensuring clear definitions when assessing the stability of any given investment, AAA rating notwithstanding.

There are other explanations for the lack of a soft landing that August.

One theory places the blame on the Bank of Canada's and the Department of Finance's refusal to intervene and their insistence that a resolution to the crisis would have to come from the private sector. Their apparent rationale was that, if the third-party ABCP market went down, Canadian banks could likely handle the liquidity calls and leave foreign banks to fend for themselves. The decision not to intervene clearly was not the cause of the crisis, although the impact could be severe on the foreign banks that had significant amounts of LSS outstanding.

A second theory was that collateral calls were already being made in August but were unanswered and unmet for obvious reasons. The only way for conduits to meet collateral calls, after all, would be to issue new paper, and clearly, there was no market for ABCP. Attempts to issue new ABCP would cause spreads to widen, triggering further collateral calls. As spreads widened, any investors rolling their paper would essentially be throwing good money after bad. Hence, not rolling the paper would have seemed to most investors to be the best decision.

There is a third possible explanation, one believed by many of those to whom we spoke: the Caisse did a double-take and backed down from its original commitment to stay the course and hold tight. Some believe that on Monday, 13 August, Caisse staffers decided they would not roll their maturing paper because they believed that failure to roll would trigger liquidity calls by the ABCP conduits; as those calls were met by the liquidity providers, the problem in the ABCP market would be resolved. Alternatively, and more likely, the Caisse may have already decided by 13 August to roll its paper only if other investors were rolling, too. Since it was clear on Monday that other investors were not rolling, the Caisse opted out of the market, and the market froze. Either way, the Caisse's decision not to roll its paper would have a serious impact on the market.

Many ABCP participants closed ranks in the wake of the crisis out of fears of litigation or fears of public scrutiny and second-guessing over prior decision making. Thus, it has been difficult to confirm which of these theories (if any) is correct. Whatever the reasons, the paper failed to roll on 13 August, and that failure precipitated the contentious liquidity calls. What had begun as an attempt to put together a quiet, cooperative solution to the ABCP problem behind closed doors quickly became a full-blown and very public crisis.

CHAPTER TWO

Not a Regional Problem

Up until the morning of Monday, 13 August, National Bank CEO Louis Vachon believed he had made a deal with the Caisse that would prevent a hard landing and save the ABCP market. But when he called up his contact at Deutsche Bank, he knew right away something was wrong: he was told not to bother making any more requests under the liquidity lines. At that moment, Vachon says, he knew the end had come. The soft landing had failed, and liquidity injections wouldn't be coming. It was, as he describes it, his first "holy shit" moment during the ABCP fiasco, the moment when he understood the bank was in dangerous waters. National Bank had been selling ABCP to retail and corporate customers, relying on the high rating from DBRS to allow clients to pile into the paper as a slow and steady place to park cash. While Vachon had known that trouble was brewing in the ABCP market and had been for weeks, the unexpected brush-off from his contacts at Deutsche Bank was a game changer: he knew that the ABCP market would collapse. That Deutsche Bank would do that, in the face of what National Bank's legal counsel had advised were clear obligations to do otherwise, was profoundly troubling. It was a sign that underlying issues could be widespread and potentially global.

The weekend before the paper failed to roll, Caisse CEO Henri-Paul Rousseau had been trying to find a way to get more information on the ABCP market in Canada. He decided that the obvious source was DBRS, which had rated the paper in the first place. So on Monday morning, 15 August, he invited representatives from DBRS to Montreal. Two DBRS analysts attended the meeting. On Tuesday, 14 August, Rousseau requested that the president of DBRS come to Montreal. David Schroeder, the firm's COO at the time, went to Montreal along with

Jerry Marriott and two other DBRS employees. These meetings provided important information to Rousseau, including – at least in general terms – the major players in the ABCP market, both investors and asset providers.

By Monday night, Rousseau had a better handle on the extent of the problem. The Caisse had already disaggregated its ABCP holdings into bank- and non–bank-sponsored paper; now it realized it was the major holder of the third-party product. Armed with this information, Rousseau was met with a possible Plan C: on Monday night, after his meeting with DBRS representatives, he received an offer from a well-known hedge fund offering to purchase all of the Caisse's ABCP for 50 cents on the dollar. In hindsight, this was a good offer, but Rousseau turned it down and decided to stick it out with the paper. The offer did, however, provide him with some insight he would use in future negotiations: he now was concerned that hedge funds could be shorting the market, affecting spreads in order to generate profits. This possibility meant that any restructuring of the market would have to involve changing current mark-to-market triggers in order to avoid collateral calls.

On Monday, when the market did not function, Vachon and Pascoe of National Bank immediately contacted Rousseau. It was essential to discuss ways to prevent a blowup in the third-party ABCP market generated by asset providers.

With insights into the ABCP market provided by DBRS, Rousseau now saw the growing crisis as part of a global problem, and he believed that the only way to address it was to bring all the key players together around a table to determine what the next steps should be. Bergeron, then head of the Caisse's legal department, describes Rousseau's response to the liquidity crisis as "instinctual" – that is, it reflected an innate understanding that to stave off a total market collapse, a quick resolution was desperately needed among all the major players in the ABCP market.

On 14 August, Pascoe started calling asset providers to invite all counter-parties to the trades to send representatives to a meeting. Meanwhile, Rousseau contacted all of the major investors along with every major bank in Canada. Pascoe and Rousseau realized that decision makers should attend: people with the business experience and the understanding of the risk that the players faced. These parties were invited to attend a meeting in Montreal to discuss the problem and possible solutions. Legal representatives were not.

Non-bank ABCP sponsors such as Coventree weren't invited to the meeting. Vachon and Rousseau knew that having asset providers and sponsors of ABCP trusts at the table would make a toxic mix – that discussions would quickly turn into squabbling, and squabbling would destroy the opportunity to find a solution with the key players. Best, then, to keep the two groups separate, they decided.

The actions of the Caisse and National Bank changed the course of the ABCP crisis in Canada and marked the beginning of a long and bumpy road to resolution. While some believe the Caisse (and others) briefly tried to go it alone, on 13 August, it quickly became apparent how very little the players knew about ABCP and how it worked. With no clear sense of the size of the market in Canada, the content of the paper, or who the other investors were, there was not enough information for individuals to make the decision to go it alone. Also, immediate action was needed on the liquidity problems facing the ABCP trusts in order to forestall legal wrangling. With time running out and information scarce, Rousseau and Vachon were eager to bring others to the table to determine a path of action.

Putting the pieces together and getting the information required a group effort, and that is what drove those initial discussions. In fact, it would take two more weeks before the Caisse and others based in Quebec realized that the problem was Canada-wide and not specifically related to Quebec. Non-Quebec players had to be involved.

What If No One Had Acted?

Many have asked what would have happened if the Caisse had decided to go it alone, to negotiate directly with the asset providers and allow the market to sort itself out independently. No one will ever know, but most of the players who ended up being drawn to the negotiation table came because they saw the potential risks of inaction. Indeed, one of the biggest risks looming was the potential for ABCP investors to launch bankruptcy proceedings against the trusts that had issued the paper. Without intervention, this would have been inevitable as holders of the non-extendible notes failed to receive their principal payments at maturity. Vachon's recollection is that Rousseau acted quickly, without having conducted a detailed cost–benefit analysis of a restructuring versus market alternatives. Because there were few reasonable alternatives, fast action was necessary. He simply picked up the phone and set in motion a series of negotiations that would take many months to resolve.

The alternative – doing nothing – could have led to a chain reaction of lawsuits, with investors suing trusts, trusts suing liquidity providers for non-performance on their liquidity arrangements, and investors suing DBRS for its ex-post (and, say some, ex-ante) inaccurate rating. Going the market solution route would have been a dicey proposition for a number of reasons.

First, given the lack of transparency of the ABCP and the constraint of contractual conditions associated with non-disclosure of the liquidity arrangements, the terms of the liquidity arrangements were not publicly available. For some of the agreements, it became clear that a market disruption that would trigger a payout was very hard if not impossible to observe. Once again, investor due diligence was deficient. While investors knew there were liquidity arrangements, they did not know the actual terms. It is likely that the courts would have respected the written terms of the restrictive liquidity agreements; however, some participants, including conduit sponsors, hoped they would have given weight to what the sponsors felt was the much broader underlying spirit or intent of those agreements. This was unlikely, since Canadian contractual interpretation is essentially based on the intent of the parties as evidenced by the words used in their contract and not on evidence of subjective intent inconsistent with the contractual language.[1] Second, the litigation would likely be protracted, adversarial, and very expensive to all participants.[2]

Probably the strongest argument against doing nothing was the threat of collateral calls on the LSS assets in the trusts, given that the bulk of the triggers were mark-to-market. If a mark-to-market trigger is breached and the conduit cannot raise the funds for the added margin, the asset provider is allowed to unwind the offending swaps, use the collateral to cover any deficiencies, and then return the remainder, if any, to the conduit. If there are enough asset providers unwinding swaps, this can lower swap prices, thus increasing spreads and perhaps resulting in further trigger breaches. Over the period leading up to the market freeze, spreads on CDS and LSS had been increasing, and there were rumours of collateral calls that had been made prior to the market freeze. If collateral calls had been made and not met, the loss of value to the investor in some of the LSS trades under a fire sale scenario could have been 100%. With 10 times leverage, a reduction of just 10% in underlying swap value would generate a 100% loss in collateral. Action was deemed necessary, and the expectation was that an agreement could be reached relatively quickly and inexpensively. Unfortunately, this was not the case.

The Standstill

On Wednesday, 15 August 2007, the major players in the Canadian ABCP market met in Montreal. Participants included all of the large Montreal investors – the Caisse, Desjardins, and the PSP – as well as the dealers, banks, and liquidity providers – ABN Amro, Barclays Bank, HSBC Bank USA, Merrill Lynch International, UBS, and Deutsche Bank, the major asset provider in the ABCP market, which two days before had made it clear it would not respond to any liquidity requests from National Bank and a number of conduits. Also, DBRS was represented by its global head of structured finance, Huston Loke. National Bank was in the unenviable position of being both head of the distribution network of ABCP for Coventree and a conduit sponsor.

Going into that first meeting, many participants at the table believed (or at least hoped) that the liquidity problems (as dealers referred to the market freeze) or market disruption problems (the investors' preferred description) were short-term – a matter of days, weeks, or a few months (certainly not the eighteen months it would eventually take to sort out the mess). They weren't exactly naive in this belief: while US subprime mortgage exposure was making headlines around the world, the exposure of non–bank-sponsored ABCPs to this asset class was relatively small and affected only a small number of trusts in any significant way. The group had good cause to hope that the problem could be resolved quickly without turning into a crisis.

On the investor side, major pension fund heads were present. So were representatives of the major Canadian banks, including those with the biggest exposure – BMO and CIBC – as well as individuals from RBC and Bank of Nova Scotia (BNS), who joined by phone. TD Bank was not at the table: CEO Ed Clark had maintained a distance from third-party ABCP after a strategic decision *not* to participate in the market. The bank would ultimately come under pressure from the Bank of Canada to help fund a solution to the mess. Mark Carney and Tiff Macklem were also involved in offline discussions with all six banks, to move along the restructuring process. Moral suasion was being used; the Bank of Canada argued that there was a more profound and wider issue – systemic risk – which could seriously affect the Canadian capital markets. DBRS also attended as the agency that had given ABCP its highest commercial paper rating.

The purpose of the meeting was to address the market disruption and allay fears in the marketplace by coming to an agreement. This would include a comforting press release that showed everyone working together to find a solution and help investors.

The meeting, co-hosted by National Bank and the Caisse, started on Wednesday afternoon. Rousseau as chair of the meeting presented a term sheet for discussion purposes. Bergeron was also present, along with Pascoe and Brian Davis from National Bank. The discussions were tough going, and by 5:30 p.m., many of those at the table were ready to walk away, having achieved very little. Rousseau knew that if the talking stopped, people might not come back. So they ordered dinner (apparently from St-Hubert) and continued discussions as they ate. In the afternoon, the group had ultimately agreed that a standstill on margin (collateral) calls was needed; this meant that the triggers in the agreements would have to be adjusted so that no collateral calls were possible. They came close to an agreement after dinner, but it was incomplete. All the ingredients were on the table, as Rousseau describes it; "however, they still did not have mayonnaise." But by 11 p.m., a tentative agreement had been struck. It would need to be approved by management and legal teams during the night, since the key decision makers had not been there to strike the deal.

The participants took a short break while Pascoe and Rousseau went into Rousseau's office and began to call the international bankers to try to negotiate with them on triggers and on increasing the maturity of the ABCP. Pascoe and Rousseau knew that the international banks had plenty of exposure in this area, and they hoped they would be open to a deal that reduced their exposure.

In the evening of 15 August, the Trust administrators were invited by Pascoe to attend a separate meeting at the Caisse's building. The purpose of the meeting was to inform them that the negotiations were taking place and that an agreement was very close. The deal would include a moratorium on liquidity and collateral calls as a prelude to further negotiations between the dealers and investors. Pascoe noted that the investors he represented who were involved in the ongoing negotiations accounted for about two-thirds of the ABCP outstanding in the trusts.

When the group of dealers and investors reconvened at 5 a.m. on Thursday, 16 August, a deal was reached and a press release was produced. At 7:48 a.m., the press release was sent to conduit administrators who had been at their meeting on the previous evening. The essence of the press release was that there would be a moratorium on collateral and liquidity calls to allow negotiations between investors and swap counter-parties (banks) to proceed. The standstill would expire on 15 October 2007. The agreement would buy the investors two months to pull everything together before the standstill agreement expired.

Even without the ABCP sponsors in the meeting, each group had conflicting interests, and that created potential for the meeting to deteriorate into complaints and rants. While that was a clear worry, it didn't happen, perhaps due to sheer force of will on the part of Rousseau or because of fear: everyone was standing on the edge of a financial precipice. On 16 August 2007, a mere three days after the market freeze, the group signed the Montreal Accord. It was the first stage in what would be a monumental effort to stave off a massive financial crisis in Canada by bringing together disparate and often competing segments in Canada's capital markets.

The first – and in some ways the biggest – hurdle had been cleared. Without the Accord, the market would most likely have collapsed. But no one knew then it would also prove to be the easiest hurdle to clear. Many other significant barriers lay ahead of the group. For one thing, not everyone had signed. None of the Canadian banks gave their signatures except for National Bank and Desjardins. DBRS was not asked to sign, since as a rating agency it was not party to agreements between conduits and dealers or conduits and investors. Those who did sign the agreement included liquidity providers ABN Amro, Barclays Bank, Deutsche Bank, HSBC Bank USA, Merrill Lynch International, and UBS. Citibank and Swiss Re subsequently joined the Accord. The Caisse and PSP were the only investors that signed. Since ABCP conduits had not attended the meeting, they were not signatories.

Although it had signed the agreement, Barclays left it in December 2007 to engage in a separate restructuring. Barclays's signing of the Montreal Accord would have important consequences for it in an action it launched in December 2009 and that was decided on 26 July 2013. That action is discussed in more detail in chapter 10.

One key thing that kept people at the table was hunger for information. Notwithstanding the information provided to Rousseau by DBRS, no one had full and clear knowledge of the state of the non-bank ABCP market – its size, its exposure to subprime mortgages, and who had invested in the paper and their total dollar exposure. But while information was a big motivator for getting people to come together, no one was willing to show their hand at the first meeting. How much ABCP each participant held remained a mystery as they negotiated a way to handle the crisis. It proved to be enormously difficult to find information from any other area of the market. Although the size of the market was known through DBRS publications, many questions remained: Was this a short-duration tempest in a teapot or a possible global-style financial meltdown? The risk of the latter motivated people to stay focused on staving off a crisis. Key players believed that doing nothing could ultimately blow up global credit markets to the detriment of all the banks. And, of course, there was the omnipresent threat of lawsuits, which loomed large over the group during the eighteen months it would take to reach a final deal.

In the negotiations, the group had to address two issues immediately. First, there was a lack of liquidity in the paper resulting from the mismatch of the maturities of assets and liabilities, with the resulting need to roll over the paper, and the associated decision by most of the liquidity providers to dispute the general market disruption clause and not provide liquidity.

At the same time, DBRS maintained that the bulk of the underlying assets in the trusts that had issued the ABCP were of strong credit quality and consistent with their AAA ratings, a necessary condition for the liquidity providers to provide liquidity. Why would they continue to think this? The underlying assets were composed of traditional assets such as credit card receivables and secure Canadian mortgage-backed securities, as well as derivative-based securities based on both leveraged and unleveraged low-risk CDSs. The CDO tranches were of low risk, given the high subordination to risk exposure of the instruments, and included portfolios that had a diversity of cash flows and average credit ratings of sub-investment grade. Despite the high quality of many of the assets, however, liquidity and asset providers refused to step in and support the trusts that held the assets and, hence, the investors, who were left on the hook for the losses.

The second issue was the use of mark-to-market triggers on LSS; these triggers could be breached as spreads on CDSs widened, lowering mark-to-market values even without any actual losses in the underlying debt issues. Of course, collateral calls could be, and were, disputed by the trusts, sometimes successfully. In fact, rumours abounded that collateral calls had already been made prior to the market disruption. An interesting story related by one trust sponsor was that the answer to his liquidity call had been a prompt collateral call by the liquidity provider/bank.

Hence, the first task facing the Accord group was to extend the maturity on existing ABCP to match the maturity of the underlying assets.

This would address the problem of maturing Class A paper and most of the Class E paper, which could be extendible for only, at most, just under one year. This step would remove the need for the trusts that had issued the ABCP to make liquidity calls, a vital part of the process given that the inability to roll the paper would result in instant default for the trusts, followed by bankruptcy proceedings.

But the maturity extension alone wouldn't solve the problem. The investor group needed a moratorium on collateral calls. Collateral calls were a huge risk to the ABCP market as long as triggers were based on mark-to-market values and CDS spreads had the potential to increase.

That the group quickly hammered out an agreement that addressed all of these problems was nothing short of a miracle, heavily assisted by pure fear of the unknown. The Montreal Accord became the framework for the restructuring negotiations that would follow.

Table 2.1. Who sponsored what? Third-party ABCP conduits and sponsors

Conduit	Sponsor	Amounts (billions)	Amounts confirmed
Apollo Trust	Coventree Inc.	0.219	0.203
Aurora Trust	Coventree Inc.	2.687	2.185
Comet Trust	Coventree Inc.	1.882	1.673
Gemini Trust	Coventree Inc.	1.486	1.323
Planet Trust	Coventree Inc.	1.803	1.515
Rocket Trust	Coventree Inc.	3.231	2.592
Slate Trust	Coventree Inc.	0.562	0.458
Structured Asset Trust	Nereus Financial Inc.*	1.372	1.143
Structured Investment Trust III	Nereus Financial Inc*	2.786	2.004
Ironstone Trust	National Bank Financial	0.764	0.584
MMAI Trust	National Bank Financial	1.403	1.192
Silverstone Trust	National Bank Financial	2.050	1.829
Aria Trust	Newshore Financial	1.499	1.376
Encore Trust	Newshore Financial	1.450	1.302
Newshore Canadian Trust	Newshore Financial	0.413	0.378
Opus Trust	Newshore Financial	1.704	1.556
Symphony Trust	Newshore Financial	1.921	1.826
Apsley Trust	Quanto	2.412	2.092
Devonshire Trust	Quanto	0.678	0.668
Whitehall Trust	Quanto	2.509	2.248
Selkirk Funding Trust	Securitus Capital Corp.	0.151	0.109
Skeena Capital Trust	Dundee Securities Corp.**	2.007	1.561

*Subsidiary of Coventree
**Not included in the subsequent restructuring

Signatories to the Montreal Accord

ABN AMRO
Barclays Bank
Caisse
Desjardins Group
Deutsche Bank
HSBC
Merrill Lynch
National Bank
Public Sector Pension (PSP)
UBS

Desjardins and National Bank Step Up

Like many of the others, Desjardins and National Bank had sold ABCP to retail and small corporate clients. In the absence of liquidity support, both institutions decided to step in and make smaller investors whole, a move that would at least mitigate some of the bad press that would surround the ABCP fiasco in the coming weeks and months. Staffers at National Bank met over the weekend of 18 and 19 August and quickly decided that it would be in the bank's best interest to buy back all ABCP holdings at 100 cents on the dollar from small retail investors and holders of money market mutual and pooled funds who had holdings of $2 million or less and who did not qualify as accredited investors under securities regulations. All told, National Bank bought approximately $2.1 billion of third-party ABCP issued by twenty-six trusts from its mutual funds, pooled funds, retail clients, and a subset of commercial and corporate clients. According to National Bank CEO Vachon, the bank decided to undertake the transaction without any direction to do so from the Quebec provincial securities regulator, the Autorité des marchés financiers (AMF), because it was "the right thing to do" and because it wanted to maintain its reputation among clients. The financial drain of this purchase – the bank might need to rebuild its capital in the event the ABCP market was not restructured – was a significant impetus for National Bank to invest heavily in time and effort to restructure the paper. During this period, the National Bank's board of directors established a special committee composed of independent directors to oversee all aspects of the bank's involvement in ABCP dealings.

Vachon himself had skin in the game: he owned $3.5 million of ABCP personally, which the National Bank board decided not to purchase back. To reduce any conflicts of interest in negotiations, Vachon had to wear only one hat – that of the National Bank, not an investor. Vachon provided a proposal to the board's special committee to address this situation: the bank would repurchase the paper at an independently established fair value (about 60% of face value), and Vachon would donate 40% of the proceeds to charity.

Desjardins followed suit, purchasing all of the ABCP held in its money market funds. The bank also had exposure for its institutional clients through security lending programs. Desjardins was the largest securities lender in Quebec. By purchasing the ABCP, Desjardins had itself become an ABCP holder. The purchase totalled approximately $2 billion, and the bank made it to uphold its reputation in the market and with clients. For the year-end 2007, Desjardins had a write-down in its ABCP holdings of $273 million, pre-tax.

The Accord Takes Shape

The signing of the Montreal Accord addressed immediate issues by setting out two main principles. First, the parties agreed that all outstanding third-party ABCP, including extendible third-party ABCP, would be converted into notes, whose interest rate would float with the payments on the underlying assets and that would mature at the same time as those assets. This matching of maturities meant that refinancing would not be necessary until the underlying assets matured. Any existing liquidity facilities were unnecessary and could be cancelled, with all outstanding liquidity calls being revoked. Second, margin provisions under LSS swaps would be revised to create renewed stability, thereby reducing the likelihood of near-term margin calls.[3]

This took care of immediate liquidity issues; it also took the heat off the liquidity providers in the short term. But an additional agreement was also created to give participants time to deal with longer-term issues. That agreement included a 60-day standstill period to end on 15 October 2007, during which signatories agreed to roll over any ABCP in which they had a beneficial interest and to encourage all other holders of ABCP to continue to roll theirs. In effect, this was a return to the aborted agreement of 11 August 2007, to roll the paper and avoid a fire sale as collateral calls arose. At the same time, counter-parties (the asset providers) of relevant assets used in third-party ABCP conduits would not pursue any existing collateral calls or make any new calls.

Conduits also agreed to drop any existing liquidity calls and to make no further calls for 150 days after the standstill period expired. Finally, the signatories agreed to encourage all other third-party market participants to take all actions to implement the long-term proposal and refrain from taking any actions that could derail those proposals.[4]

The termination of liquidity calls under the Montreal Accord applied to *all* liquidity providers – including all Canadian banks – not just those who signed. Most of the liquidity providers, such as Deutsche Bank, were foreign entities.

During the negotiations, CDS spreads were widening at a worrying pace as the financial crisis unfolded. This ramped up the risks to the dealers if they decided to forgo collateral calls. By agreeing to stay collateral calls for 60 days, the asset providers introduced substantial risk to their financial positions. If there was an increase in CDS spreads at the end of this period and collateral calls were not met, liquidating the assets could generate significantly less than the current value at the time of the standstill agreement.

What motivated the dealers to agree to a moratorium on collateral calls? There were two main factors. First, with the deteriorating markets, the dealers had their own ABCP structures that were in trouble: collateral calls and liquidation in an illiquid market could increase spreads and possibly unravel the market. Those increased spreads would translate into lower mark-to-market values for the structures on the dealers' financial statements.

Second, there may have been pushback by legal and other risk management groups within the dealer organizations. All of the dealers had to be wary of lawsuits from not meeting liquidity calls, with a resulting loss of reputation. Perhaps the dealer banks were also worried about involvement by their domestic central banks in this problem. Their decision to agree to the moratorium would ultimately lead them into a difficult negotiation position as spreads widened later in the negotiation process.

Having successfully negotiated the Montreal Accord structure on 15 August 2007, the participants now had to dig into the more difficult task of completing the road map set out in the Montreal Accord. The speed with which the Accord was hammered out must have given the participants some expectation of difficult but not brutal negotiations. After all, the Montreal Accord had been completed over a period when CDS spreads on the CDX IG 10-Year Index increased from about 60 to 70 bps in mid-July to more than 100 bps at the end of July. Between 13 and 15 August 2007, the spread ranged from 90 to 97 bps. With what was considered at the time a large increase in spreads, it's no wonder collateral calls were being made. The success of signing the Accord in the face of such increases in spreads must have buoyed the investors and asset providers.

Unfortunately, the global financial world would not cooperate, and the hope of a speedy resolution to the problem would soon be dashed. The Montreal Accord problem facing the Canadian ABCP market was the result of a reduction in liquidity due to a crisis of confidence in the underlying paper. This had precipitated the difficulty in rolling the paper. But to the asset providers and the sponsors, the real problem was LSSs and collateral calls.

A Peek at the Future

Fundamental to the negotiations were the spreads on CDSs – the underlying valuation driver of the LSS transactions. The CDS spreads reflected credit conditions for the underlying debt of companies refer-enced in the index; this in turn depended on the strength of the econ-omy and on credit conditions. Increases in spreads can lead to collateral calls as well as difficulties for both investors and asset providers. As in any market, changes in market values (spreads) can precede actual events due to expectations of future events. Unfortunately, problems with spreads happen when liquidity dries up, so changes in prices can be very dramatic.

Just how challenging things were about to get for the negotiators dur-ing the next phase of the restructuring can be seen in the daily spread value for the CDX IG 10-Year Index over the period from 1 January 2007 to 30 January 2009 (Figure 2.1). The latter date followed the closing date of the restructuring agreement. The horizontal axis shows the date; the vertical axis indicates the spreads measured in per cent. A value of 1.0% is equivalent to 100 bps.

Until about July 2007, spreads were reasonably stable, ranging from 50 to 60 bps. Increasing threats to financial institutions in the United States and globally (save Canada) from the subprime market were reflected in higher spreads. From around the end of July to early

Figure 2.1. CDS spreads during restructuring period: CDX IG S5 10-Year Index (matures on 20 December 2015)

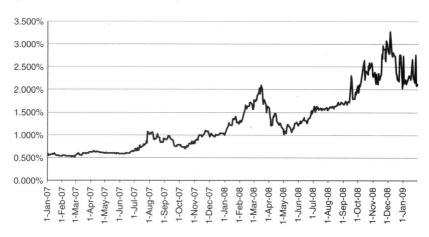

Source: Bloomberg

August, the spreads increased from 100 to 110 bps. The market freeze and the Montreal Accord negotiations occurred with spreads around 90 to 97 bps.

However, look further along the figure and a very frightening scenario emerges that the negotiating participants could not have expected. From about mid-October 2007 to 14 March 2008, spreads increased from about 73 bps to 210 bps. Leading up to 14 March, there were serious problems around the world with government guarantees and central bank actions. On 11 January 2008, Bank of America bought troubled Countrywide Financial, the largest US mortgage lender. On 14 March, J.P. Morgan provided funding to Bear Stearns; two days later, it bought Bear Stearns.

A period of relative calm then prevailed until early May, at which point the declining spreads began to increase again. During this period, the US government-supported mortgage entities Freddie Mac, Fannie Mae, and Indy Mac were put into conservatorship. On 14 September, Bank of America bought Merrill Lynch. On 16 September, Lehman Brothers filed for bankruptcy and the CDS spread reached 230 bps. Between 6 and 10 October, the Dow Jones Industrial Average lost 22.1%, the worst week on record; thus, it was down 40% from its record high of 13,165 on 9 October 2007.

Figure 2.2. First difference

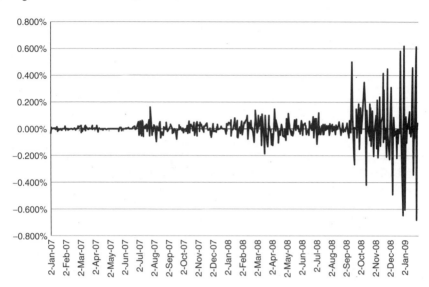

Source: Bloomberg

This proved disastrous for CDS spread levels, which, in late November and early December, further increased to a level of 327 bps on 5 December 2008. During this period, the final touches were being made to the ABCP restructuring agreement. It's very clear from this picture that risk was increasing on LSS transactions that had pure mark-to-market triggers. The restructuring needed to move away from this type of trigger and introduce mechanisms that would reduce the likelihood of collateral calls and that would make it possible for those calls, if made, to be answered with little or no disruption.

A more dramatic picture of the future problems facing the negotiating parties is provided in Figure 2.2, which presents the daily changes in spread levels. These changes show the volatility of the spreads facing the negotiators.

It does not take a financial engineer to understand the importance of this diagram. The left-hand side shows that until about 29 June 2007, CDS spreads are stable – there is very little in the way of spread changes. The period from the end of June 2007 to the end of August 2007 becomes more volatile. The large spike in this period reflects a change of 16 bps. Roll forward and you observe the volatility increasing.

By mid-September 2008, there are very large changes in spreads. For example, on 15 September 2008, the change is 50 bps. On 24 December, it is 58 bps. But there are large changes in both directions. For example, there is a 62 bps increase on 1 January 2009, followed the next day by a reduction of 60 bps. For 26 January, there is an increase of 61 bps, followed the next day by reduction of 68 bps.

The daily spread changes demonstrate the risk that faced the negotiating parties during the period. Would the restructured entity have enough safeguards to protect both parties to the negotiations after the deal was signed? As the spreads changed, the relative bargaining power of the negotiators would change. This behaviour of spreads also explains why it was necessary to have daily negotiations on standstill arrangements between the investors and the asset providers during the latter part of the negotiations. The observed volatility over the last period was probably exaggerated somewhat by the illiquidity in the CDS market, but it was still real for the participants.

The "War Room"

Getting information about the scope of the ABCP market in Canada was a big challenge from the beginning: no one could see the extent of the crisis. Without a clear view of the size and scope of the market, it was impossible to stave off a bigger crisis. From that first "holy shit" moment on 13 August, National Bank's Vachon knew that the group would have to piece together the ABCP puzzle by gathering information and data. He and his team set up a "war room" at the bank and packed it with documentation on prospectuses, contracts, liquidity arrangements, and other related material. This helped bring trust-related information to the players in the Montreal Accord, but there were still huge gaps in understanding the ABCP structures and who held the paper. This difficulty was the result of the lack of transparency in the underlying trusts.

As those in the war room sifted through the information they had been given, it became clear how extensive the third-party ABCP market had become. Vachon and Rousseau realized that the paper was widely held across Canada. They were also getting a glimpse of a new and even more troubling group of investors: Canaccord and Credential had been selling ABCP to their retail client base, a fact that came as a surprise and shock to many involved in the Montreal Accord. Of course, both National Bank and Desjardins had already dealt with some of their own retail ABCP clients. But this was just the tip of the iceberg.

Mark Maybank, Canaccord's COO at the time, was at a barbecue in Toronto when he heard the news that the commercial paper market had frozen. New to his role, he didn't know about the ABCP that had been sold to investors. He would soon be visited by a J.P. Morgan representative, who would explain the paper he had inherited when he took over the position.

It wasn't just Maybank who had to learn this new ABCP language. Representatives from many of the major players caught in the freeze-up would have to read up on exactly how the products worked and what was "under the hood."

Information would be crucial in helping affected investors understand what had transpired and how to resolve the problem. The Caisse set up its own war room to obtain detailed information on the trusts and counter-parties. With such a large exposure to ABCP and with so many trusts, a large number of people were dedicated to the task. Since information was so important and cooperation among parties so crucial, the Caisse and National Bank shared information. This was another example of collective action superseding a go-it-alone strategy.

As they began to understand the scope of the crisis, Vachon and Rousseau, along with Alban D'Amours, president and CEO of Desjardins (a group referred to as the "three musketeers" in the press), travelled to Ottawa to alert Dodge and Carney, who at the time was senior associate and deputy minister at the Department of Finance. Rousseau and D'Amours were adamant that the federal government had to do something to resolve the crisis. They came armed with suggestions that ranged from having the Department of Finance enforce the liquidity arrangements to allowing ABCP to be used for collateral purposes in order to provide liquidity to the investors. But as they would soon find out, little or no help would be coming from the powers in Ottawa.

A Regional Problem

In the late spring and early summer, Dodge had viewed the unfolding ABCP issue as a somewhat limited problem. He and the Bank of Canada did not appreciate the scale of the problem at the time and hence underestimated its potential to develop into a national financial market crisis. Dodge said that the Bank of Canada initially saw the issue as a securities market problem and that the "qualified investors" who made investments in opaque ABCP-structured investments were responsible for their own actions. As the crisis developed, he said, the role of the Bank would be to take action to preserve the overall liquidity of the financial system; it would not be to intervene directly in the resolution of specific securities. As David Dodge explained to us, "not only would direct support of these troubled ABCP securities have been beyond the normal scope of action of the Bank of Canada, the provision of direct support would have created both the incentive for inappropriately risky behavior by banks to sponsor this type of opaque structured product and a disincentive for investors to do their due diligence." This latter behaviour is often referred to as "moral hazard."

Dodge's dilemma was a portent of the choices that would face the US government a year later as it worked to bail out select financial institutions under the Emergency Economic Stabilization Act of 2008. The Bank of Canada, led by Dodge, opted for a different route: a hands-off approach that would see the Bank of Canada and the Department of Finance monitoring the situation from a distance, with regular updates from the Caisse.

Undaunted by their failure to move Ottawa to action, Vachon, Rousseau, and D'Amours headed back to Montreal determined to push forward with a longer-term agreement between ABCP investors and asset providers. Sure, the Montreal Accord had been relatively easy to put together, but could the group keep all the players at the table for longer than just sixty days, if necessary? And could they do it in the midst of what was proving to be a global liquidity crisis among all of the world's biggest banks, many of which had also signed the Montreal Accord?

Strength in Numbers

As Vachon's war room unearthed more and more information on ABCP and its holders, it became clear that the original group of Montreal Accord signatories was only a drop in the ocean relative to the vast numbers of note holders in the Canadian marketplace. There were many others, dispersed across Canada. At the first meeting of the Montreal Accord investor group, which included the Caisse, National Bank, Desjardins, and the PSP, the investors realized that they needed more committee members to accurately reflect the national scope of the problem. It was not, as Dodge had thought, a regional Quebec problem: it was a national financial crisis, and they needed more members to illustrate this.

To help them identify other investors and undertake needed administrative work for the group (such as posting of documents and maintenance of a data room), the committee hired Ernst & Young International (EYI). The group asked EYI monitor Pierre Laporte to identify who the holders of ABCP were. Larger holders were relatively easy to source; finding the smaller investors proved to be a bigger problem.

In another effort to boost national representation, signatories of the Montreal Accord held a conference call on 19 August seeking to attract other holders of ABCP who wanted to participate in the process and abide by the standstill agreement. The call brought other investors into the fold, including larger, financially sophisticated investors, such as the pension funds of NAV Canada and Canada Post. However, the information about the call failed to reach a host of smaller retail, corporate, and institutional investors – a group that was hard to reach and hard to find. Yet that group would ultimately end up holding all of the cards at the most important point in the negotiations.

As information uncovered in the war room identified more holders of ABCP, these holders were asked to contact Laporte and fill out a form detailing the extent of their holdings, and also to indicate whether they would support the standstill. By 23 August 2007, members of the Accord knew that 77% of the outstanding investors had contacted EYI and signed the agreement or at least indicated their support. The level of support was greater than two-thirds in eighteen conduits and between one-half and two-thirds in three conduits.

To further boost the size of the investor group, Bergeron approached Laporte and obtained the names of investors who might be interested in joining the Investors Committee. He called them individually, with some becoming voting members and others becoming observers to keep on top of the process. These members were sophisticated investors who held substantial amounts of ABCP.

Finally able to put some of the puzzle pieces together, the investor group was hopeful that a deal could be reached quickly. It was now time to bring another set of players into the ABCP crisis: the dealers, who up until now had been excluded from the discussions. The growing group of investors felt they needed to come to the discussions from a position of strength and size. The dealer group, which included global giant Deutsche Bank, required the investors to come to the negotiations with "big guns." By far the biggest "gun" in the investor group was the Caisse. As the investors' ad hoc leader, the Caisse had the clout and skin in the game to take the lead in the negotiations.

Beginning in August 2007, many of the dealers approached the Caisse. The Caisse met many of them in one-on-one discussions, looking for information on the underlying contracts and their structures. The purpose of these discussions was to negotiate a settlement on a trust-by-trust basis. The idea was to provide each trust sponsor with an agreement that had been made by the investors and the asset providers and have the ABCP sponsors implement the negotiated structure with each individual trust. The agreement involved creating substitute notes for the ABCP notes that met the requirements of long maturity and revised triggers. For many trusts that had underlying assets that were primarily traditional and perhaps modestly exposed to credit derivatives, the restructuring would be relatively straightforward. The problems would arise for trusts with significant exposure to subprime and derivative assets. This approach dealt with the restructuring as a collection of individual trust problems, and not a market problem. However, ABCP *was* a market problem, according to the rest of the investors – and fixing it would require restructuring the entire ABCP market.

Why the Government Didn't Step In

As investors scrambled to determine how deeply they were embedded in ABCP, many still believed that liquidity providers could be made to step in and honour the agreements they had been well paid to provide. That didn't happen. Deutsche Bank and Barclays both refused to pay, relying on the restrictive terms of the Canadian-style liquidity clause that was at the heart of those agreements (and that made them largely worthless). So why didn't the federal government step in? It was a question asked by many, including Alban D'Amours, Desjardins' president and CEO until March 2008. D'Amours would later criticize the feds' role in the ABCP crisis in an interview with the Montreal *Gazette* in May 2009. Had a general market disruption been called by federal authorities, he said, the crisis would have been averted and foreign banks such as Deutsche Bank and Barclays would have had to step in and pay. Investors on the committee who expected government intervention were sorely disappointed, he explained: "The party line came in fast, and everyone fell into line quickly." It became clear that a private market solution would have to be found and that no intervention would come from any federal bodies.

Another member of the investors group who spoke to us anonymously describes his disappointment at the lack of action on the part of the federal government: "I wouldn't have asked for a government bailout," he told us. "I would have asked for government backbone to protect Canadians. I would have asked them to play hardball with the banks. Instead, the banks got away with it."

Though the frustration of the participants is understandable, it is not entirely clear how, as a matter of law, the federal government could have easily mandated a non-bailout resolution. In other words, the government could, of course, have provided money to effect a resolution. The issue here is, how could they have simply "mandated" a solution to a problem created by private agreements?

The suggestion that the government could somehow have called or deemed the occurrence of a market disruption that would have bound the liquidity providers under their respective privately negotiated contracts is especially problematic. Interpreting private contracts is the domain of the judicial branch – the courts – *not* the executive, and certainly not other federal government agencies. It is not clear how a unilateral decree by the federal government that a market disruption event had occurred could necessarily bind the parties to a private contract (which contained the parties' own privately negotiated market disruption) absent, perhaps, an Act of Parliament to that effect. And for Parliament to attempt to rewrite – or unilaterally interpret – the contracts of private parties would be an extraordinarily intrusive – indeed potentially dangerous – exercise of state power in a market economy, even assuming that Parliament would have had the necessary constitutional authority to legislate in respect of contracts, since contract law generally falls within provincial legislative authority.

This is not to suggest, of course, that the government was powerless. Clearly, it wasn't. The federal government has many powerful indirect levers it can use to persuade financial institutions to take, or to refrain from taking, actions. Reasonable people may differ on whether the government should have made greater use of these levers to try to craft a speedier resolution. The only point to be made here is that the suggestion that the government could have easily and unilaterally compelled the enforcement of private contracts – without the intervention of the courts – in accordance with the government's own preferred interpretation of those contracts, is highly problematic.

The Investors Committee on Montreal Accord

John Crichton, president and CEO, NAV CANADA
Alban D'Amours, president and CEO, Desjardins Group
Gordon J. Fyfe, president and CEO, PSP Investments
Doug Greaves, vice-president, pension fund, and chief investment officer, Canada Post
Rowland Kelly, interim CEO, Credit Union Central of British Columbia (representing Credit Union Central of Canada)
Karen Kinsley, president and CEO, Canada Mortgage and Housing Corp.
Mark Maybank, president and chief operating officer, Canaccord Capital Corp. (Canadian operating subsidiary)
Dave Mowat, president and CEO, ATB Financial
Ricardo Pascoe, co-president and co-CEO, National Bank Financial Group
David G. Patterson, chair and CEO, Northwater Capital Management
Henri-Paul Rousseau, president and CEO, Caisse de dépôt et placement du Québec
Jim Scopick, president and CEO, Credit Union Central Alberta

CHAPTER THREE

Enter Purdy Crawford

It was ultimately Purdy Crawford who was selected to take over as chair of the Montreal Accord investors' group. He brought with him some much-needed leadership and focus. The Montreal Accord had been the result of ad hoc meetings and generally failed agreements to act (i.e., the failure of everyone to stick to the plan and roll the paper), and it now needed full-time help. It was David Dodge who first suggested Crawford to Rousseau. Dodge pointed out that a number of individuals at the Bank of Canada (including Mark Carney) and at the Department of Finance felt that Purdy was the one person with enough credibility to bring together the various conflicting parties to arrive at a market solution to the problem. People at the Bank and at Finance felt that Purdy understood well the difficult public policy issues involved and that he could steer the banks and investors to a solution that would also be acceptable to the government. The Bank and the Finance Department were very lucky he was willing to take on the task. Rousseau, for his part, felt that Crawford's track record and friendly demeanour – which concealed a tough and canny negotiator – would fit the bill perfectly. Crawford, a veteran Bay Streeter, was a long-time corporate and securities lawyer who had helped the federal government deal with Dome Petroleum's debt crisis in 1982. In Rousseau's view, Crawford had shown he could handle tough negotiations and gain consensus among individuals with sharply diverging interests. A former CEO of IMASCO, he had been active on boards of directors and had been chair of a number of influential committees, including the Five Year Review Committee to review securities legislation in Ontario (the Crawford Report).

Few people thought Crawford would say yes to the job, according to Rousseau. So he surprised almost everyone when he agreed; perhaps he thought the task would be relatively straightforward and quick. Crawford admits he thought the negotiations would be over within months. What he didn't realize was how technology would change the game. "I'd never been involved in negotiations where instant communication would predominate to that extent," he explained. "If I was to keep control of what was going on, I had to get a BlackBerry and learn to use it in a hurry," he says of his first weekend on the job. Immediacy and a changed media space would also come to dominate in another area of the negotiations: dealing with wronged retail investors.

The Caisse chief was convinced that the discussions and deals made would now be viewed as more objective and more representative of investors across Canada. Critical to this would be Crawford's reputation for getting the job done and for reaching consensus with committees around contentious issues. He was well connected, and ultimately, he would leverage his connections to hammer out a deal just when things looked darkest. He took over as chair of the Investors Committee on 5 September 2007 and went about setting up shop at the Toronto law firm Goodmans, which became the legal adviser to the committee. It was at Goodmans that Crawford undertook his first task: gathering the disparate band of informal group members and establishing a formal committee that would represent all ABCP investors: large pension funds, institutional holders, Crown corporations, and smaller corporate holders. Crawford and his legal team began by giving the committee a name that would position ABCP not as a regional problem but as a national one. The scope of the problem was captured in the rather wordily titled Pan-Canadian Investors Committee for Third-Party Structured Asset-Backed Commercial Paper (PCIC). The PCIC was born.

Joining Crawford in the growing ranks of consultants and experts hired to solve the problem was Pierre Laporte of Ernst & Young International (EYI), the accounting firm appointed monitor responsible for the daunting amount of administrative work that the PCIC would require. Laporte would be responsible for operating another, bigger data room than the one originally set up by National Bank: it was a high-security, fortress-like space, opened a week after Crawford came on board (12 September), that contained all known ABCP-related data. Nothing could be removed from the room or passed on to non-approved recipients.

Anyone who wanted to see data related to ABCP had to provide evidence of ownership of the affected paper and sign a confidentiality agreement. On the surface, the agreement ensured that the user of the information would not be able to trade on it. But it was directed mainly at the signatories of the Montreal Accord, note holders, swap counter-parties, liquidity providers, and credit enhancers. Some institutional holders, on the advice of counsel, chose *not* to sign the agreement in case it jeopardized their right to sue – an approach that still was fore-most on the minds of many investors.

Those who succeeded in clearing all of the legal hurdles so that they might actually view the ABCP data now had to wait. Collecting that data was a slow process hindered by the necessary involvement of DBRS, which had much of the data and was slow to release it owing to contractual terms with the asset providers. And that data, once acces-sible, came in a format that was difficult for most to interpret: a paper dump of poorly organized information without any of the important parts highlighted. Anyone seeking help interpreting it was out of luck.

All of these factors added significant time to the process of reaching a deal.

The PCIC's mandate was to provide a workable solution to the ABCP liquidity problem. Its approach, which was to be built on the Montreal Accord, would reflect a set of underlying principles for a solution that was fair and equitable and in the best interests of all investors, and that would avoid the value destruction that could result from a forced liqui-dation of trust assets. The committee wanted to see ABCP converted to floating rate notes with maturities that reflected those of the underlying assets, and in order to create liquidity, it wanted greater transparency regarding what those assets were.

To help ensure that the solution met these criteria, the PCIC looked for a financial adviser that could bring financial expertise to the restruc-turing of the ABCP trusts. No Canadian firms stepped up to take the job. Among the US firms responding to the request for proposals was Lehman Brothers; had it been hired, there would have been even greater headaches after its bankruptcy in 2008 – the largest bankruptcy filing in US history. Without a financial adviser during a particularly bumpy period in the negotiations, the restructuring would likely have been doomed. Another US firm vying for the job was J.P. Morgan, which was ultimately hired. J.P. Morgan had expertise in the area, and it had not been involved in the ABCP market in Canada – an added bonus. At the same time, J.P. Morgan did not face a conflict of interest. Vachon recalls that J.P. Morgan had staff who were involved in the Resolution Trust restructuring, and Rousseau personally called Jamie Dimon, chair of J.P. Morgan, to tell him the firm had the job – but only if Timothy Ryan, who worked on the Resolution Trust restructuring, would be leading the team. Ryan would ultimately leave the firm, however, and Buffalo, NY–born Andrew Kresse would take his place at the negotiating table as the lead representative from J.P. Morgan. A younger man, Kresse had spent a lot of time in the border city of his birth, and that, he believed, helped him understand Canadians. Importantly, he understood that Canadians could behave differently than US investors, especially when it came to litigation – Canadians are less inclined than Americans to litigate.

The protracted negotiations to identify and hire the financial adviser should have signalled to the investor group that a solution would not be quick. The dealers preferred that an accounting firm and not an investment banker act as the financial adviser. Whatever their reasons for taking this position – perhaps an investment banker would know all the tricks of the trade, including tough negotiation strategies – there was a delay in getting the financial adviser in place so that the problem could be resolved.

PCIC members held approximately 66% of the outstanding $35 billion of ABCP by book value. DBRS, the Department of Finance, and the Bank of Canada had observer status. From the beginning of the ABCP crisis, Gar Emerson, a partner at Fasken Martineau, served as consultant to the Department of Finance and Bank of Canada. This included, now, being their observer on the PCIC. Some investors, such as the Ontario Financing Authority, stayed out of the restructuring since they could not obtain provincial permission. Others remained out for other reasons, including concerns about impeding future lawsuits against the dealers and conflicting interests between the larger and mid-sized investors.

As noted earlier, at the time of the market freeze, corporate and pension fund investors did not know who else held ABCP, and there was no information available on what was happening in the market. In fact, a corporate CFO describes the situation as "short on facts and long on rumours, and the way everything was starting off wasn't terribly comforting for all but the largest investors in ABCP." Many CFOs reviewed the original term sheets to determine what assets were in the trusts they held. But the term sheets were of little assistance. Obviously, they should have known what was held in these trusts, and in this regard, they were not the only players in the dark.

Many of these companies and pension funds were angry at not being asked to join the PCIC, although at that time the committee was also trying to determine who held the paper. Informal networks were established among pension funds and corporate holders based on historical relationships, and many telephone calls were made in attempts to obtain any information on what was happening with the ABCP. For example, based on existing relationships, Toronto Hydro, Ontario Power Generation, and the Greater Toronto Airports Authority discussed these issues and shared what little information they had.

After the Montreal Accord was signed, a number of large ABCP investors approached Jeff Carhart and Jay Hoffman of Miller Thomson, and the Ad Hoc Committee was formed. The group of investors represented by this committee grew over the negotiations period up to the time of the Companies' Creditors Arrangement Act (CCAA) application in March 2008 until it represented approximately $2 billion worth of ABCP, and was ultimately recognized by the Ontario Superior Court of Justice. The Ad Hoc Committee played an important role in the final structure of the global third-party liability releases under the CCAA – releases that were crucial to resolving the crisis.

The companies and pension funds belonging to the Ad Hoc Committee chose not to join the PCIC for a number of reasons. First, some were still upset that they had not been invited in the first place. Second, the Caisse was the moving force behind the Montreal Accord, had the largest holdings, and would have significant input in the negotiations. Thus, the outcome might not represent the aspirations of some of the Ad Hoc Committee members. Some of those members, especially corporate investors, wanted their money back right away – anything less was unacceptable. Finally, to join the PCIC, they would have to sign a waiver stating they would not use the information they received for trading purposes. On the advice of legal counsel, some institutions chose not to join in case it jeopardized their right to sue. Furthermore, it was not clear that they would have been free to trade their securities, given that they would have seen the information. Clearly, those who did not join the PCIC would, as individual note holders, have little influence either within or outside the PCIC tent unless they banded together.

Other investors did join the PCIC, however, which expanded from the initial four participants in the Montreal Accord to twelve members as of 6 September 2007. The membership now included credit unions from British Columbia, Ontario, and Saskatchewan. However, there were two groups that were not represented: corporate holders of ABCP, and retail investors, although Maybank of Canaccord Capital was there as the retail investors' representative. While it was recognized that corporations held significant amounts of ABCP – typically for working capital needs or for parking funds temporarily in "risk-free" assets – the extent of the holdings of retail investors was not appreciated. To create a better balance of investor interests, Magna was invited to join the PCIC to represent the corporate holders. The global automotive company reported ABCP holdings of about $134 million and was open to being at the table to reach a solution. Magna's willingness to negotiate set it apart from other corporate holders, many of which remained adamant that they wanted their funds back immediately and were unwilling to negotiate; the latter group included large companies such as Jean Coutu and Air Transat. For them, the legal remedy – a lawsuit – was the appropriate solution.

Just Like GICs

As the war room generated data and more and more investors came out of the woodwork, it became clear that a large – to many, surprisingly large – contingent of small retail investors had been sucked into the ABCP fiasco. While pension funds and to a much lesser degree corporate investors commanded space at the negotiating table, retail investors were experiencing the crash in isolation. Like the Caisse and other major players, they had to work to understand what it was they were left holding and what it meant for their finances. For them, information was sketchy and hard to access. For example, on 15 August, Brian Hunter, a fifty-three-year-old engineer, got a call from his broker at Canaccord Capital. Hunter had recently cashed out his equity investments to get his retirement savings out of what he thought was a "crazy" market. At his age, he thought, stocks were getting too risky for him. Instead, Hunter wanted to put his money somewhere more secure. So he put $750,000 into what, Hunter says, his broker had told him was a T-bill type of investment that would keep his money as safe as it would be in a GIC and yield him a modest 4% interest rate on the term. Needless to say, he was surprised to find out during the 15 August phone call with his broker that his account had been frozen because of a liquidity event related to his investment.

   As Hunter sought more information in the weeks following, he began to understand what he had actually been sold. And because he had never heard of a CDS, he was surprised to learn that instead of buying something similar to a T-bill, "I had actually sold insurance contracts to banks," he says. Hunter had purchased the paper on a recommendation from his long-time broker and had not felt the need to do his own due diligence. Now, after the fact, he looked through the sales documents and realized that even if he had tried to do his homework on his own, there was nothing to indicate these products were so risky. Moreover, Hunter says, the rate of return did not strike him as being suspiciously high: it was only slightly higher than what T-bills were yielding at the time. "It's not like I was getting a 24% return or anything crazy like that," he says.

A few weeks later, Hunter finally received a politely worded letter from Canaccord executive vice-president Bruce Maranda explaining that the firm had no legal obligation to reimburse him or anyone else. The financial crisis, explained Maranda, was an event that no one could have foreseen, and Canaccord had relied on the DBRS credit rating given to ABCP. Wrote Maranda: "At the time of purchase, there was no indication that the R1 (high) rating was inaccurate or that the market might experience a disruption that could impact upon the repayment of such highly rated ABCP."

A second client communication, dated 30 August 2007, seemed to take a different tone: Canaccord explained its role in the newly formed Montreal Consortium. In the closing paragraph of that letter, the firm positioned itself as more of an "updater" or equally wronged party than the dealer who had sold the investors the paper in the first place. Maranda wrote: "We wish we had more concrete information at this time, but it appears that the 60-day process outlined by the Montreal Consortium is going to have to run its course. We will continue to provide you with regular updates as information becomes available."

With little information about what had happened or whether he would ever see his money again, Hunter decided to fight back. His decision to do so led to one of the most interesting and compelling pieces of the ABCP story, as retail investors – brought together by Hunter – shared information and ultimately banded together to get a place at the negotiating table when a solution was being put together. While retail investors were the smallest holders of ABCP by dollar amount outstanding, they were the most vocal. They would also become among the most innovative in finding ways to connect and communicate, exploiting social media and working their legal team to get in front of the PCIC and make sure their needs were brought to the negotiating table.

For its part, Canaccord Capital had the most clients holding ABCP: about 1,430 retail clients with more than $138 million worth of the paper (roughly 1% of its total account base). National Bank had sold ABCP to 340 clients, totalling $170 million when the market froze. Credential Securities had sold ABCP to about 335 individual investors, who held about $48 million. It did this through a network of investment advisers across 135 credit unions in British Columbia, Alberta, Saskatchewan, Manitoba, and Ontario. Institutions such as National Bank and Desjardins stepped in early to make investors whole, acquiring all the ABCP held by mutual funds, pooled funds of the bank's subsidiaries, their individual retail clients, and other corporate clients at 100% of the acquisition cost plus accrued interest for amounts less than $2 million per client. However, other retail investors were not as lucky: Canaccord and Credential did not have the deep pockets to fund a full bailout, and this left their clients with frozen and worthless paper.

Hunter had been a Canaccord client for years. His experience mirrors that of many other retail investors who ended up holding ABCP. In countless stories, investors claimed that brokers had described ABCP to them as being like a GIC or T-bill. An e-mail sent on 1 August 2007 by Canaccord vice-president Mark Hewitt directly compared Planet Trust ABCP to GICs. Under the subject line "Money Market Rates – Higher Than 1-year GICs," the e-mail implied that the ABCP issued by Planet Trust was, in some ways, preferable to GICs: "This paper offers the following: Liquidity: You can sell the Planet Trust at any time before maturity. GICs are non-redeemable. Protection of the capital. The rating on the Planet Trust is AAA credit. GICs are only ensured up to $100,000 [sic]."

Coventree's Ching says he was shocked when he learned that ABCP had been sold to retail investors. Coventree Inc. was Canada's biggest issuer of non-bank ABCP and the sponsor of Planet Trust (the issuer of the Planet Trust paper referred to above). In his view, the product his firm sold was aimed at sophisticated institutional investors only. For him, it was absurd that it had been sold to retail investors.

But despite the fact that ABCP was inappropriate for unsophisticated investors, it was being widely sold to them. Indeed, it was being sold to some of the most vulnerable clients: baby boomers and retirees moving cash from businesses or home sales and seeking a place to park their savings – in many cases, life savings – for a short term. Although just $600 million of the $32 billion in frozen ABCP was held by retail investors, their losses were perhaps the most profoundly felt. ABCP was routinely being marketed and sold as an alternative to GICs – as a very low-risk savings vehicle that offered a bit more interest than the alternatives. But in fact, ABCP was nothing like GICs. An article in the *National Post* by John Chant put it clearly: "ABCP trusts were essentially hedge funds, albeit with capped returns. They offered investors high risk together with low returns. All in all, they were totally unsuitable for investors seeking a safe haven and would have had few takers had their true nature been known. A broad market developed through a combination of limited information, forbearance from securities administrators, and positive credit ratings."

According to a report by Investment Industry Regulatory Organization of Canada (IIROC), beyond e-mails and conversations with advisers, there was little or no marketing material – investors relied on their advisers to guide them. It's clear that they were often given misleading information from trusted sources. For example, Mike and Wynne Miles from Victoria had almost half their retirement savings in T-bills in July 2007. When it came time to roll them over, their long-time broker claimed she was unable to find T-bills in the Canaccord system. The Miles say she put their money into ABCP on 26 July, just two days after the Coventree memo was sent to Scotia outlining the product's subprime exposure. The Miles claim they did not find out they owned anything other than T-bills until after they began receiving notices in their statements from Canaccord explaining that Structured Investment Trust III (SIT III) had experienced problems. Mike Miles says that after a few such notices, he called his broker and was surprised to learn that almost half their retirement savings had been put into ABCP without anyone consulting them. "She said don't worry about it," he says. How did they end up with ABCP? "Our broker saw that there were no T-bills for sale," he says. According to Mike Miles, she claimed that what was available was "ABCP with an R-1 (high) credit rating and a liquidity guarantee, and she rolled over our T-bills into that. The change was done without our knowledge or consent."

During our conversations with those involved in the early stages of the negotiations, many maintained they were in the dark about the extent to which ABCP had been sold to retail investors. But it is difficult to understand how they could not have known, especially given Canaccord's role at the centre (remember that Maybank was brought in relatively early in the discussions). Canaccord was a retail-focused firm, and it must have been obvious that at least some retail investors had been sold ABCP. Indeed, Crawford invited Canaccord to join the PCIC to represent retail interests during the negotiations. Crawford believed that Canaccord, having sold 95% of the outstanding retail ABCP, was in the best position to bring the voice of retail investors to the table.

This was, in part, true: Canaccord arguably had the most at stake, and without a resolution to the ABCP crisis, the firm would be financially destroyed. Crawford believed this financial imperative was a strong motivator for Canaccord to participate actively in the process. Since the possibility of using the CCAA was proposed early in the negotiations, it remains a mystery why the PCIC didn't anticipate early on how strong a force retail investors would become down the road.

The Perimeter Sideshow

An early decision agreed to by the PCIC was a moratorium on trading the original paper to prevent it from being acquired by hedge funds; the committee believed that hedge funds could derail the deal if they acquired a sufficient position in the paper. They worried that hedge fund activity could lead to prices breaching triggers in the underlying LSS transactions. This moratorium was not binding on investors outside of the restructuring – they remained free to monetize the paper, provided they could find someone to buy it.

And that led to Jonathan Polak's big idea. An employee at Perimeter Financial, Polak wanted to provide a traditional option for locked-in investors. Doug Steiner, the CEO of Perimeter and former CEO of VERSUS Technologies and E*TRADE Canada, had a reputation for introducing new and challenging ideas into the capital markets. Polak's concept caught his attention. On 8 November 2007, Perimeter, an operator of electronic markets, announced it would launch a market in ABCP notes starting 14 November 2007. Perimeter's market would allow trading in all conduits except Skeena Trust, which was being restructured outside of the Montreal Accord. All trading would be done on an anonymous counter-party basis. Perimeter intended to make public all-limit prices and post-transaction prices for the ABCP notes but not the dollar-value-traded.

Polak started by building a list of ABCP holders. This was an arduous task. He used Bloomberg to identify public company CFOs. Also, there were newspaper articles on companies and funds that held ABCP. After compiling the list, he took the direct approach – he called them to determine whether there was any interest in selling the frozen paper. Polak clearly recalls the hostile reaction from the individual he contacted at the Caisse, the biggest holder of the frozen ABCP.

What is interesting about Perimeter's attempt to establish trading in the ABCP notes is that the original backers and partial owners of

Polak's firm, Perimeter, were National Bank Financial and the Caisse, both members of the PCIC.

The opening of this market, three months after the ABCP market froze, generated controversy. Crawford stated that the market was an attempt to exploit vulnerable investors or, as he put it, "to exploit the needs of some investors for liquidity and induce panic in the market to acquire ABCP at a distressed price." He added that the lack of interest in the market (his comments were made four days after the market opened) "would seem to confirm their understanding of the motivation behind its purveyors."

The subtext of his comments related to the standstill arrangement under which investors agreed not to trade any of the ABCP. In addition, the PCIC used its influence to try to ensure that trading by investment dealers was not undertaken.

Steiner responded to Crawford's comments by stating his belief that the Montreal Accord was self-serving and paternalistic. Regarding the lack of trading in the ABCP (which had then been open for only five days), he added that "it takes a while to develop a market." This same sentiment would be echoed by Crawford less than two years later. When asked in August 2009 about the low trading volumes and prices in the market for the new restructured notes, Crawford would respond: "But a market develops over time."

The Perimeter market was doomed from the start. The first and most important reason was a lack of transparency in the underlying assets in each of the conduits. Since the underlying assets were not all the same, and since they were opaque to any potential buyer in the Perimeter market, bids were unlikely. In fact, any bids would probably be very low as prospective buyers attempted to steal the paper (such bids are referred to as "stink bids" – familiar to those in the housing market). At the same time, the major investors had all agreed to a moratorium on any trading in the paper.

A number of corporations had used ABCP for working capital purposes. They needed the funds, but now they were frozen. These companies were irate with the banks that had sold them the paper. The banks found themselves between a rock and a hard place – they had agreed not to sell any of the paper under the standstill arrangement, but their clients needed to obtain funds.

To address this issue, the banks lent money to these corporations, accepting the borrowers' ABCP as collateral for the loans. These transactions resolved the problem facing the banks and their clients (albeit at a cost for the latter), but they also reduced the potential supply of ABCP for trading. However, not all corporate clients were able to make a deal with their bank, and some were unhappy with the proposed terms. When those bank clients traded their ABCP in a market transaction, the banks were very upset, since there was a moratorium on such transactions, and let Perimeter know about their displeasure.

As a result of all of these influences, if there were any trades, the pricing would have been a best guess. And while for some investors a price based on a best guess may have been better than frozen funds, it was no way for most investors to obtain cash for their notes. However, there were serious concerns about trading the ABCP notes.

First, there was no doubt that the prices of the transactions would be well below par – some had speculated about 50 cents to the dollar. This crystallization of the value of the paper, as uncertain as the price was, could send negative signals to the market and potentially worsen the crisis.

Second, the reduction in prices could cause problems when the paper was valued for accounting purposes. For investor companies subject to mark-to-market accounting, a fall in observed market prices could require them to write down the book value of any ABCP they held for financial statement purposes.

Notice the conditional *could*. The accounting profession had provisions to deal with asset prices that were generated from poorly functioning markets or fire sale situations: they permitted the accounting entity (the companies holding ABCP) to provide an independent valuation of the asset.

With all of these challenges, it was no surprise that the decision to start a market in the ABCP was greeted with hostility by banks and other parties to the restructuring negotiations. As a result, there were not many trades in the original ABCP notes. It is equally surprising that transactions occurred even with the moratorium in place. Given what was perceived as fragility in the market, the Bank of Canada wanted to block trading on the ABCP notes in order to forestall what it considered a negative impact of low transaction prices on the outlook of investors in the paper, the negotiations in the Montreal Accord, and the presentation of financial reports.

When Perimeter started trading in the market, there was an offer of about 91 cents on the dollar – a dream valuation – but only for a small dollar quantity (a mere $300,000). However, there was no great interest in this market. Eventually, there were bids at 70 cents on the dollar – these remained outstanding for some time and, in hindsight, were an excellent value. In 2008, there was a trade of a small amount (in the area of $5 million) at 70 or 71 cents on the dollar. This was the only trade. An interesting sidelight of this transaction is that it occurred while there was a moratorium on trading and credit markets had again deteriorated, breaching triggers in the underlying agreements and triggering collateral calls.

Adding to the difficulty in trading these ABCP notes, they had been removed from the clearing corporation, leading to a problem in settling the transaction in the market. The transfer agent was National Bank Financial, which held a substantial amount of the original ABCP notes based on purchases from retail investors. Consistent with the moratorium on trading of which it was a signatory, National Bank refused to settle a transaction. This obstruction led to threats to publicize the bank's position, which ultimately resulted in a trade settling.

The Perimeter transaction prices would have been listed, but there was no such price transparency when transactions occurred between buyers and sellers outside of this market. It has been suggested that a number of these transactions between investors in ABCP and distressed-debt hedge funds did occur. Westaim Corp., a public company in Alberta, held $17 million of ABCP, which it wrote down to $14 million. It then agreed to sell half of its ABCP holdings for $6 million. This transaction amounted to an almost 30% write-down on the paper that was sold. Additional off-the-market transactions were occurring between investment houses and their angry clients, some of whom had threatened to sue. The investment houses purchased the paper at par and sold at a lower value, eating the loss. Finally, GMP Capital was purchasing paper from investors in an attempt to set up a fund composed of the original ABCP paper.

Overall, an audacious attempt to inject liquidity into the ABCP market while the paper was frozen was unsuccessful. The reasons are many, and as noted, the probability of success was small to zero.

Other Decent Proposals

The Caisse's early proposal to extend the duration of the ABCP issues wasn't the only proposed fix to the crisis. From the beginning, the PCIC heard proposals for many possible solutions, some of which were too complicated for members to fathom. One such complex proposal came from Coventree's David Allan. Crawford says he did not understand Allan's idea. Allan was keen to help the committee find a solution and tried to join the PCIC. The door remained closed to him, however, because the PCIC reasoned there could be concerns about conflict of interest. However, no one knew the underlying assets better than Allan and his team at Coventree. He tried to help, offering a number of "messages in a bottle" outlining potential solutions and ideas from his isolated place outside the circle.

Not all of Allan's messages were complex. One of those bottle messages was quite intriguing and got him a meeting with the Caisse. Allan proposed a "goodwill strategy" that would see the PCIC members buy out the smaller investors and leave the negotiations to the major players that had the most money at stake. This buyout approach could have been extended to the small corporate and pension funds as well. Despite the initial interest, no one followed up on it, Allan says. Later on in the negotiations, as the retail investors threatened to scuttle the deal, Allan's proposal would, in retrospect, have been an excellent one. It did, however, have a major drawback: it required a significant amount of cash to fund the buyout. The smaller investors who would have been bought out were primarily clients of Canaccord (and, to a lesser extent, Credential). While a buyout would have solved the retail investor problem, Canaccord did not have the money to pay them.

PART TWO

The Art of the Possible:
Hammering Out a Deal

CHAPTER FOUR

A Proposal Is Born

As smaller investors reeled behind the scenes, the PCIC struggled to find the best way to restructure the paper and make sure everyone was at the table. For the most part, dealers, asset providers, and large investors were willing to back the deal. Crawford, at the centre of the negotiations, faced the monumental task of listening to and balancing everyone's needs and views. To do this, he would need to spend much of his time getting to know the players and working to understand what each wanted out of the negotiations. He reckoned that by gaining insight into everyone's disparate needs, he would stand a better chance of shaping a deal that gave *all* the players something they wanted, if not 100% of their money back on the spot. Central to the negotiations was Crawford's knowledge that their outcome would be shaped by "the art of the possible." It was a phrase he repeated in his conversations with all of the players, a message he used again and again to drive home the fact that the fate of the deal was in their hands. In short, everyone would need to compromise.

Through all the ups and downs of the negotiations, Crawford was confident a deal would be reached, and given the restructuring participants' heightened fear of being sued, he had good reason to believe they were driven to resolve the crisis quickly and quietly. As he pushed committee members to compromise and reach a deal, he pointed to a potentially grim alternative: without the required support from committee members, investors in the trusts would be "on their own," left to battle creditors for any remaining assets in trusts that were being liquidated. While the large investors were certainly able to bring actions in court, it was a dark alternative that everyone wanted to avoid.

No one involved in the PCIC discussions was naive enough to believe that the restructuring would be straightforward. From the outset, they faced monumental challenges, not the least of which was the amount of money at stake in the frozen $32 billion ABCP market. Crawford and his committee faced sixty-six LSS trades, forty-seven series of individual trusts, disgruntled investors sitting on the committee, a lack of transparency in the ABCP structures, stressed-out asset and liquidity providers, and the looming threat that dealers would decide to call for additional collateral from the trusts. This last point was becoming a bigger risk every day. Spreads on CDSs and on super seniors widened as the financial crisis began to spread in mid-October 2007. Those widening spreads would ultimately throw the whole process into disarray. To top it off, the wronged investors at the table had very little appetite for compromise: nearly all of them wanted 100% of their money back and were unwilling to waver.

The trusts themselves were a tangle of disparate, opaque vehicles and trades, all of which had to be restructured. The questionable quality of the assets underlying the frozen ABCP was a huge concern for Crawford and the PCIC. Of the entire $32 billion ABCP market, $7.5 billion was made up of good or traditional cash flow assets, but there was another $1.4 billion in US subprime mortgages whose quality had deteriorated to the point that default risk was soaring every day. Compared to the rest of the pool, subprime mortgage debt was a relatively small amount, and most of the trusts had no exposure to it whatsoever (Ironstone Trust was the only one that had 100% subprime exposure). The subprime assets – Ironstone's included – sported AAA ratings from DBRS. DBRS had accepted the ratings on these assets from its respective US rating agency.[1] A large percentage of the market – about $20 billion – comprised a combination of leveraged and unleveraged synthetic CDOs. And, of course, some of the paper was sound, with CDSs that were AAA rated and unleveraged, presenting no potential for collateral calls.

The worst of the market by far was the highly leveraged LSS portion, which had sixty-six trades that still needed to be negotiated with the asset providers. With the bulk of the triggers based on mark-to-market valuations, the risk of collateral calls was significant because of the massive amount of leverage involved. If triggers were breached, asset providers could call for collateral from the conduits that had issued the ABCP – collateral that the conduits clearly could not produce unless, of course, the dealers were constrained by a standstill arrangement.

In short, the ABCP crisis during the fall of 2007 looked like a house of cards loosely constructed of competing interests: angry investors on the PCIC vied with asset providers, which in many cases also acted as liquidity providers. Both groups feared litigation by clients, pensioners, and shareholders – a fear that kept people riveted to the table throughout even the toughest times. Standstill agreements were pivotal to the process: everyone involved in the negotiations agreed they would not trade ABCP and would not make any draws under existing liquidity arrangements. This moratorium related to all liquidity providers and asset providers; asset providers also agreed they would not make any collateral calls during the existing standstill period, which would expire on 15 October 2007. However, the risk of collateral calls was already playing out among asset providers that had not signed on to the Montreal Accord.

While the standstill agreements were essential to ensure that a market in the notes did not develop, they had to be renewed several times during the negotiations between the PCIC and the dealers, and this was a constant source of tension and stress in the months after the freeze-up. The first standstill agreement, which was part of the Montreal Accord signed on 16 August 2007, was valid for just 60 days, a period the PCIC felt would leave plenty of time to reach an agreement and restructure the market. But as it turned out, it took months to develop a proposal, and those standstill agreements had to be renegotiated again on 15 October and yet again on 14 December.

Negotiating the standstill renewals was never easy. The restructuring was taking place during the tumult that was the financial crisis, and market events were triggering increased spreads and slowing progress in the renewal discussions. For example, it was challenging to renew on 15 October because CDS spreads had increased to reflect the ongoing problems in the US economy in late September and early October. At this time, the signatories to the Montreal Accord agreed to extend the standstill for 60 days as long as the conduits that had issued the troubled ABCP signed the accord. This requirement was met, and the standstill was extended. The S&P 500 Index, which had been coming back from its low on 17 August, started to fall again. And, on 15 March 2008, a standstill had to be renegotiated at the same time as the purchase of Bear Stearns by J.P. Morgan to prevent its bankruptcy. The market had an impact on what was being negotiated, especially the triggers. What saved the restructuring was a clear alignment of interests among all parties: everyone was in trouble and was ultimately better off cooperating than going it alone.

But negotiations became harder and harder as the months wore on. As asset providers rode out market gyrations, some observers of the restructuring suggested that they had made a tactical error by accepting the standstill. Back in August 2007, spreads had left plenty of available collateral – providers could easily have called for collateral if triggers were breached and could have merely liquidated the LSS transactions. Most likely they would have received full value for their swaps. But by accepting a standstill, asset providers had eliminated an important bargaining tool. The trade-off, of course, was significant: in agreeing to the Montreal Accord, asset providers avoided reputational and litigation risk even as they lost their window for a quick and potentially less financially painful exit from the market.

The risk of litigation loomed large over the PCIC, and indeed, lawsuits would become a reality over the coming years, despite everyone's best efforts to avoid them. The City of Hamilton went on to sue Deutsche Bank Securities, which had sold $9.9 million in Devonshire Trust notes to the city. In July 2009, the city retained Henry Juroviesky, whose Toronto firm specialized in class action suits in the financial services industry. Hamilton wanted its money back, and hoped Juroviesky could get it. (As an aside, the City of Hamilton turned around and sued Juroviesky in 2011.[2]) With plenty of aggrieved investors, the threat of more lawsuits was a very real one – and something the asset providers were desperate to avoid.

The CCAA

As the PCIC struggled to put together a solution to restructure the paper and appease angry investors, it also had to figure out a plan for dealing with the looming threat of litigation. It needed a plan that would make sure the final deal didn't fall apart in a barrage of lawsuits. Steve Halperin, a key adviser to the PCIC, had an idea. After speaking to Gale Rubenstein, the solvency lawyer on the legal team, he concluded that an arcane legal tool might just pull the players together in a final deal. The Companies' Creditors Arrangement Act (CCAA) was presented to the PCIC by Halperin in the early days of the negotiations. Enacted by Parliament during the Great Depression, the CCAA allowed for the reorganization of debt rather than a fire sale of assets. The CCAA allows creditors and debtors to negotiate a compromise. It has been used in many high-profile Canadian restructurings, including Air Canada, Stelco, Eaton's, Dylex, and Nortel. It is meant to prevent creditors from pushing debtors into bankruptcy by allowing both groups additional time to reach a compromise in the face of insolvency – a time period called a "stay." There are few hard-and-fast rules with CCAA – as a piece of legislation it is relatively bare bones, and judges have traditionally played a key role in interpreting its use (often quite liberally).

Even so, applying the CCAA to the ABCP crisis would test the limits of the legislation. The trusts subject to the ABCP restructuring weren't even eligible for the CCAA, whose use is limited to corporations. Moreover, the CCAA was intended to help restructure individual businesses, not an entire market. Clearly, applying the CCAA to the ABCP restructuring would involve legal acrobatics never before seen in Canadian legal history. Using the CCAA would also create the biggest and most high-profile hoop that participants in the restructuring would have to jump through: the voting process. The CCAA requires a restructuring plan to be approved by a double-majority of creditors, meaning a majority of voting note holders who collectively own two-thirds of the total value of the affected ABCP. If an ABCP vote by number of note holders failed, the stay would be lifted and the market would tank, leaving investors empty-handed and asset providers running for cover as they tried to liquidate the swaps.

The participation of the major Canadian banks was needed to ensure a successful restructuring, and their participation hinged on a legal release clause being included in the plan. The banks contemplated that the release clause would include an absolute exemption from liability for all matters concerning the ABCP market for *all* players: ABCP conduits and sponsors, satellite trust parties, administrative agents, financial services agents, asset providers, issuer trustees, indentured trustees, Canadian banks, liquidity providers, asset originators, ABCP dealers, issuing and paying agents, note holders, the rating agency, directors, employees, auditors, financial advisers, and legal counsel. Everyone who touched the paper in some way!

There would also be no liability for those involved in the restructuring process. The banks wanted a blanket release that included a release from liability for fraud. The releases were crucial to many on the PCIC who were threatened by potential lawsuits from disgruntled customers and whose financial reserves were limited – in particular, Canaccord and National Bank.

Throughout the restructuring process, the legal releases sought under the CCAA turned out to be the most contentious part of the deal. Putting legal releases in place meant that parties that were instrumental in the ABCP market failure would be completely immune from legal recourse. Unfair? Perhaps, but without those releases, argues Halperin, the restructuring – and hence the market – would have collapsed. Without those releases, banks and dealers would, ultimately, not have provided the cash needed to fund the credit facility that would become a central pillar of the proposed deal. Furthermore, without the "carrot" of legal releases, there would not have been the shift of triggers away from mark-to-market towards a more investor-friendly structure. Obtaining releases meant that the PCIC could achieve what it wanted: a successful restructuring of the ABCP market in Canada. It wasn't perfect, but it did align with Crawford's vision of the "possible."

This controversial use of the CCAA would, as Halperin had argued, pave the way to a solution, as PCIC members gave up the right to sue, thereby lifting the threat of litigation. But it would also open a very large can of worms, creating other problems as negotiations went on, especially when it came to appeasing legions of retail investors, the majority of whom were completely unknown to the people involved in those early months of the restructuring.

CHAPTER FIVE

Putting It Back Together Again

As PCIC pondered the implications of using the CCAA to reach a final deal, it was simultaneously considering proposals for restructuring the actual paper. More than ten different proposals were submitted to the PCIC, asset providers, third parties, and J.P. Morgan. But it wasn't until J.P. Morgan was finally able to access complete information in the database that it could really begin to value each series of the beleaguered ABCP. In the end, the valuations were not market values – rather, they were indicated or theoretical values, based on the best modelling tools available. A market valuation was impossible: the market was illiquid, and if there were observable transaction prices, they most likely did not represent a true value that could be applied to the entire group of assets.

So what did the PCIC do? The original idea was to restructure each trust series separately – the Caisse's original preference. Under this approach, there would be no liquidity calls, and the maturity of the restructured series would reflect the maturities of the underlying assets. The negotiations would have to include changes in trigger levels for the LSSs and some facility to meet potential margin calls. This approach had clear benefits for those investors in higher-quality assets because trusts with traditional assets would be deemed less risky, while those with subprime or LSS assets would be set apart. But for obvious reasons, investors stuck with the more risky assets preferred a pooled approach. Dumping the poor assets in with the less risky ones would spread the risk, with lower-risk entities subsidizing higher-risk ones.

Skeena: A Light at the End of the Tunnel?

As investors wrangled over the best way to approach the restructuring, one deal did manage to get done: on 16 October 2007, Skeena Capital Trust became the first successful restructuring. Arguably the easiest of the trusts to restructure, Skeena had been able to refinance most of its maturing notes during the freeze-up on 14 August 2007, except for $39 million of class A notes that weren't funded. Skeena then issued a market disruption notice to all of its liquidity providers: ABN Amro, BNS, HSBC, and RBC. Positive responses came from ABN Amro, BNS, and HSBC, all of which made funding available for note holders. RBC, however, turned Skeena down, arguing that the liquidity provision had been written before July 2006, when DBRS tightened its requirements for liquidity provision. For RBC, Skeena's problem was not a general market disruption. Under the terms of the contract, two conditions had to be met for a market disruption: (1) two-thirds of non-bank ABCP issuers had to be unable to roll, and (2) 90% of Canadian bank conduits had to be unable to place their paper. The latter was not the case. Without RBC on board, Skeena couldn't roll.

Although it was announced by Crawford on 20 December, 2007, the restructuring of Skeena Capital Trust was done outside of the PCIC by ABN Amro, HSBC, BNS, Dundee Securities (the administrative agent), and Edenbrook Hill Capital (the creator and funder of Skeena). The president of Edenbrook Hill was Mark Adams, who was with DBRS until late in 2005 and was purported to have been the first to use Canadian-style liquidity in third-party ABCP structures. The Skeena deal was ratified by approximately 99% of the outstanding ABCP holders. Under the restructuring, all note holders (A, E, and F), representing about $2.1 billion, received approximately 98.7% of principal and interest as of 15 August 2007. The funds were obtained by the issue of new long-term floating rate AAA-rated notes from a newly established trust. These notes were issued to large financial institutions, with ABN Amro and BNS taking small positions.

For some, the successful restructuring of Skeena was proof that the Caisse's original proposal for a trust-by-trust solution could work. But in the end, Skeena's situation was not representative of what could be done with the other trusts, since most of the underlying trades were more conservative than those found in other conduits. These unique attributes made it possible for ABN Amro and BNS to succeed in the restructuring. What happened with Skeena could not be applied to the rest of the market. In the end, the pooled approach to restructuring won out.

A Proposal Takes Shape

On Friday, 14 December 2007, the day the 15 October standstill expired, Rousseau left a Toronto meeting of investors and asset providers believing that a deal had been done. He returned to Montreal to attend a Christmas holiday party at work. After addressing the group, he sat down to enjoy the festivities. His cellphone rang, and he left the room to take the call. For him, at this point, the festivities were over: the foreign banks had rejected the deal. Why? There are three possible reasons for this change in position. First, the foreign banks believed there was too much legal risk under the structure, since they could still be sued by Canadian banks. Second, there was concern that in the event of a collateral call, some investors would be unable to access the needed liquidity. Third, some asset providers were not happy with the specific structure of the new triggers. Rousseau returned to the room and encouraged his staff to enjoy the party, but it was back to work on Saturday.

On 14 December, a new standstill was put in place to permit continued work on the deal. On the following day (Saturday), the Caisse staff worked on alternative approaches that would satisfy the foreign banks' concerns while at the same time benefiting investors. On Monday, the Caisse presented a revised proposal to the investors' group, which was ultimately agreed to by both investors and asset providers.

The idea was to split the PCIC into two groups: those that had the liquidity to meet collateral calls, and those that did not and so would have to rely on some form of collateral "insurance." The former group would self-insure. The split would clarify the extent of the collateral insurance required as well as its cost. This revolutionary proposal was presented as an approach that would benefit the collective by permitting a deal to be done.

But a number of building blocks had to be put in place before the proposal could be presented to the asset providers. First, the large corporate holders of ABCP had to be persuaded of the benefits of the proposal. As part of the negotiation, National Bank had to explain what it would do for its corporate clients that held ABCP. Second, the collateral insurance had to be found, and the most likely candidates were the Canadian banks. Crawford and Rousseau took on "good cop, bad cop" roles in their discussion with the banks and eventually convinced them it was in not only Canada's best interests but also their own to become involved.

Two days before Christmas, on 23 December 2007, the PCIC released details of the restructuring plan. As the press release stated:

> "After a thorough analysis of a broad range of alternatives, key stakeholders have agreed to support a comprehensive restructuring proposal that addresses the fundamental issues which have affected the ABCP," said Purdy Crawford. "The restructuring reflects compromise and contribution by the dealer bank asset providers and investors, coupled with the support of margin lenders in the event that additional collateral is required to support the structure in the future. In particular, certain of the major investors represented on our Committee have shown leadership and commitment, facilitating our restructuring."

Details included an eight-page term sheet that had been prepared for the investors and asset providers – a bare-bones look at the deal and hardly the comprehensive plan that everyone was looking for from the PCIC. In reality, the hard work had yet to begin.

The document was light on details because the exact structure of the deal had yet to be finalized. But by December, everyone had a general idea of what the restructured market would look like. At the centre of the reformed market were two master asset vehicles (MAVs), which would pool the assets of all the conduits and issue new long-term floating rate notes in exchange for existing ABCP notes. Holders in MAV I – mainly banks and other big financial institutions – would self-insure their exposure to collateral calls in exchange for a higher coupon rate. MAV II participants would rely on what, at the time, was expected to be a $14 billion senior third-party–backed margin funding facility (MFF). Holding the whole thing together was the CCAA plan, which imposed a general stay of proceedings on everyone involved. And everyone who signed on to the plan would also be signing comprehensive releases from liabilities. No one could be sued in the future – not asset providers, liquidity providers, trustees, dealers, agents, or the PCIC.

Clearly, the plan was complicated and full of details that needed to be hammered out. The first major wrinkle was the funding facility for that second MAV. Crawford himself didn't believe a funding facility was needed, given that the restructured notes reduced and most likely eliminated the possibility of a collateral call. Dealers, however, weren't convinced. They wanted assurance that, in the unlikely event of a collateral call, funds would be available to meet it. One proposed solution was to "cross-collateralize" the LSS assets – in other words, a collateral call on one transaction could be met by collateral from other transactions, thereby reducing the impact of a call. The decision to introduce an MFF meant that cash would be available in the event that existing collateral was not sufficient following a collateral call. The MFF was expected to be in the $5 billion to $6 billion range – not $14 billion, as had first been estimated. In taking a position in the MFF, the backers, in essence, were writing an insurance policy similar to the questionable liquidity arrangements but without any doubts how it would be triggered. But this insurance policy meant that investors would have to pay an insurance premium.

The big question was, Who would be the third parties to back the funding facility? The current posted collateral for all LSS trades and unleveraged collateral was approximately $25.7 billion on an LSS notional of $216.8 billion. Even though he didn't think an MFF was needed, Crawford eventually found that putting the required commitments together had become one of the biggest challenges he would face. He started out by approaching everyone involved to put in money to float the facility. By and large, the response was to pass the buck. The most common response, Crawford said, was that he should "approach those institutions that were involved in the market." Those approached by Crawford included DBRS (which clearly could not afford to make the commitment), conduit sponsors, asset providers, and Schedule 1 Canadian banks.

The asset providers ultimately agreed to put up some funds to the tune of approximately $4 billion. That left about a $2 billion difference to make up. The Government of Canada had already made it clear it would not provide any funds to resolve a private sector problem. Crawford's solution was to convince Canada's biggest financial institutions (the Schedule 1 banks) that it was in their best interests to put money on the table. Crawford had to convince and satisfy them that it was a good deal for everyone, including them.

Shortly before Christmas 2007, Crawford approached the Department of Finance and the Bank of Canada for help in convincing the big banks to fund the MFF. Clearly, the banks weren't beating down the PCIC's door to help – perhaps the Bank and the Department together could exert some pressure on them to become involved. After all, RBC had been one of the banks that turned down Skeena's call for liquidity, relying strictly on its rights as it understood them under Canadian-style liquidity.

The MFF would be needed only if the new triggers were breached and the existing collateral was considered insufficient. Moreover, the movement to new triggers was intended to reduce dramatically the likelihood of a breach and a resulting collateral call. And, of course, Crawford didn't even think a collateral call was possible. With no possibility of a collateral call, the question remains: Why would banks, if they agreed to be involved, be receiving a 160 bps standby fee for the MFF, especially when the same organizations were prepared to provide liquidity arrangements under the previous paper for about 10 bps? When adjusted for maturity differences between the average maturities of the LSS transactions, which was less than that of the MFF, the MFF fee was equivalent to 222 basis points. It has been suggested that the 160 bps rate also took into account that, as the swaps approached maturity, they would become less risky: something like an average risk level over time reflecting a high starting risk level and a lower amount as the swaps approached maturity.

Perhaps not taken into consideration in the structuring was an unsatisfying side effect for investors. As the transactions were fully amortized, cash would become available, but it could only be paid out to investors if the members in the MFF agreed to release it. In other words, the cash had to be left in the collateral pool until the assets reached final maturity. Thus, the leverage and collateral risk of MAV II would fall as the collateral value increased. Both of these effects would reduce the risk to the funding facility members. This benefit to the MFF participants was a cost to investors who had their funds locked in the pool and could only access funds from their MAV investments by selling the paper in a market that was not certain to develop.

The deal was a tough sell for one bank in particular – TD. At the time of the market freeze, while TD did have its own ABCP conduits, these did not include LSSs. TD did not hold any of the third-party ABCP. Ed Clark, the bank's CEO, had made a point of publicly announcing that. In the early days of ABCP, he'd made a decision to avoid the non–bank-sponsored ABCP market, believing, correctly, that his inability to understand how it worked meant that the bank shouldn't own any of it. The bank had also reviewed the liquidity arrangements and did not have confidence that they would be available when needed. Clark did state that TD would consider measures to support attempts to resolve the liquidity issues, but he also emphasized that it would not be in the best interests of TD's shareholders to take on added risk for activities in which the bank was not involved. In this vein, the easiest sell was the

National Bank, which had been greatly affected by the ABCP crisis and was an important participant in the negotiations. National Bank, in its role as conduit sponsor and seller of ABCP to investors, had the most to lose in the event that a deal could not be consummated and litigation ensued.

As the banks mulled over their options, Crawford announced on a conference call during the week of 24 December that a foreign bank was prepared to top up the funding facility and fill the gap. This announcement was quickly seized upon by the financial press, which reported that the mystery buyer was J.P. Morgan. Including J.P. Morgan as part of the MFF would have been a serious problem for the restructuring process. As a financial adviser and negotiator for the restructuring, J.P. Morgan would have been subject to a major conflict of interest, for it would be placing itself in the position of an investor. J.P. Morgan agreed to search for an investor for the MFF. An unanswered question is, where did the original press report identifying J.P. Morgan come from? Another way to look at the question is, who in the restructuring process had something to gain from releasing this story to the press?

On 4 February 2008, four of the large Schedule 1 banks finally agreed in principle to participate in the MFF along with National Bank, and a non-binding letter to this effect was received on 13 March 2008. However, certain conditions were attached to their participation. For example, CIBC would conclude an agreement in April 2008 with the PCIC on three CDSs related to two ABCP trusts. This was a precondition of the bank's participation in the funding facility, in return for which, it was reported, CIBC was prepared to provide approximately $300 million. What really enticed the major banks to join the funding facility were those releases promised under the CCAA: the banks would no longer run any risk of litigation for their actions and roles in the ABCP crisis. Another major lure: big profits, and, if Crawford was correct, a very small risk of collateral calls. In a 14 March 2008 report, J.P. Morgan calculated a market-related fee for the bank's standby position in the range of 695 bps.[1] This was significantly more than the 160 bps negotiated in the agreement and appeared as a concession by the banks to expedite the agreement. However, with an illiquid market in the swaps, J.P. Morgan's calculated standby fee was unlikely to be realistic.

Ultimately, TD also joined the MFF. What changed Clark's mind? Aside from the 160 bps fee for providing the funds (a tidy sum), there are two additional theories that have been the subject of speculation. The first involves the long-standing business relationship between

Crawford and Clark, which some believe finally swung the deal in Crawford's favour. Crawford had been CEO of IMASCO and had hired Clark for IMASCO's subsidiary, Canada Trust (which ultimately merged with TD). While consistent with some views of the interconnected nature of the corporate world in Canada, this relationship would, at least, have provided Crawford with access to Clark. The other theory is that governor of the Bank of Canada, Mark Carney, used moral suasion to convince Clark that it was in Canada's, TD Bank's, and its shareholders' best interests to contribute to the MFF. Whatever the reason, TD's participation was essential to reaching a final deal and making the restructuring possible.

In the end, the exposures of the Canadian banks to the MFF were roughly proportional to their exposures to the ABCP market – all except for TD. Given that it had no exposure to ABCP, TD's exposure of $50 million was disproportionally large. Among the Canadian banks, the largest positions were about $300 million each from the Bank of Montreal and CIBC. The Canadian banks invested in aggregate about $1 billion. The remainder of the total MAV II MFF of approximately $5 billion was provided by the foreign banks and asset providers, with Deutsche Bank leading the way with about $2.4 billion. Of course, it was the asset providers that could initiate a collateral call, and as members of the MFF, they would be required to meet such a call, assisted by the other members of the MFF. The asset providers would be paying themselves. This was clearly a bizarre situation, unless the likelihood of a collateral call was remote. The MAV I structure did not use a funding facility – the investors provided self-insurance up to an amount of approximately $8.5 billion. In the end, however, all the banks, including TD, ended up making money on the restructuring of a market they had helped to create and, in the case of those that did not meet legitimate liquidity calls, to destroy.[2]

The final composition of the MFF is presented in Table 5.1.

The Collateral Exposure

Starting with the total of all the new notes, there was a notional amount of LSS swaps of $216.8 billion. This amount is shown in Table 5.2 under the heading "MAV total." Collateral for the overall MAV structure of $39 billion was found as the sum of the current posted collateral for the LSS trades, the unleveraged collateral, and the total margin funding of $13.7 billion. This value is the sum of the final amount of the

Table 5.1. MAV II margin funding facility lenders and exposure

MFF lender	Original commitment (billions Canadian)
Citibank	0.200
Deutsche Bank	2.400
HSBC	0.400
Swiss Re	0.200
Merrill Lynch	0.835
Bank of Montreal	0.300
CIBC	0.300
National Bank	0.112
Royal Bank	0.100
Bank of Nova Scotia	0.200
TD	0.050
Total	5.09

MFF negotiated for MAV II ($5.2 billion) and the self-financed facility of $8.5 billion for MAV I. This left a residual of $177 billion. The resulting leverage in the total MAV structure was 5.5 times (the notional divided by the collateral $39 billion (i.e., $216.8/$39), resulting in a leverage rate less than the average 10% used in LSS structures and dramatically below the 40 times in some of the LSS structures. The residual amount of $177 billion was the amount that would be at risk for the dealers and reflected the potential loss to dealers if liquidation of trades was required under a collateral call and the proceeds were less than the amount of the collateral.

The table also shows the allocation of collateral to the two MAV structures. MAV I is larger than MAV II, and the collateral amounts are in proportion to the relative notional exposure.

Notice that for MAV I, the investors were self-insuring up to $8.5 billion, and the residual of $110 billion was the asset providers' risk in the

Table 5.2. Collateral arrangement in the MAV I, MAV II, and MAV total structures (in billions)

LSS swap notional	MAV I	MAV II	MAV total
	134.2	82.6	216.8
Current posted collateral	10.6	6.6	17.2
Unleveraged collateral	5.1	3.4	8.5
Margin funding facility	8.5	5.2	13.7
Total	24.2	15.2	39.4
Residual	110.0	67.4	177.4
Leverage	5.5 times	5.4 times	5.5 times

event of a collateral call. For MAV II, the MFF would be responsible for $5.2 billion in the event of a collateral call that exceeded the cash collateral of $10 billion ($6.6 + $3.4).

The Restructured Notes

While rumours of subprime mortgage exposure created a panic in the ABCP market, the ultimate source of the paper's downfall was embedded deeply in its flawed structure. Poorly understood liquidity arrangements weren't honoured by providers, leaving conduits holding the bag while participants debated competing views on what a market disruption looks like. Beyond that, however, the ABCP market was built on a fatal flaw: a significant mismatch between the duration of the underlying assets (long-term) and the duration of the paper itself (short-term). While this structure is not unusual – banks use it all the time – the crucial difference is that banks have a strong liquidity provider in the event of a problem: the Bank of Canada. The trusts, however, were left in limbo.

The restructured paper had to resolve both problems in order to create assets that better matched the duration of the underlying securities. Equally important was the establishment of more workable triggers. This change required the negotiation of an alternative to the mark-to-market triggers found in almost all of the LSS structures.

The decision to pool the assets and not structure them trust by trust (the Caisse's preference) meant that trust assets would be thrust together and exchanged for new paper in a totally restructured entity. This had its benefits and drawbacks, depending on what kinds of assets each trust originally held. Pooling all the assets might mean combining gold-plated traditional assets and synthetic CDOs with junk-like subprime assets. For investors who'd originally been stuck holding trusts with risky assets, this was very good news. But for investors whose assets had not been tainted by subprime exposure, this was a maddening possibility.

To fashion new notes, the committee decided to divide the underlying assets in the existing ABCP trusts into two major groups: Group A and Group B. Group A assets included trust series with any synthetic asset exposure – those problematic super senior structures. The trust series included in the pooling could be 100% synthetic or a hybrid – a combination of synthetic and traditional assets. In some instances, the trust series included subprime exposure referred to as "ineligible" assets. These problematic subprime Group A assets were placed in a separate MAV III vehicle, created to house these ineligible assets. Assets in MAV III were not pooled but hived off. A separate ineligible asset tracking note was to be exchanged for each asset series. Ineligible asset tracking notes would have a maturity equal to that of the assets and would have a floating interest rate based on the actual yield of the assets. Thus, some investors in the trusts would be holding these tracking notes. It was hoped that to obtain liquidity in these notes, investors would trade in an over-the-counter market. However, given the high risk of these assets, it was unlikely that the values would be high or that a market would develop.

Since the restructuring process was driven by the goal of fairness, the PCIC also decided to remove trust series with 100% high- and 100% low-risk assets from the pool and move them to MAV III. These assets were the Group B assets. In some cases, the series included only subprime exposure. For example, all assets in Ironstone Trust were based on subprime exposure. The 100% low-risk assets included only traditional assets. Given the disparate risks, these traditional assets and the subprime assets would not be pooled. Group B investors would receive ineligible tracking notes for their trust assets just as Group A investors would receive for ineligible assets. Investors in trusts with only traditional assets would have their paper exchanged for traditional assets tracking notes. For all of the tracking notes, the interest rate floated with the actual returns on the underlying assets. There was no pooling of assets; they were siloed.

Those MAV I and MAV II structures contained the trusts from Group A. The two MAVs were created as tranched sets of securities, with each tranche bearing different risks reflecting their differing exposures to priority of cash flows and principal repayments. In fact, the structure closely resembled that of a CDO.

Investors were free to choose which of the two MAVs they wanted. The large investors who had the financial capacity to bear the margin funding risk (self-insure) chose MAV I. Smaller investors selected MAV II, which was supported by the bank-sponsored funding facility. For both MAVs, LSSs were the largest underlying asset at approximately 67% of the total value.

ABCP investors would exchange their paper for a combination of securities that were tranches of the respective MAV. The notes were referred to as A1, A2, B, and C notes. In fact, all investors would obtain C notes, and almost all would receive a combination of A1, A2, and

B notes. These notes are expected to mature on 20 December 2016, but they could mature earlier if the principal is received and paid out sooner. The A1 notes have the highest priority of payments; the C notes, the lowest. Those C notes are the equivalent of equity, and it is possible that with default losses in one or more of the debt issues underlying the CDS index, the amount of interest and principal recovery for them could be small to zero. In the MAV I structure, the A and B notes are floating rate notes and receive interest at 3-month CDOR plus 30 bps, whereas for the MAV II, the interest is the maximum of (1) CDOR minus 50 bps or (2) zero. The difference of 80 bps compared to MAV I reflects the self-insurance and attendant risk that the investors in MAV I are taking – a risk that the investors in MAV II have removed through the MFF (at a price). If the amount of funds available for interest payments is not sufficient in any period, it is accrued and paid when available – hopefully, in the following period.

For the MAV II A and B notes, the risk that they would not receive any interest payments if the CDOR rate fell to 50 bps or lower was not hypothetical The CDOR rate was about 5% (500 bps) at the end of July 2007, the beginning of the crisis in Canada. The rate had fallen to about 1% (100 bps) by the end of January 2009 when the Montreal Accord was signed. CDOR rates then languished at 40 to 50 bps until March 2010. The first payments to investors under the new structure were made in April 2009. Neither A1 nor A2 note holders received interest payments. The B class will receive no interest payments until interest and principal payment requirements are made in full to the A1 and A2 notes. The C class notes are the residual tranche, whose holders receive payments only after the B class note holders are satisfied.[3]

In Figure 5.1, we provide a schematic of the Group A proposed MAV II structure. We focus on MAV II since information on MAV I is not available and the major difference is the funding in the event of a collateral call.

On the left-hand side are Group A assets that have been allocated to MAV II. Note that in order to be included in the MAV, the trust series have assets that are either all synthetic or a hybrid of synthetic and traditional. These assets are then pooled and become the base for MAV II. The bottom of the diagram reflects the exchange of the subprime assets (ineligible assets in any of the trust series that have been removed from the pool) for ineligible asset (IA) tracking notes. To the right of the MAV II block is a block that shows the exchange of ABCP for the MAV II notes, classes A1, A2, B, and C. These notes have a payment that arises from

Figure 5.1. Group A: MAV II Structure

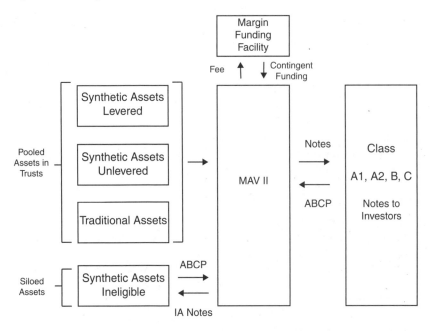

the cash generated by the assets. Finally, there is a block that reflects the margin funding facility (MFF), which has the first claim on cash flows from the ABCP assets included in MAV II.[4] As noted in the diagram, the MFF provides contingent funding in exchange for an "insurance" fee.

It was the PCIC that decided which trusts would be part of the pool and which would not. While the decisions regarding subprime and traditional assets were simple, there are always shades of grey for trusts that have both traditional assets and synthetic assets, including leveraged and unleveraged super senior exposure. For example, Rocket Trust series E had 6% unleveraged synthetic assets. The rest of the series consisted of traditional, low-risk assets. Greg Allderdice, an investor, asked the PCIC during a pre-vote conference call whether it would be possible to place this series in the traditional asset group as a separate tracking note (i.e., to keep it out of the pool). Andrew Kresse responded that a line had to be drawn somewhere and that it had been subject to negotiation by a number of parties in the restructuring. The chosen solution was that, if there was any synthetic asset exposure in the trust, it would be pooled. However, note holders in trusts with a lower proportion of these trades would receive a greater amount of the lowest risk A1 notes. This pooling solution was easy to implement and tried to meet the standard of fairness. Even so, the decision had a significant impact on the investors. If Allderdice could have had a tracking note for his low-risk trust investment instead of having it pooled in the MAV II notes, he would have been better off than with the pooling, in which he received a combination of A1, A2, B, and C notes.

Another goal of the restructuring was to eliminate the risk of collateral calls – something that the standstill agreements had done in the months leading up to the Montreal Accord and during the negotiations. This was probably the most complex part of the restructuring. To achieve this, the trigger mechanisms that could lead to a collateral call on a leveraged super senior trade had to be renegotiated. Since 67% of the assets were LSSs, this was paramount. The committee decided to use "spread-loss" triggers to replace the mark-to-market triggers used in the ABCP. Spread loss triggers require a combination of losses and spread changes to lead to a trigger event. Mark-to-market triggers are far more risky for investors than they are for asset providers because those triggers are set to reflect general market conditions in the CDS market. Thus, if spreads increase in the market, LSS mark-to-market values will fall, potentially triggering a collateral call even if there are no actual losses in the underlying CDS portfolio.[5] The other widely used mechanism they could have chosen would have been loss triggers – that is, triggers that reflect experienced or realized losses (net of recoveries) in the reference companies in the reference index. These are more risky for dealers than they are for investors because the market values of the underlying assets can fall dramatically even while the losses experienced in the index remain below the trigger level. The negotiated position was a spread-loss trigger, reflecting a trade-off between investor and dealer risk. Most important, however, the investor's risk under this trigger would be lower than under existing mark-to-market triggers. This trigger is explained in more detail below.

The choice to replace mark-to-market triggers with spread-loss triggers addressed the risk of collateral calls, because the new triggers would be tied to a matrix of spread values and net losses in the event of defaults. In other words, a collateral call could be made only under certain combinations of spread and loss.

Since this trigger was a major departure from those used in the original LSS structures found in the frozen ABCP, we present an example

Table 5.3. Spread-loss triggers for MAV II notes

	Spread-loss trigger matrix: 10 year CDX7, maturity: 12/20/16									
	Remaining years to maturity									
	9	8.67	8	7	6	5	4	3	2	1	0
Loss %										
0	3.70	3.93	4.34	5.51	6.86	8.96	9.46	10.89	14.86	15.94	17.42
2	3.45	3.65	4.03	5.11	6.34	8.75	9.14	10.78	14.76	15.82	17.30
4	3.19	3.37	3.72	4.71	5.83	7.58	8.88	10.65	14.07	14.57	15.94
6	3.17	3.33	3.66	4.31	5.24	6.64	7.88	9.70	12.86	13.37	14.62
8	2.23	2.48	2.98	4.18	4.90	5.61	6.79	7.42	10.68	12.89	14.04
10	2.05	2.14	2.31	3.87	4.36	4.61	5.92	6.82	10.59	12.73	13.95
12	1.72	1.91	2.29	3.06	3.44	3.62	4.78	6.08	9.92	11.98	13.14

of the spread-loss trigger mechanism using the trigger matrix of one of the underlying indices. The spread-loss matrices presented in the J.P. Morgan Restructuring Report were determined after consultations with DBRS and the asset providers.[6]

In the restructuring document that was part of the CCAA application, six spread-loss trigger matrices were referenced, reflecting spreads and losses on portfolios of high-grade company CDS transactions. Three of the six trigger matrices used the five-year CDS index maturities; the other three used 10-year CDS maturities. The spread-loss trigger matrix applicable to a specific LSS transaction depended on the relationship of the characteristics of the underlying CDS in the LSS structure to the particular CDS index. The assets in the LSS CDOs had characteristics similar to the index used – for example, similar maturity dates of assets in the specific index and similar location of companies whose debt was referenced in the index (North America or Europe). An example is given in Table 5.3, which references the 10-year spread-loss matrix for the CDX7 index used in the restructuring. The matrix values are based on a closing of the CCAA case in April 2008.

Holding loss constant, as the transaction approaches maturity, the spread needed to trigger a collateral call becomes wider, reflecting the lower risk of the transaction as it approaches maturity. For example, if the loss is 0%, a collateral call can still be made, but only when the spread is sufficiently large – say 10.89% (1,089 bps) for the CDS with three years to maturity. Holding years to maturity constant, the spread needed to trigger a collateral call is smaller as the loss rate increases, reflecting the increased risk of the underlying index and the potential loss to the dealer if liquidation is needed. For a six-year to maturity CDS, the spread falls from 6.86% at zero losses to 3.44% (344 bps) if there are losses of 12%. Unfortunately for the investors, the mark-to-market trigger risk was not completely removed, since under the agreement, if there were two spread-loss trigger events, mark-to-market triggers would be reinstated.

Under the spread-loss triggers proposed in the restructuring, the prospect of a collateral call was significantly reduced. With the traditional mark-to-market value triggers, a collateral call could occur if the mark-to-market value of the swap transactions decreased by 56%. By comparison, under the new proposed spread-loss triggers, the equivalent mark-to-market value of the swap transactions would have had to decrease by 80% on average before a collateral call could occur. Thus, when the spread-loss trigger approach was applied, the prices of the underlying swaps would have to fall much more than under a straight mark-to-market trigger. This was of benefit to investors but clearly a negative to dealers.

Finally, spread-loss triggers increased transparency for investors: with mark-to-market triggers, the value of the swap transaction was left up to asset providers to model, leaving conduits and investors unsure whether the models were indeed tilted in favour of asset providers. With spread-loss triggers, by contrast, the triggers were based on public and observable indices of portfolios of CDS spreads and realized losses.

Why did the dealers agree to switch away from the more dealer-friendly mark-to-market approach? It is difficult to look at only one element in the negotiations in isolation – it is the overall outcome that is important. The prospect of obtaining those legal releases should not be underestimated: dealers could see themselves free and clear of future litigation.

Once the PCIC and dealers had agreed on the triggers, they also needed to agree on which specific indices to use in the triggers as well as the actual combinations of realized losses and spreads. DBRS was asked to provide an opinion on the reasonableness of the spread-loss trigger matrices proposed by the dealers and the PCIC. This request was part of the mandate to rate the new notes.

In its promotion of the restructuring proposal that was to be the subject of the CCAA vote, the PCIC relied heavily on the existence of a market for the new notes. In the conference call prior to the CCAA vote, Crawford pointed out that, on accepting the plan, even though retail investors would receive notes and not cash, they could convert the notes to cash. Unfortunately, investors would have to be patient, given that the market could take time to develop. This, among other issues, made the deal a very hard sell.

Distributing the Notes

To meet the criterion of fairness to investors, an appropriate method was identified to allocate the new notes in MAV II to the underlying trusts' investors. To do this, some kind of "value" had to be determined for the paper of each underlying trust. J.P. Morgan, which was assigned this task, estimated the value of all eligible assets in the trusts. With these amounts, it was able to calculate a value for each trust based on its holdings of eligible assets. Once values were obtained for each trust, the allocation required that the trust with the greatest value as a percentage of its notional value (i.e., that with the lowest risk) receive the greatest percentage of the lowest-risk paper in MAV II (i.e., A1). The procedure started with each investor in a trust receiving C-tranche paper as 3% of the notional value. Thus, for every $100 of notional value, each trust investor received $3 worth of C paper. The remaining 97%, or $97 per $100 of notional value, was allocated by formula among the three remaining tranches: A1, A2, and B. In this way, the least risky trusts would receive higher proportionate allocations of the least risky tranches, A1 and A2. As trust risk increased, the allocation of B tranche would increase.

The word *value* in this case isn't value as we would normally refer to it. In other words, it is not an amount that can be obtained in a functioning market – rather, it is a calculated value based on a model, not on transaction prices. Given the illiquidity of the market for the assets and LSS swaps underlying the trusts, market values were next to meaningless and could be influenced by an attempt to sell a large position. Thus, J.P. Morgan's calculations were referenced as "indicative value" to distinguish them from market values.[7]

As an example, consider Table 5.4. Rocket Trust Series A was the least risky of all of the trusts being considered. With its weighted average indicative value of 93.48%, the A1 allocation proportion was set at 97%. This was the highest possible value, since 3% was needed for the C class. The highest-risk trust was Aria Trust Series A, which had an indicative value of 23.48%, reflecting its holdings of LSS. Based on the procedure used by J.P. Morgan, 24.4% was allocated to A1 notes for investors in Aria Trust Series A and the remaining 72.64% was allocated

Table 5.4.

Trust	Indicative Value (%)	Allocation to MAV II securities by tranche (%)			
		A1	A2	B	C
Rocket A	93.48	97.0	0.0	0.0	3.0
Aria A	23.48	24.36	61.97	10.67	3.0

*source: J.P. Morgan report, March 14, 2008

to A2 and B, with a larger allocation to A2.[8] Thus, the procedure used by J.P. Morgan was consistent with the concept of fairness, since lower-risk trusts received higher allocations of the least risky tranches in MAV II.

During this period, companies were preparing financial statements, and those that held ABCP had to deal with the presentation of these investments in their financial statements. With thin trading in the ABCP markets, it was difficult to calculate a valuation for the trusts held by various companies. The indicative values were not intended to be used as market values for financial statement purposes; the companies would have to use established accounting principles to provide value estimates for financial statement purposes. This point was emphasized during a series of meetings with accounting bodies and securities regulators, which caused another slowdown in the process.

CHAPTER SIX

Selling the Deal

The MAVs were constructed to adhere to principles of fairness – the goal of the Montreal Accord. But not everyone thought the deal was fair. Many investors large and small felt that participants should be sued or punished in some way for their part in the crisis. And there were legions of smaller retail investors whose voices were largely unheard by Crawford and the PCIC, and for whom the new notes – with maturities of 9 to 10 years – were wholly inappropriate. These dissenting voices threatened to bring the deal to a crash landing: without their votes under the CCAA, the entire house of cards could quickly fall, with investors being left to the vagaries of litigation. To make the deal happen, the PCIC would have to hear from and somehow appease major dissenting groups: a large and well-organized contingent of retail and corporate investors, the court-appointed ad hoc group of investors, and a second ad hoc committee of retail investors composed of a number of corporations. The latter two committees were opposed to signing the deal, but as ultimately became clear, each had its own distinct reasons.

The specifics of the deal were complex. As a starting point, Crawford organized a cross-Canada "road show" to help present and explain details of the deal to investors in Toronto, Montreal, Calgary, and Vancouver. The plan was to use this tour to communicate to Canadians how it would work, but instead it disintegrated into a venue for aggrieved investors to voice their concerns and vent their anger to the committee.

Retail Investors Rise Up

As banks, pension funds, and investment dealers involved in the ABCP crisis gathered behind closed doors to negotiate a way out of the crisis, some 1,800 retail investors across Canada were left struggling in isolation to get more information. During the negotiations, Crawford insisted that he did not know the full extent of the retail exposure to ABCP. Certainly, he had no idea how many people had been misadvised to put their life savings into this paper as a short-term alternative to risk-free GICs.

For the proposal to succeed under the terms of the CCAA, a double-majority of note holders would have to sign on to the agreement – that is, a majority in number of note holders, holding notes with a collective value of at least two-thirds of the total amount outstanding. This voting requirement gave the retail investors an extraordinary advantage. Though retail holders represented only $360 million of the $32 billion ABCP market, the majority approval requirement meant that their potential votes were more than enough to dominate the voting process and scuttle the deal. The question was, could they band together and make their voices heard?

Brian Hunter became the informally appointed leader of this group. He had spent weeks trying to work things out with Canaccord Capital from the time he received the call from his broker telling him $750,000 of his life savings was now frozen and unavailable. He understood that Canaccord's Maybank was at the table supposedly bringing the voice of retail investors to the discussion. But as time passed, Hunter's trust in Canaccord to represent his interests eroded. In fact, as he learned more about the kind of paper that had been sold to him as a low-risk short-term place to park his money, he had less and less trust in the financial services industry generally. "It turned out the stuff I had was in synthetic CDOs," he says. "I didn't know that." To add insult to injury, the ABCP wasn't generating extraordinary rates of return in exchange for the risk he had unwittingly assumed. "It's funny to learn that I had actually sold insurance contracts to banks."

For its part, Canaccord worked to help affected clients understand the paper they held and how it worked in the wake of the freeze-up. It hired Daryl Ching, an ex-Coventree staffer, to meet with investors like Hunter and walk them through the ABCP puzzle.

But as the summer drew to a close, investors' patience wore thin. Many, like Hunter, saw financial institutions and pension funds at the table, working to hammer out a deal, and they wanted to make sure that retail investors' voices were heard. They didn't want to be left on the sidelines, especially when so much was at stake for them. "I was not willing to lie down on this," Hunter says. By the fall, he was writing letters to everyone he thought could help, including Crawford and Carney, asking them to make sure they considered compensating retail investors whose money had been unfairly put into ABCP, often without their knowledge. Crawford responded to Hunter's e-mail and so too did Carney, who explained to him that the Bank of Canada and the Ministry of Finance weren't getting involved. Hunter's efforts were noticed by many of the players involved. During the process, Hunter became the informal representative of the retail ABCP holders, winning respect from key members of the PCIC and from the investors who were banding together with his help.

Canaccord was offering assurances that retail investors would have a say in the final deal, but Hunter had his doubts. By December, when it was announced he would have to wait years for his money to be returned, he had declared all-out war on the system that had sold him the junk paper. As he saw it, the restructuring proposal was designed to meet the needs of big banks and institutional investors – those that could afford to wait a decade to get their money back. For the hundreds, perhaps thousands, of retail investors, whose life savings were tied up in the paper, this was an entirely unacceptable solution. A furious Hunter began firing up a PR campaign and leveraging his knowledge of other Canaccord clients, with the goal of bringing them to together to ensure that retail investors' concerns were front and centre.

He started by trying to connect with other Canaccord clients. An adviser at the firm had accidentally sent an e-mail to Hunter on which another twenty-one retail investors had been Cc'd instead of Bcc'd. Those twenty-one names became the seeds of a growing list of retail investor contacts. This enabled Hunter to engage in a sort of brinkmanship. He started to get the upper hand as the threat of hundreds of *no* votes to the CCAA proposal became possible.

To expand his contact list (and thereby win more potential *no* votes and establish leverage vis-à-vis the PCIC), Hunter turned to social media. He'd been a Facebook user for some time already, using it to keep in touch with family and friends. In February 2008, he launched an ABCP Investors Facebook page, posting a couple of newspaper articles to start. He didn't expect much from the page, but it eventually became a pivotal point of contact for aggrieved investors, especially once Hunter began drawing attention to the page while speaking with major newspapers such as the *National Post* and the *Globe and Mail*.

Soon, Hunter's name was everywhere, and so was the plight of ABCP's retail investors. He compiled a long list of investors willing to show up and vote *no* to the proposed restructuring, and that list gave the group real power to wield. "It was about brinkmanship," he said. "The more investors they thought had banded together, the more likely that we would vote the proposal down and they wouldn't get the deal or the releases they needed." PCIC members started to get nervous.

Hunter's organizing efforts with disgruntled retail investors would culminate in the outcry and widespread investor rage unleashed on Crawford and his team when they set out to explain exactly what was in the proposal to restructure the Canadian ABCP market.

The Road Show

In early January, just after the proposal was released, Crawford announced his intention to arrange a cross-Canada tour to explain it to investors in Vancouver, Calgary, Toronto, and Montreal. His goal was to inject some transparency into the process in order to quell the fears of investors who'd been involved in the ABCP debacle. But those fears would not be quelled.

Crawford prefaced each meeting by saying that the committee had not created the crisis but was working hard to fix it. That did nothing to calm frustrated investors who had seen their savings frozen overnight. He soon became the target of their months of pent-up anger and disappointment and their mounting fear. Crawford tried in vain to explain the details of the plan, so much of which was incomprehensible to most of the people in the audience. "This thing is thicker than the Bible," griped one aggrieved investor who attended the road show in Vancouver. To investors, only one thing in the three-hundred-page document was clear: the Montreal Accord didn't include a plan to give them back their money any time soon.

The Vancouver meeting was particularly rancorous. Hundreds of investors came to jeer and heckle the committee as it made its presentation in a hotel ballroom. Those who had been banded together by Hunter's Facebook page wore pink carnations to identify one another. During the heated meetings, Halperin insisted that "I am just the messenger here" as the crowd vocally balked at his description of the legal releases the committee was seeking from all investors. "It was something we had no choice about," he said. Tensions were high, and Crawford finally said to the crowd, "I think there's sunshine over the hill for you." Knowing there was no explicit plan to make small investors whole, Crawford was clearly moved by the stories he heard. He must have also realized the extent of retail holdings of ABCP and the power of these many small retail investors to scuttle the deal. A new plan would have to be developed, one that would see those investors taken care of.

Investors had a right to be angry, and some were enduring extreme hardships without their money. Crawford was receiving threats, hate letters, and a host of pleading calls from desperate retail investors. Some investors were giving in to despair – by now, there had been one suicide and several threats of suicide. One lawyer for the Ad Hoc Retail Investors Committee, Arthur Jacques, said he had talked to one investor who called him threatening to jump off a bridge in Vancouver. Crawford himself was receiving e-mails from suicidal investors who had lost their family's savings or their own life savings – e-mails that he dealt with personally. According to some, it was the news of these suicides and suicide threats that finally pushed the committee to address the needs of retail investors. The committee began seeking a workaround that would see those investors paid instead of being folded into these 9- and 10-year notes.

Meanwhile, lawyers were beginning to gather around the road show, eager to sign up clients for class action lawsuits. Juroviesky and Jacques were two such lawyers. Though from different firms, they would team up to help ensure that retail investors got a decent deal, working in tandem with Diane Urquart – an independent consultant who had been hired by some ABCP note holders as a financial adviser – to understand and scope out exactly how the paper worked and how it had been sold to the retail investors.

Hunter, for his part, is cynical about the lawyers and consultants who stepped in to help retail investors, making good money in the process. He maintains that he spent eighteen unpaid months of his life trying to get his money back, and all the while, many others were making small fortunes from the sufferings of the retail investors.

After the road show, the PCIC members put pressure on Maybank to fix the mess. During one meeting, Crawford turned to Maybank and asked point blank what he planned to do. Clearly, the retail investors had to have their paper bought back, but Canaccord did not have the money to do that. It needed a partner with deeper pockets – a firm such as the Caisse or National Bank. This was a replay of Allan's goodwill strategy as had been proposed early in the PCIC negotiations.

On 9 April, Canaccord stepped up with a relief program for its beleaguered clients. The deal would see the firm buy back $138 million worth of ABCP at 100 cents on the dollar from clients with $1 million or less invested in the paper. The buyback was contingent on an approval of a market restructuring under the CCAA. In other words, only a majority vote would ensure that retail investors got their money back. Within days of Canaccord's announcement, Credential announced that it would provide similar relief to its retail clients. When all was said and done, investors like Hunter went along with the proposal. "I just wanted my money back," he says.

Hunter's persistence and his ability to rally together other investors impressed Crawford, who has said that in his mind, Hunter was almost a member of the committee. The two men came to respect and even to admire each other under the immense pressure of the negotiations.

Yet the question remains: Who helped Canaccord buy out most of its clients' ABCP holdings at par? Had Canaccord tried to do it on its own, the firm would most certainly have failed. It has been said that the Caisse stepped up as the "mystery investor," since it had the most to lose in the event of no agreement. Unfortunately, while we heard this and other rumours about the buy-out and who was involved, we could not find any sources that would speak to us on the record and confirm it.

The Ad Hoc Committees

Court hearings associated with the CCAA application offered a platform for other groups of disgruntled investors who felt that the committee's proposals fell well short of their needs. One was the court-appointed Ad Hoc Committee Investors' Group, which included the GTAA. A second and smaller ad hoc committee was composed of smaller corporate ABCP investors, such as Transat and Jean Coutu – referred to by some in the PCIC as the "renegade group." Both used the hearings to voice their concerns with respect to the releases. This smaller group was also known as the Ad Hoc Retail Investor Group. The former group wanted to introduce "carve-outs" for certain items, while the latter wanted the releases to be removed entirely and to get their money back.

The conference calls to the initial Ad Hoc Committee in the fall of 2007 were not helpful. Several of the investors participating in those calls still wanted to remain anonymous, possibly due to their embarrassment over purchasing what had turned out to be poor investments. The callers would participate without knowing who was on the call. As one member of the Ad Hoc Committee noted, "after the call, you wondered why you even picked up the telephone to listen." All of the participants were groping in the dark. By the fall of 2007, the members of the Ad Hoc Committee were being asked to sign various extraordinary trust resolutions, as noted in an article by the legal counsel to the Ad Hoc investors committee. These were considered sufficiently problematic regarding the ability to take legal recourse in the future that many ABCP holders refused to sign them.

From the beginning, the Ad Hoc Committee placed little trust in the process and in some of the firms involved. It hired its own independent financial adviser to help the members understand the structure of the new paper and to interact with the J.P. Morgan representatives preparing the final relative valuation document. Throughout, the Ad Hoc Committee had its doubts about J.P. Morgan, which, so it felt, was talking only to the "big bucks" investors at the table and putting its own needs first. So instead, it turned for help and guidance to Price-WaterhouseCoopers, whose fees were ultimately paid, in part, by the PCIC (or, as a practical matter, from the ABCP cash flows). In the end, it accepted J.P. Morgan's report and valuations.

The main goal of the Ad Hoc Committee in voicing its dissent and hiring an independent adviser wasn't to crater the deal. It knew that without a deal, litigation would be possible. Rather, the goal was to ensure that investors didn't end up with nothing. By banding together and questioning the PCIC's actions, it created an element of doubt, thereby making its power to scuttle the deal felt throughout the process. Some members of the group also wanted to change the releases, which under the restructuring would protect from litigation all parties associated with the distribution and sale of ABCP and the efforts of the PCIC.

On 22 April 2008, a motion was brought before Justice Campbell seeking to have the scheduled 25 April meeting adjourned, the proposed releases declared overly broad and illegal, and the corporate and individual note holders treated as separate classes for voting purposes. At that hearing, Ad Hoc Committee members argued that releases should be included but with a carve-out for fraud, gross negligence, and wilful misconduct. The boards of the companies that were members of the Ad Hoc Committee, it was argued, would not be prepared to approve any restructuring without the fraud carve-out. This position, it was hoped, would result in some further movement by the dealers and asset providers in terms of paying out cash to members of the Ad Hoc Committee. In fact, some of the institutions that were on the retail investors' committee left to join the Ad Hoc Committee before the original plan was voted on. However, the Ad Hoc Committee had to walk a fine line. At the same 22 April hearing, the so-called "renegade" group was arguing that no releases should be given. If this argument were accepted, it would kill the deal and pave the way to litigation.

Justice Campbell denied the motion, ruling that the 25 April vote should proceed as scheduled and deferring consideration of the releases until the ultimate fairness/sanction hearing, which would take place after the vote. He also declined to reclassify the note holders for voting purposes. That too, he noted, would require an unacceptable postponement of the vote. It would also grant an effective veto to some note holders that would likely ensure the plan's defeat – an outcome, he said, that he did not think was "a desirable result for any of the parties associated in any way with the plan or for those who participate or observe the financial markets in Canada."

Thus, the 25 April vote was held as planned. Then, following the vote, on 12 and 13 May 2008, the original CCAA sanction hearing was convened. By this time, the membership in the Ad Hoc Committee had grown from fourteen parties holding approximately $1.2 billion in ABCP to thirty-one parties holding approximately $1.8 billion. The jump in ABCP holdings was the direct result of a migration of retail investors who held in excess of the $1 million upper limit imposed on the Canaccord and Credential conditional buybacks of ABCP paper.

The Ad Hoc Committee members didn't have the clout of the retail investors, even though they had far more money invested. They certainly had the ability to annoy and disrupt the process, but since they were not a separate class of investor, they simply didn't have the voting power of the more than 2,000 retail investors, each of whom was entitled to a vote and thus retained the ultimate power to derail the deal.

As for the renegade group, it argued strongly against releases – and the members wanted their money back, 100 cents on the dollar. By taking a hard line, they hoped to get a better deal. They didn't really care if their actions cratered the deal, since they believed they could do better in a subsequent round of negotiations or through litigation and potentially a settlement. The Ad Hoc retail group believed that, as unsophisticated investors, they should be treated in the same way as retail investors: they should get their money back in full.

Another example that suggested that a litigation threat was a successful approach arose from Barrick and Sun Media, which held Ironstone Series B notes, which were valued by J.P. Morgan's report at approximately 13 cents on the dollar of face value. There were $750 million of notes outstanding in both Series A and Series B. The series had 100% subprime exposure through US CDO holdings. The companies argued that they had not been told of the subprime exposure when they purchased the paper. Barrick Gold threatened to sue CIBC, and it is reported that, ultimately, political pressure was applied on CIBC by Finance Minister Jim Flaherty.[1]

Some of these ABCP note holders subsequently disappeared from the battle. A good number, such as Jean Coutu, Transat, Aeroports de Montreal, and Société générale de financement du Québec were from a Montreal group of companies represented by James Woods of Woods LLP. This group of companies represented approximately $1 billion is outstanding ABCP. In its 2008 annual report, Jean Coutu's management stated that "the Company is assessing its alternatives and recourses to receive the full value of these ABCP." These companies settled directly with their bank, National Bank, and were able to obtain lines of credit or loans on a non-recourse basis using their ABCP as collateral. This was an attempt by National Bank to maintain a positive relationship with its clients, and those settlements ultimately reduced the size of the retail Ad Hoc Group. However, the group continued to appear at subsequent hearings and appealed Justice Campbell's sanction order.

The Ad Hoc Committee ended up playing a positive role in the process by pushing for a fraud carve-out in the releases, without jeopardizing the restructuring plan. It did not end up increasing payouts to members, however, and many have since sold the notes they received through the reorganization in the secondary market, thus removing them from their balance sheets altogether.

At the end of May 2008, Rousseau announced that he would be leaving the Caisse at the end of August to take a position with Power Corp. He was replaced on the PCIC by Claude Bergeron, the Caisse head of legal affairs, who had been working on the file. At that time, the economic indicators were consistent with an improving market. The S&P 500 had increased from its low in March, and CDS spreads on the 10-year Investment grade North American Index had decreased from their high of about 200 bps in March to a value of about 100 bps at the beginning of May. Rousseau thought that the worst was over and that it was a good time to move on. There were no indications of problems, and the Lehman Brothers disaster wasn't on anyone's radar screen that month.

Putting the Paper Together

With apparent clear sailing in the markets, the group turned its attention to appointing an administrator – a firm that could complete the restructuring by pooling the assets and issuing the tranched securities. The chosen firm would have to invest and reinvest the collateral until its release to the waterfall and also oversee the financial statements, giving notice if any triggers were breached. But perhaps its most important task would be to generate any possible revenue for investors during the process.

A five-member subcommittee of the Investor Group was struck to identify a set of eligible companies and make a recommendation on the final candidates. Thirty-five proposals were submitted, one of which was from Coventree. Who better to deal with the structures, after all, than a company that had arranged them and that knew what assets were included. Brendan Calder, chair of the Coventree board at the time, prepared the bid and believed his firm was in the running. Being selected as administrator would have staunched somewhat the bleeding at Coventree. But hiring Coventree would have sparked an outcry from those investors who were troubled that the firm would gain financially as administrator from a crisis it had helped create or at least facilitated. Coventree's proposal highlighted to the subcommittee issues that would have to be included in any final contract, including indemnity arrangements.

The subcommittee whittled down the original list to five proposals, and a "beauty contest" was held. The participants in the process explained to us that in the end, the final choice was between two firms – Blue Mountain Capital LLC, a US private investment company that had the right experience, and BlackRock, a more acceptable choice to participants, which had less experience in the area. Coventree was not one of the two considered. The PCIC went with BlackRock, which had tendered the lower bid and was ultimately recommended for administrator in February 2008. The specifics of the contract later changed somewhat through renegotiations with BlackRock based on the services to be provided and the amount of risk BlackRock was prepared to accept. This negotiation proved to be extended and frustrating, at least for some members of the PCIC. BlackRock's fee was set at 4.5 basis points per annum (0.045%) on 20 March 2008, to begin at the plan implementation date. In the January 2009 Administrative and Management Agreement, the fee is 5 bps (0.05%), paid quarterly. That fee is applied to the outstanding MAV II notional balance. The notional balance is reduced as any notes are terminated.

Yet in the end, the committee did turn, at least indirectly, to Coventree for help by hiring TAO Admin Corp., a company staffed by five former Coventree senior employees: John Abraham, Eugene Fong, Chris Pocock, Manuela Popescu, and Kenneth Toten.

TAO had been hired to deal specifically with the traditional asset structures that were part of the deal. The firm was helpful on two fronts: it provided a smooth transition from Coventree conduits to MAV III notes, and it brought with it a deep knowledge of the deals. The hiring of TAO by MAV was described by DBRS as non-standard for an administrator of the new note structure. The concern was that because TAO had been hired directly, the MAV and its note holders would be exposed to TAO risk – TAO was a thinly capitalized entity that did not meet DBRS's requirements for administrators in AAA transactions on a stand-alone basis. BlackRock noted that it would, in limited circumstances, step in and administer the assets if TAO was unable to perform its duties. TAO was paid a set of fixed fees and a 10.5 bps annual fee payable quarterly on the assets of each seller program,[2] plus a retention fee designed to ensure the company remained staffed with key employees. Since the structures were still uncertain and there could be risk, the indemnity reserve fund was designed to protect the employees in case of error.

Getting It Rated

The PCIC's next task was to obtain a rating, or preferably two ratings, for the tranches of the new paper. Ratings were of paramount importance for committee members, especially given the less than stellar investment analysis they put into the original ABCP. The new paper turned out to be much more transparent than the original trusts when it came to identifying risks and clearly stating triggers, but ratings were still required. Banks could hold unrated paper, but the regulatory capital charges on unrated paper would be so punitive that it is likely they would not invest. Also, many pension funds require minimum ratings to hold fixed income securities.

But who would rate it? US rating agencies wouldn't touch it: they had refused to rate the LSS swaps with mark-to-market triggers. In fact, none of the agencies in the United States or Europe were interested in rating the product. The PCIC was politely told by agencies that they were not looking at new products at the time.

One reasonable explanation was that there was no upside for the agencies to rate the paper. They had never rated Canadian third-party ABCP to begin with, they had limited experience with spread-loss triggers, and the transaction was complex. All of these factors suggested high levels of risk. High risk, along with the possibility of being sued, was not a winning combination. Plus, the timing was off. Many rating agencies were already beset with serious legal problems in the United States because of their ratings of the subprime paper.

In the end, the PCIC turned to DBRS – the only agency that would step in and rate the paper.

CHAPTER SEVEN

The Plan Gets Approved

After a disastrous road show and much last-minute negotiation, the final hurdle was cleared: on 25 April 2008, an overwhelming majority of creditors approved the plan, with only 3.6% of note holders, representing $1.2 billion, voting against it. Despite the support, however, the plan could only become effective under the CCAA if it was sanctioned by an Ontario Superior Court judge, following a hearing. That hearing was an opportunity for the dissenting note holders to persuade the court that, despite the overwhelming majority vote, the plan was neither "fair" nor "reasonable" – the legal standard that courts apply when evaluating CCAA arrangements.

The final sanction hearing began on 12 May 2008. The presiding judge, Colin Campbell, had issued the earlier 17 March order providing for the 25 April note holders' meeting as well as the "stay" order, the initial order under the CCAA aimed at giving the parties "breathing space" to negotiate a restructuring by staying any existing proceedings and preventing the commencement of any other proceedings or enforcement processes against the conduits, their trustees, and various related parties. At the 12 May hearing, the Ad Hoc Committee took particular aim at the sweeping legal releases that had been included in the plan. The court recognized the unusual nature of this particular arrangement. The releases were especially important to the banks and asset providers, and those parties were crucial to the deal because they were providing lending facilities that were essential to the arrangement. Much more was at stake here than the fate of a single company, Campbell observed. Here, there was "risk to the whole financial community." Desperate times, in other words, might well call for desperate measures.

But did the comprehensive releases, even in light of these extraordinary circumstances, simply go too far? The argument put forward by the Ad Hoc Committee opposing the broad releases was based on an alleged lack of information: without a claims process (i.e., a process that would allow the court to figure out who could sue whom, for how much, and on what basis), the court could not confidently say what was being released. Also, at such an early stage, the investors did not have enough information about the marketing, sale, funding, and sponsorship of the ABCP market to know what they were releasing. Given this lack of information, the investors argued, a blanket release was not reasonable. They suggested that there should be a carve-out from the releases to leave claims of fraud, gross negligence, and wilful misconduct on the table for aggrieved investors possibly to pursue in later proceedings.

Other investors advanced a more technical legal objection. The CCAA, they noted, did not expressly permit releases for most third parties (i.e., parties other than the CCAA debtor itself). The CCAA explicitly authorized only one type of third-party release: a release of claims against a debtor company's directors, subject to specific limitations. Investors argued that since the CCAA referred to one, and only one, type of third-party release, it must be inferred that the CCAA forbade any other type of third-party release. This argument evoked a well-known if somewhat simplistic approach to statutory interpretation known by the impressive and lawyerly Latin maxim *expressio unius est exclusio alterius* (the expression of one thing is the exclusion of another).

Between 12 and 13 May, Campbell heard arguments focused on objections to the blanket release from liability. Then on 16 May, he decided to adjourn the approval hearing and send the parties back to the drawing board to revisit the release question. As he explained, "I am not satisfied that the release as part of the plan, which is broad enough to encompass release from fraud, is in the circumstances of this case at this time properly authorized by the CCAA, or is necessarily fair and reasonable. I simply do not have sufficient facts at this time on which to reach a conclusion one way or another."

Campbell was clearly troubled by the prospect of releasing all claims for fraud. Such a release was very different from a release from negligence claims. Yet comprehensive third-party releases of claims were said to be crucial to the arrangement. Without them, it was feared, the entire arrangement might break down. Aggrieved plaintiffs, who had agreed to release specific parties from claims, might later attempt to make an "end run" around those releases. For example, a plaintiff who had expressly granted a release to a bank might then sue a dealer who in turn might launch a third-party claim or seek indemnity or contribution from that same supposedly "released" bank. Plaintiffs would, in other words, be able to do indirectly what they had expressly agreed not to do directly: extract payments from parties to whom they had granted a full release.

Worse still, these cross-claims and third-party claims might trigger a huge litigation chain reaction. Campbell was not persuaded, however, that fraud claims necessarily presented the same threat of triggering this sort of disruptive litigation cascade as negligence claims. Fraud, after all, is highly personal in nature, so the justification for unlimited third-party releases for fraud was less compelling.

The Carve-Out

The parties eventually responded to Campbell's directions by producing a narrowly crafted fraud "carve-out" to the blanket third-party releases. The proposed carve-outs would work this way. First, in any subsequent fraud claim brought by a buyer of ABCP, only the ABCP dealers that sold the specific third-party ABCP that was the subject of the claim could be sued. There was a further limitation: a claim could be pursued only where fraudulent representations had been made directly to the investor by the dealer's representative at the time of sale. In other words, as Campbell acknowledged, it could actually happen that, "as drafted, the permitted fraud claims would preclude recovery in circumstances where senior bank officers who had the requisite fraudulent intent directed sales persons to make statements that the sales persons reasonably believed but that the senior officers knew to be false."

Moreover, the fraud carve-outs limited the amount of damages a successful plaintiff could receive. Total damages in any permitted fraud claim could not exceed the principal amount of the notes together with interest, less any amounts distributed as part of the plan. Finally, any investor who chose to launch a fraud claim would open him or herself up to possible counterclaims by the defendants. Perhaps due to these formidable legal barriers, no such fraud claim has yet been commenced as of the writing of this book.

Campbell was satisfied that the releases, with the narrow fraud carve-out, were "rationally related to the purpose of the plan and necessary for it." He approved the plan – an approval later upheld by the Ontario Court of Appeal.

Some of the investors did try, unsuccessfully, to persuade the Court of Appeal to follow a different line of reasoning based on a 1993 decision of the Quebec Court of Appeal. The Quebec court had held that the CCAA – as worded in 1993 – simply did not permit third-party releases as part of an arrangement. The CCAA was amended a few years after that decision with added language expressly permitting releases in favour of a debtor's directors, but otherwise made no mention of permitting third-party releases. If Parliament had wanted to reverse the Quebec decision in its entirety, the argument ran, then surely the new language added to the CCAA would have expressly permitted all third-party releases – not just releases in favour of directors.

Justice Robert Blair, for the Court of Appeal, rejected this argument. In his view, everything about the CCAA indicated that it should permit third-party releases: the flexibility of the CCAA, the act's broad definitions of "compromise" and "arrangement," and the twin protections afforded by the double-majority voting requirements and the requirement of court approval, all supported the conclusion that third-party releases could be permitted in appropriate cases. He rejected the argument that, by adding wording to the act permitting releases in favour of directors, Parliament had somehow intended to exclude the granting of releases to any other third parties. He did acknowledge that releases that extended to some claims of fraud might be "distasteful." However, the legal position was clear: these releases were authorized under the CCAA as long as they were reasonably connected to the proposed restructuring. Campbell had ruled in the lower court that, in this case, the releases were indeed a necessary part of the arrangement, and Blair deferred to his finding on this point.

The overwhelming support of the note holders was also a compelling factor. Campbell's trial-level judgment emphasized the 97% majority vote obtained from the note holders. He conceded that it was impossible to satisfy every affected party, but he noted that "[t]he size of the majority who have approved [the plan] is a testament to its overall fairness." On appeal, Blair quoted this statement with approval. Some investors argued that allowing most fraud claims to remain within the release provision was unfair and unreasonable. Blair noted, however, that there was no legal impediment to granting the release of a pre-existing claim in fraud and that "parties are entitled to settle allegations of fraud in civil proceedings ... and to include releases of such claims as part of that settlement." ABCP investors must be understood to have evaluated the costs of giving up their right to sue, and balanced those costs against the benefit of having a restructured market in the notes.

The Supreme Court denied leave to appeal the Court of Appeal's decision on 19 September 2008, and the Plan Implementation Order went into effect on 12 January 2009.

Unanswered Questions

Even following court approval of the arrangement, however, a few interesting legal questions remained unanswered. For example, would the Ontario court's approval of the controversial releases ensure their effectiveness across Canada and around the world? Hy Bloom, a Montreal-based businessman, who had purchased $12 million of ABCP notes, tested the Canada-wide effectiveness of the order. He commenced a court action in the Quebec courts against National Bank, which had sold him the paper, arguing that the third-party releases were not effective in Quebec. Justice Richard Wagner of the Quebec Superior Court (as he then was) flatly rejected his claim and dismissed his suit.

But what if an investor simply went to the United States to commence a private action against one of the parties to get around the third-party releases? There was indeed a real concern that dissenting investors would try to get redress in the United States. EYI, the court-appointed monitor, pre-empted this manoeuvre. They petitioned the US Bankruptcy Court for the Southern District of New York to effectively adopt the plan in the United States – including the controversial third-party releases – under Chapter 15 of the US Bankruptcy Code. To do this, EYI sought to have the Canadian CCAA proceedings recognized as a "foreign main proceeding" under the US Bankruptcy Code and to have the Ontario courts' sanction orders enforced in the United States. EYI's application succeeded.[1]

Accounts of the process that Crawford went through to obtain approval for the plan demonstrate that it was not easy for everyone affected to swallow. People wanted to retain the right to sue those who they believed had wronged them and caused them to lose their investments. However, there was an element that counterbalanced the argument that they ought to be left with this avenue of redress: their assumption of risk in making the initial investment. This consideration dealt the banks the necessary card of compromise. The court acknowledged that, in any restructuring under the CCAA, both sides would likely lose out in some way. Both sides had to compromise in order to come to the best solution. So when investors recognized this reality and voted for the plan, the court did not, and was not required to, look behind their vote to examine their motivations.

CHAPTER EIGHT

It Almost Falls Apart

While negotiations on the substance of the deal were over, everyone was still engaged in negotiations during the summer on the "papering" of the deal – a slow legal process that involved putting into writing all the minutiae of the agreed-upon deal terms. By this point, investors should have been "icing the champagne," preparing for a big closing party. That was not to be. Storm clouds were gathering in the form of the global financial crisis. In early April 2008, spreads in CDS markets started to increase and reflect volatility. (This foreboding is visible in the spread figure we presented in chapter 2.) Everyone involved in the papering discussions began to get very nervous about the impact that increasing spreads could have on the agreement.

Their worries were well founded. By the end of August 2008, five-year investment grade CDS spreads had increased to approximately 170 bps, reflecting uncertainty in the credit markets. Then in September, a series of events showed that the risks in the marketplace weren't limited to a few companies – rather, they were systemic risks related to the entire global economic system. Furthermore, these risks were no longer related to the liquidity crisis but had become a true credit crisis.

Too Big to Fail

As a precursor to the spate of massive failures to come, Indy Mac, a large savings and loan company in the Los Angeles area and a large mortgage originator specializing in Alt-A mortgages (mortgages that are typically larger and of a quality above subprime), was faced with a large number of non-performing loans. The company required a capital infusion that was not forthcoming. Following a bank run starting on 26 June 2008, Indy

Mac was placed into receivership by the Office of Thrift Supervision on 11 July 2008.

The next casualties were two government-sponsored enterprises, Fannie Mae and Freddie Mac, which reported sharp losses for 2007 and for the first quarter of 2008. On 7 September 2008, Fannie Mae and Freddie Mac were placed under conservatorship by the US Treasury. The previous "soft" government guarantee of their financial obligations was converted into a hard guarantee with the backing of their insurance by the full faith and credit of the US government.

Following significant losses from subprime exposures in 2007, Lehman Brothers Holdings Inc. filed for Chapter 11 bankruptcy protection on 15 September 2008. The Lehman bankruptcy was the largest bankruptcy filing in history.

As Lehman failed, Bank of America decided to acquire Merrill Lynch, and parts of Lehman were ultimately sold to Barclays PLC and Nomura Holdings. After the Lehman bankruptcy, volatility increased and values fell in the stock market, credit default swap spreads widened, and T-bill yields decreased dramatically as investors fled to safety. Spreads reached 240 bps on 16 September 2008.

Then, on the same day, the Federal Reserve offered insurance giant AIG assistance in the form of an $85 billion loan secured by AIG assets in exchange for an equity position just below 80%. AIG was a major player in the CDS market. Following a debt rating downgrade, AIG was required to increase its collateral on CDSs and credit default obligation trades. AIG was unable to meet this collateral requirement and faced a choice: bankruptcy or bailout. The Federal Reserve reluctantly provided AIG with support.

A week later, on 25 September 2008, Washington Mutual was placed in receivership by the Federal Deposit Insurance Corp., resulting in the largest US bank failure in history. The receivership was the culmination of a bank run in which approximately $16 billion in deposits was withdrawn over a 10-day period. The Washington Mutual banking subsidiary was sold to J.P. Morgan for $1.9 billion.

The shattering of global financial markets was reflected in increases in the volatility index over this period, with growing CDS spreads and reductions in yields on Treasury bills and high-quality debt. The Canadian volatility index (MVX) – known as Canada's "fear index" – went from a value of 18 in March to a peak value of 88 in December 2008 as equity investors responded to roiling markets.

For the PCIC, this period should have been the home stretch of the final deal. But rising CDS spreads had ushered in a nightmare scenario.

With the increasing spreads came heightened risk to the dealers as well as a higher probability of collateral calls and difficulty in renewing standstill agreements, both problems for the ABCP investors. As the spreads increased, the Caisse and Deutsche Bank entered into discussions about a possible deal where, in the event of collateral calls, the Caisse would get back its original collateral and replace it with Caisse paper. The result would be that the Caisse would put the financial instruments on its balance sheet but would not have to face the task of finding liquidity to meet the collateral call. Caisse management continued to believe that the problem was not the quality of the underlying assets in the ABCP, but the overall market. However, the decision to take on the assets would result in a very risky position for the Caisse. These discussions between Bergeron of the Caisse and John Pipilis of Deutsche Bank did not lead anywhere, but the concept would re-emerge later in the process.

As the broader global crisis spread, the risks to both sets of parties in the restructuring mounted. Dealers suddenly wanted to reduce their risk by shortening or even removing the duration of any standstill agreements. These agreements, which were measured in months in 2007, became weekly and daily in late 2008 as spreads reached their highest levels and increased the threat of collateral calls.[1] The need to renegotiate standstill arrangements with dealers resulted from the CCAA proceedings, which ordered a stay of proceedings against CCAA debtors (preventing the enforcement of claims against them) but not against the synthetic derivative contracts. Those contracts were considered "eligible financial contracts," and, under s. 11.1 of the CCAA, as it was then worded, no order could be made "staying or restraining the exercise of any right to terminate, amend, or claim any accelerated payment under an eligible financial contract." This put intense pressure on the PCIC to successfully renegotiate daily standstills.

The Caisse Has Second Thoughts

But did the shorter standstills truly reduce dealer risk? If the dealers made collateral calls that were not met and tried to sell the swaps in the market, the values obtained would be dramatically less, and the collateral wouldn't be sufficient to cover their losses. Although the dealers could sue for the differential if permitted in the CDS contract, they would likely be unsecured creditors in the event of a default of the trust and receive cents on the dollar. But the real problem in the deal stemmed from problems at the largest ABCP investor – the Caisse. The pension fund's troubles were beginning to reach far beyond ABCP. Rousseau, the architect and negotiator of the Montreal Accord, having announced in May 2008 that he would be leaving the Caisse, departed on 1 September 2008, as the credit market situation was deteriorating. His replacement, Richard Guay, had been the chief investment officer of the Caisse. He was aware of the transactions that were causing trouble and faced intense pressure to fix the situation.

The Caisse reported a $40 billion loss (a −25% rate of return) for 2008. Some of the losses were the result of mark-to-market accounting; even so, the impact on the Caisse both financially and politically was significant. That loss didn't just reflect the pension fund's ABCP investment – it also showed the cost of currency-hedging strategies in various portfolios in the face of a declining Canadian dollar. Also, equity markets had decreased dramatically from October onward. Adding to this problem was the impact of the Quebec Mondial product, an index futures strategy using Quebec and Government of Canada bonds as collateral. Over this period, the benefit from global diversification disappeared as all global stock markets moved in the same direction: down. Big negative stock returns meant margin calls on the futures contracts. With all the Caisse's short-term liquidity tied up in ABCP and therefore frozen, the Caisse was in a serious bind. It didn't have the cash to fund the margin calls if required to do so. The value of liquidity calls that had to be met was potentially large – approximately $5.7 billion.

Following Lehman's bankruptcy in late September, Caisse management became understandably nervous about the possibility of future collateral calls; spreads on five-year CDS had increased from 169 bps on 1 September to 230 bps on 16 September 2008, when Lehman filed. As Bergeron, the Caisse's negotiator, noted, the Caisse was ultimately "the match that started the fire after Lehman." The "fire" was a movement to renegotiate the deal. And the Caisse was the most important party to the CCAA process – without it, there would be no deal.

Bergeron notified Crawford that the Caisse was having second thoughts on the current deal. Its concerns revolved around triggers, the need for liquidity in the event of collateral calls, and the value of underlying CDSs, especially in the event of a forced liquidation in an illiquid market. In addition, all MAV I investors were becoming concerned about the deal. Crawford was not prepared to renegotiate the transaction: it had been a long and difficult road to this point, and renegotiations were unacceptable.

While driving to Quebec City, Guay and Bergeron discussed the Caisse situation and potential solutions to it. Bergeron asked Guay whether it would be a good idea to call John Pipilis, Deutsche Bank's main negotiator in the ABCP negotiations. They wanted to find out if Deutsche Bank was open to a renegotiation of the deal approved under the CCAA. Bergeron had had previous discussions with Pipilis and believed he had developed a good relationship with him. From the tenor of the discussion, Bergeron felt that Deutsche Bank would be compelled to change something in the deal to get it done. Rising spreads were not a good thing for asset providers either.

What followed was a meeting with Deutsche Bank, Merrill Lynch, and HSBC, the main dealers in the ABCP transactions. The discussions concerned the possibility of the Caisse obtaining an option to put the transaction onto its own balance sheet – the same approach discussed in May 2008 – under specified situations. As Bergeron noted, this attempt to avoid liquidity calls would be highly risky. Bergeron began discussions with the Caisse board regarding this "put" in order to have a "Plan B" ready in the event that the deal could not be renegotiated.

The MAV I investors were unanimously of the view that there was now added risk to them and to those that relied on the funds invested with the members' organizations, and that renegotiations were essential. They were ready to "go to war" to obtain changes to the deal. The added risk concerns were observed among the MAV II investors as well. Of course, since the Caisse was a major lender to the MFF of MAV II, without the Caisse, there would be no deal. If the Caisse were to get cold feet, the MAV II investors would be left the most vulnerable.

The underlying argument for a renegotiation from MAV II's pension fund investors was that, as fiduciaries, they were required to consider pensioners' interests and did not want to be in a position post-deal with risks that were higher due to the possibility of collateral calls, even with spread-loss triggers. The rising spreads added fuel to their concerns. In addition to the collateral-trigger problem, investors were loath to add any more money to the pot. Throwing good money after bad was not a good investment decision even for parties that had bought ABCP without doing due diligence.

Negotiations were difficult not only between the PCIC and the dealers, but also among the members of the PCIC. This dynamic was not surprising, given the different goals each was trying to achieve, the amount of money each had at stake, and the personalities of the individual representatives. When the renegotiation of the original deal became a strong possibility, the PCIC needed to have an acceptable negotiating position. Of course, time was of the essence, since the ABCP solution had been in the works for an unreasonably long time.

Claude Bergeron was given the task of dealing with the other members of the PCIC. The most difficult to deal with was the Montreal-based Public Sector Pension Plan (PSP). As it had been from the beginning, PSP was very tough in its negotiations, and now it delayed the process. Fortunately, Bergeron knew some of the people in PSP from their time working at the Caisse, and this helped him move the process forward. It has been suggested that PSP's intransigence was only fully removed by the intercession of the federal government, which sponsored the pension plan. The government wanted the deal to move forward.

The PCIC members now wanted to change the deal completely. Some investors returned to arguments made in the negotiations for the initial deal in 2007–8, (i.e., "give us all of our money back now or eliminate all triggers"). This request had been a non-starter in the first set of negotiations and was completely off the mark in the financial environment faced by the dealers in late 2008 and early 2009.

The no-trigger part of the request was more realistic if it referred to the elimination of mark-to-market triggers and their replacement with loss-only triggers. The investors were concerned that, with the spread-loss triggers under the current deal, there could be a collateral call even if there were no losses and a substantial increase in spreads. Given the volatility of CDS spreads in the current past, the latter was a serious concern. At the time of the discussions, there was a standstill in place, so no collateral call was possible.

A good example of the problem that may have provided fodder for the investors in their subsequent negotiations occurred on 10 October 2008. The Royal Bank of Scotland, which had not signed the Montreal Accord and was not bound by the standstill, delivered a collateral call that day to a satellite trust of Structured Investment Trust III (SIT III) relating to a $230 million leveraged CDS. The call was for $60 million of collateral to be provided by 3 November 2008. The call was based on a spread-loss trigger, and when spreads subsequently narrowed, the collateral call was withdrawn. However, based on the specifics of the contract for this transaction, any subsequent trigger event would be based on a mark-to-market trigger, even though the first trigger event was rescinded. This flip over to a mark-to-market trigger in the event of previous collateral calls was what all PCIC members feared; they believed the new structure would not protect them as CDS spreads widened. Furthermore, with an illiquid market, the asset providers could value the transactions based on their models – a valuation method that likely would be in the best interests of the asset providers and not the investors.

Table 8.1. LSS Providers in the restructuring of the Canadian non-bank ABCP market

Bank (asset provider)	Number of transactions	$ Notional (billions)	$ Initial funded collateral (billions)
Deutsche Bank	31	50.4	4.2
Merrill Lynch	13	8.5	0.7
UBS	3	6.5	0.2
HSBC	6	6.4	0.6
Swiss Re	3	5.5	0.3
Citibank	3	4.3	0.3
CIBC	2	0.9	0.09
Royal Bank of Canada	2	0.2	0.07
Total	63	82.7	6.5

Source: J.P. Morgan Canadian ABCP Restructuring Overview, January 2009

The dealers were not prepared to give in to this pressure. With losses mounting towards the end of 2008 and spreads increasing dramatically, many dealers were prepared to take a loss on unwinding the LSS transactions rather than give in to the demands. They relied on the concept that "a deal is a deal." Negotiations continued during this period, since the failure of the deal would expose dealers to litigation and potentially large losses. In addition, the foreign banks (all of them – see below) were crucial in the negotiations as LSS asset providers.

Deutsche Bank was by far the largest asset provider in the LSS transactions area. Of the sixty-three transactions, Deutsche Bank had thirty-one, representing $50.4 billion, or 61% of the total notional value. The average attachment and detachment points for all of the transactions were 19.6% and 64.2%, respectively, and the average maturity date was June 2014. However, the longest maturities were for CIBC, HSBC, and RBC: 20 December 2016. Table 8.1 displays the notional amounts of LSS outstanding by asset provider. The initial amount funded reflects the funds invested as collateral. A comparison of notional amount to funded amount shows the extent of leverage in the structures. For example, on average, across all asset providers, leverage was 12.7 times (i.e., 82.7/6.5). Some asset providers were particularly highly leveraged. UBS, for example, had a leverage rate of 32.5 times.

During all the turmoil, discussions, and renewed threats of litigation, the plan termination date – the final extension of 30 December 2008 – was fast approaching. Clearly, time was running out, and the pressures to get a deal through were enormous.

With the final deadline looming, a meeting was held on 10 December 2008, in the Toronto offices of the PCIC lawyers, Goodmans. Dealers, PCIC representatives (including the Caisse, Crawford, Halperin, and Kresse), and representatives from the Bank of Canada and the Department of Finance met for two days as all parties felt the pain and struggled to get something in return. The art of the possible was back on the table.

During the meeting, Bergeron presented a new solution: Why not change the nature of the restructuring by introducing the concept of the "put"? This idea was familiar to some of the dealers at the meeting. The "put" was the Plan B that the Caisse considered and held in reserve in May 2008.

All investors in MAV I, MAV II, and MAV III would be presented with this option. As he presented this proposed solution to the dealers, Bergeron saw in their faces looks of surprise and even horror. Both Bergeron and the dealers knew that any new approach to the restructuring would drag out the process for at least a year. The dealers just wanted to get the deal done. The global financial market problems were becoming an overwhelming issue for them.

Whether or not the introduction of the "put" concept was a bargaining ploy is unknown, but its introduction refocused the discussion on a revision of the current deal. On 11 December 2008, the PCIC announced that an agreement-in-principle had been reached that would result in improvements in the restructuring plan. The announcement stated that the process to complete the restructuring would start on 19 December 2008 and be completed in January 2009. The proposal contained two key elements. First, there was to be an initial moratorium period (fourteen months) in which there could not be any collateral calls. Next, some spreads in the spread-loss triggers would be widened and one spread-loss matrix would be eliminated.

It was also clear that the MFF, as originally structured, had become inadequate. CDS spreads had increased to levels over 250 bps – the highest level attained over the negotiation period had been 327 bps on 5 December 2008 – and there was significant volatility in the spread levels, as shown in chapter 2. An increased funding facility was needed. As a first pass, the dealers wanted the increase to be in the amount of roughly $90 billion and to not include any exposure to them. Ultimately, they agreed to an additional MFF of $9.5 billion, which would rank senior to the other MFFs and would be called upon as a last resort.

While the fourteen-month moratorium and the change to the spread-loss triggers helped investors, this new "senior funding facility" (SFF) benefited asset providers and gave them more comfort that, in the

event of collateral calls, there would be adequate proceeds from liquidating the swaps as well as access to the funding facilities if needed.
And they would not be providing margin funding to themselves.
But the big question was how to fund this additional facility. The Caisse
and National Bank were not prepared to put in more money. With the
well seemingly running dry, the Caisse was, at this point, adamant that
government(s) had to come up with some funding or it would walk away.

The PCIC was also being pressured by corporate and large retail
investors with more than $1 million of ABCP that did not qualify for
the initial payouts. These investors had approved the CCAA restructuring in April 2008, yet they still hadn't received any of the frozen funds
and had been without access to their money for approximately sixteen
months. In addition, many retail investors were waiting for the approval
of the restructuring so that they could access their frozen funds. At the
Caisse's urging, the first order of business for the PCIC was to finally get
the federal government on board and get the deal done.

While the feds had been interested in helping behind the scenes and had
attended PCIC meetings as observers, their active participation in the specifics of the deal, including providing funds to a new funding facility, was
not assured. At least one member of the PCIC gave a presentation to an
unnamed government group on the importance of the new funding facility.

Progress, however, was slow, and the negotiations appeared to have
been taken out the hands of the PCIC and taken over by Finance Canada
(under Macklem) and the Bank of Canada (under Carney). At this point,
negotiations on the investors' side needed a strong hand. The process was
stalled, spreads were very high, and the risk of the negotiations falling
apart was significant. At one point, negotiations deteriorated to the point
where the foreign banks left the table and PCIC members were left sitting
on their hands, waiting for a resolution of the standoff. The feds had taken
over negotiations with the dealers, and the PCIC was on the sidelines.

A signal that there would be greater involvement of the Bank of
Canada and the Department of Finance was the hiring of Credit Suisse
First Boston as the government's financial advisers near the end of the
process when it looked as if the government would be needed to realize a successful outcome to the negotiations. Credit Suisse's expertise
in evaluating the plans, the size of any additional funding facility, and
the consequences of doing nothing would be useful in the discussions
of and negotiations for the restructuring.

The first issue that held up the negotiations between the PCIC and
the dealer group and that led to the entry of the government into the

negotiations was the request from the PCIC that the government finance the new funding facility to the tune of $9.5 billion. The original request for this "senior funding facility" (an additional layer of insurance in the event of a credit crisis, referred to as the SFF) was reviewed by federal Finance Minister Jim Flaherty and the finance ministers of Ontario, Quebec, and Alberta – the provinces affected by the ABCP issue.

During this turbulent period, Crawford approached Flaherty to ask him whether the government was willing to become involved in the senior funding facility. Flaherty replied, cryptically, "We are engaged." Since politics has its own vocabulary, the interpretation of "engaged" was elusive. Would the government step in or would it not? For Crawford, it was a good sign and the first and only time he would speak directly with Flaherty.

This new SFF financing was brought up as a discussion issue at a meeting of finance ministers in Saskatoon on 17 December 2008. However, some provincial finance ministers had already signalled their opposition much earlier. A spokeswoman for Quebec's finance minister, Monique Jerome-Forget, said the province had done its part by financing collateral through the Caisse in the original plan. Furthermore, Quebec was unwilling to further expose taxpayers to additional risk. A spokesperson added: "We feel the federal government has the tools and is the best-positioned with the Bank of Canada [to help out]." The province of Alberta was equally unhelpful, citing that it had already done enough and had supported ATB Financial by increasing ATB's borrowing limit and changing regulations that would permit ATB to hold the restructured notes. Alberta's finance minister stated it as follows: "Federally regulated banks had a major role in the origins of this problem, so we think it's really one for the federal government to address."[2]

Getting It Done

The federal finance minister was already on record saying that the ABCP crisis was a private problem that should be resolved without government financing. This position was an important political statement, given the amount of taxpayer funding that had been used in the United States and other countries to bail out banks and the financial system. Was the ABCP market also "too big to fail"? The answer came on 17 December 2008, from Carney, who said publicly: "Canada can afford to see the failure of a proposed rescue of $32 billion of ABCP that has been frozen for sixteen months."

It was a clear message to the dealers that they had best get back to negotiations to resolve the deal. On 18 December 2008, the dealers, including Deutsche Bank, Merrill Lynch, and Citigroup, came back with a lightly veiled threat delivered by their counsel, Peter Howard of Stikeman Elliott. Howard stated that they would pull their support for the plan if the deal, including the $9.5 billion additional backstop facility, wasn't signed by 22 December 2008 (the following Monday). He added that, barring a resolution on Monday, an option for the dealers was the "unthinkable" – walking away from the restructuring and potentially issuing collateral calls.

The behind-the-scenes work began in earnest. Not only was a deal needed to get provincial and federal support for the additional margin facility, but the dealers also had to agree to accept the changes to the original deal, some of which were to the benefit of the investors in ABCP. The Bank of Canada and the Department of Finance obtained input from a few sources on the new funding facility's size: Was the $9.5 billion value correct or was it too much? Clearly, the Bank of Canada and Department of Finance advisers gave their opinion, as did others, including senior officers at the National Bank and Credit Suisse. The advice was that this new margin facility, the SFF, did not have to be the $9.5 billion requested by the dealers. Moreover, and most important, any funding by the Government of Canada would be purely symbolic – the facility was an attempt by the dealers to ensure that the feds would be at the table in the event there was a serious problem after the deal's completion. The level and volatility of CDS spreads during the latter part of the negotiations signalled the potential for serious problems. Based on the CDS spreads and the presence of the feds at the table, negotiators believed that the dealers would accept a much lower SFF amount to get the deal done.

Still, the question remained: How was this lower, but still significant, amount to be funded? This was the last hurdle that needed to be cleared; it was also where politics entered. The provinces had to be part of the solution, since they were involved in its benefits as well as its risks. The prime minister and the premier of Quebec had a difficult time resolving this issue. Quebec being the province where more than 50% of the ABCP was held, there was discussion about the relative contributions of Quebec and the federal government. On 20 December 2008, Carney discussed this issue with Premier Jean Charest.

There was very slow progress in gaining the federal government's agreement on the SFF. Canaccord played a role in resolving the issue when it hired lobbying firm Hill + Knowlton to work on the file and convince the political decision makers that financing the funding facility was good politics. Michael Coates and Lou Riccoboni (then at Hill + Knowlton), together with Canaccord's Scott Davidson, worked on gathering the relevant people in the Prime Minister's Office and the Department of Finance to talk through the issues associated with the proposed solution. At a time when the federal government was dealing with many problems, including the global financial crisis and its impact on Canadian and global banks, the importance of resolving the ABCP debacle had to be made clear. However, it is likely that the agreement of Charest was the crucial element.

By supporting the SFF with a federal guarantee (not a US-style bank bailout), the federal government could ensure that 2,000 investors wouldn't lose their money. This industry-led solution would involve little risk exposure for taxpayers. That was a very good political trade-off. In the end, the government agreed to back the facility and the deal was done.

On 22 December 2008, it was announced that a $4.45 billion backstop facility had been created: $3.5 billion was to be provided through a SFF funded by the government of Canada and the provincial governments of Quebec, Ontario, and Alberta, which had provincially owned entities that held ABCP and the Caisse. The funding participants were to receive a fee for the insurance they provided through this facility. The added $1 billion would come from the original MFF providers on a pro rata basis. The guarantee amounts by participants in the SFF are presented in Table 8.2.

On 24 December 2008, the terms sheets were presented that included the changes in spread-loss triggers, the removal of one spread-loss matrix, and the moratorium on collateral calls – changes that were intended to help the investors and provide some relief to the dealers.[3] But even with these changes, the Caisse was still concerned there could be a breach of a spread-loss trigger without an actual loss or even with a small loss. It wanted a longer moratorium. In response, the moratorium on collateral calls was extended from 14 to 18 months, thus ensuring that, even if there could have been a collateral call with increased spreads, there would not be a collateral call for one-and-a-half years.

The changes noted above were the direct result of intervention by the Bank of Canada and the Department of Finance. Together, Carney and Macklem used persuasion, both subtle and overt, and numerous telephone calls to cut a deal with the dealers regarding proposed changes

Table 8.2. Senior Funding Facility (SFF) ($ billions) – Total and by MAV

Entity	Total	SFF-MAV I	SFF-MAV II
Canada	1.30	0.67	0.63
Alberta	0.30	0.15	0.15
Ontario	.25	0.13	0.12
Quebec	1.3	0.67	0.63
CAISSE	0.3	0.15	0.15
Total Facility	3.45	1.8	1.7

Source: Senior Funding Facility, government commitment letter, 28 December 2008

in the contract. At the time of these negotiations, global credit markets were roiling in response to the collapse of US banking institutions. Had the deal failed, a flow of CDS assets would have been released into the CDS market and further instability could have resulted.

At this point, there was international cooperation among the major central banks to deal with the credit crises in their markets. Canada was an important player in this area and in a strong position to put pressure not only on some of the foreign asset providers but also on the central banks in the countries in which they were domiciled. With its large presence in the LSS transactions and its lead role in the negotiations for dealers, Deutsche Bank (and its CEO, Josef Ackermann) became the main target of Bank of Canada persuasion. Ackermann would also be sensitive to any concerns raised by the Bundesbank, Germany's central bank. Since Deutsche Bank's presence in Canada was a relatively small part of its global operations, it's unlikely it would have been moved by threats to its continued operations in Canada. Any strong intervention would have to be from the Bundesbank.

The Bank of Canada also wanted assurances that it would not be asked to step up and provide funding at a cost to Canadian taxpayers, although it would be available as a funding facility on paper. The SFF was a form of insurance that was being provided at a price to the investor group. The hope – and perhaps through the construction of the facility and the restructuring of trigger arrangements, the *reality* – was that the guarantee would be of low risk. To this end, the following provisions were established.

First, the maturity of the SFF was 19 months following the closing of the deal, and the moratorium on collateral calls would extend for 18 months from the date of the agreement. Thus, the government would be exposed for approximately one month to a potential collateral call that could exceed the capacity of the junior funding facility. This exposure

Table 8.3. Revenues and Expenses for MAV II (CAD$ billions)

	July 2014	July 2013	July 2012	July 2011	July 2010
Total revenue	16.9	41.0	45.1	46.3	26.7
Administrative costs	0.7	1.7	1.8	1.7	1.8
SFF	2.0	5.0	4.9	4.7	4.9
MFF	5.0	12.7	14.8	14.3	15.0
Interest A1	3.9	9.8	9.6	10.1	0.7
Interest A2	2.9	7.5	7.3	7.7	0.5

Source: Blackrock MAV II website: www.blackrock.com/X/CMAV2/public/index.html

to funding a collateral call was symbolic: if there was a major problem in the market following the agreement, the Government of Canada would have to be at the table to help resolve it anyway.

Second, the standby fee for the facility was to be 119 bps per annum, payable until 20 December 2016, the maturity date of the longest LSS swap. Thus, the government would be receiving payment while being exposed to minimum risk.

Like all of the participants in the SFF, the government would in effect be clipping coupons. From the perspective of the governments and organizations that had signed on, the SFF was essentially a risk-free bond.[4] If it was used, the fee would be either the Canadian Bankers Acceptance (BA) rate or LIBOR, depending on the form of the advance. Finally, the facility was senior to the other MFF and would be called on only under very dire credit market circumstances that in all likelihood would not materialize. With the increased CDS spreads moderated by the revised triggers, the moratorium on collateral calls, and the short maturity of the SFF, the Department of Finance had shrewdly negotiated a good deal for the participants and taxpayers and was able to move the deal forward.

Government intervention in the ABCP crisis might have been driven by the growing global financial crisis and fears about the stability of Canadian financial markets; that said, those who ultimately stepped in to backstop the SFF will profit handsomely.

Backstopping the restructured notes was profitable for everyone involved. Banks that agreed to provide funding for the first MFF took on slightly more risk than the SFF (even though collateral calls were highly unlikely) and were paid 120 bps for their commitment.

To indicate the payments to the funding facilities, we present Table 8.3 (above), which shows revenues and costs associated with the MAV II notes for three-month periods ending in July for years 2010 to 2014.

Look at July 2012. The total revenue, which depends on the notional amount outstanding and the level of CDOR, is $45.1 billion. Remember that the revenue will fluctuate based on CDOR. From this revenue is deducted administrative costs and the two funding facilities: the SFF amount is $4.9 billion, or about 11% of revenue, and the MFF amount is $14.8 billion, or 33% of revenue. In July 2014, the revenue is down dramatically due to the reduction in the notional amount outstanding following the unwinding of some of the swap transactions.[5] More about this in chapter 9, where we discuss the activity in the market for MAV notes. The SFF and MFF, which are based on the notional amount outstanding, are lower, but as a percentage of the revenue, they remain relatively similar to the July 2012 levels.

J.P. Morgan Threatens the Deal

Throughout the restructuring, J.P. Morgan had been a crucial player in developing the models for the MAV structures, generating the relative valuation estimates, and negotiating with dealers and margin funding parties. These services did not come cheap. While the total amount they were paid is unavailable, based on contractual arrangements and information in the CCAA ruling, it appears that J.P. Morgan received in the range of US$87 million. More interesting, however, is exactly how it ended up charging that amount and the wrangling that led to it – wrangling that became yet another threat to the final deal.

It all began on 1 October 2007, when J.P. Morgan was officially hired as the financial adviser. The original terms of engagement spelled out an end date that hinged on the deal closing on 31 December 2008, with no obligation to provide further support beyond this termination date. There was an initial instalment of US$10 million; two additional payments were provided on closing the deal (or by February 2009, whichever came first). The second and third instalments would see J.P. Morgan taking in $17 million and $6 million, respectively; the latter was referred to as a "discretionary fee." The contract was straightforward, except for an additional services section not well defined in the contract that some participants on the PCIC had assumed was a success fee. But this wasn't clear, and in fact, conflicting interpretations of that section turned out to be an interesting wrinkle in the deal.

As the restructuring dragged on, J.P. Morgan's costs grew and the quick job that perhaps had been expected turned out to be much more complicated – and billed as such. With 2008 drawing to a close, no deal in place, and credit spreads ballooning, J.P. Morgan presented a bill that included a startling US$23 million charge for added services in line with the additional services section in the contract. When asked by the PCIC to explain the hefty and unexpected charge, J.P. Morgan claimed it reflected its success in finding participants for the MFF and the SFF.

If the bill was not paid, J.P. Morgan would withdraw its services, leaving the PCIC – and the deal – in limbo. After all, according to the contract with the PCIC, J.P. Morgan had no obligation to continue working after February 2009.

The bill hit the PCIC hard, and it generated disagreement among members, at least one of whom didn't think J.P. Morgan was entitled to the money. One member was upset enough to threaten to walk away from the deal – a credible threat, given that negotiations were still fluid and final agreement had yet to be completed.

The reality was that J.P. Morgan had the PCIC over a barrel. If it wanted to keep J.P. Morgan at the table (and ensure that the deal finally went through), it would have to pay the bill and negotiate yet another contract for continued services. To add salt to the wound, J.P. Morgan sent two additional letters to the committee on Christmas Day 2008 reiterating the conditions of the official engagement letter and confirming the PCIC's agreement to pay the $23 million fee for additional services.

This payment was to be made on the earlier of the closing of the restructuring plan or 1 January 2010, which was the termination date for the new engagement letter. The letter concluded with a segment confirming the end of the contract. The second letter provided the specifics of the new engagement. Payments were to be US$5.5 million per month for January and February 2009, paid in advance. The same monthly payment was also required beginning 1 July 2009, and ending the earlier of the closing of the plan or 1 January 2010. Payments were for advisory services going forward. These letters were a Christmas gift that showed participants in the restructuring that investment banking firms have a lot of experience playing hardball. Without a viable alternative, the PCIC signed.[5]

On 12 January 2009, the PCIC announced that Justice Colin Campbell of the Superior Court had granted the plan implementation order and that the implementation of the plan was imminent. It was expected that the plan would be implemented on 16 January 2009, although the actual implementation date was 21 January. Apart from the changes noted above, the features of the structure detailed in the March 2008 restructuring report remain the same.

PART THREE

ABCP Afterlife:
How Has the Market Performed?

CHAPTER NINE

Evolution of a Liquid Market

I believe that the implementation of the plan will lead to a healthy secondary market in the new notes over time and thereby provide investors with liquidity.

Purdy Crawford

The goal of the restructuring was never to make investors whole. That would have required at a minimum the payment of principal and any interest forgone during the restructuring process. Retail investors were off the table when it came to getting their money back until they banded together in a vocal effort to assert their power, threatening to scuttle the restructuring. For the rest, however, the best they would ever get was the face value of the replacement securities at the maturity date, June 2017, which was the first payment date on the maturity of the last LSSs.

Barring repayment in full, the realistic goal of the restructuring was to establish a viable secondary market in the MAV II notes. This would give investors the option of selling their holdings in the individual notes (A1, A2, B, and C) or in the collection of the notes called a "strip,"[1] or holding them to maturity.

The investors in the MAV notes weren't there willingly. From their perspective, an original investment in ABCP short-term notes had become a long-term illiquid investment with uncertain payouts based on the fluctuations of the CDOR rate. A well-functioning secondary market would give investors a chance to get out and recoup at least some of their losses, depending on market conditions – a fact emphasized by Crawford in discussions with investors during the restructuring process. It would provide liquidity for the many investors not covered by the retail investor buybacks or by the offline transactions of corporations with financial institutions. Without a well-functioning liquid secondary market in the restructured notes, the 18-month restructuring journey would be only a partial success, and investors would be required to hold the new paper until maturity.

But while the idea of a liquid secondary market was great in theory, ABCP still bore the stench of the original tainted notes, and potential investors in the secondary market had big questions about whether an investment in the restructured MAV II notes could actually be profitable.

Performance of the Market

The question remains: Has anyone actually made money by investing in the restructured notes? Some certainly have. In July 2014, Bloomberg reported that Canadian fund manager Fiera Quantum noted that one of its most profitable investments was the Canadian ABCP Fund. Fiera Quantum is the adviser to the fund. The original MAV II securities in the fund were purchased in 2009 for 65% of their face value. Subsequent purchases and sales during the period from the fund launch on 5 November 2010 to 31 December 2014 resulted in a 59.5% return[2] – a hefty gain over the Merrill Lynch US High-Yield Index over the same period. On 18 January 2013, Fiera Capital announced an agreement to purchase the ABCP fund as one of a number of funds of GMP Capital Inc. Since its inception, the ABCP fund has traded more than C$7.5 billion of MAV paper on behalf of the unit holders – about C$3.9 billion purchased and about C$3.6 billion sold for a current net holding of C$300 million.

The market has done well, but it was slow taking off. From 1 January 2009 until the end of November 2009, trading was almost non-existent. The price for A1s was about 52 cents on the dollar, for A2s about 44 cents on the dollar. No one was interested in purchasing the notes in the market, possibly because most didn't understand what was in them. But despite these obvious hurdles, the price improved – markedly so. As Figure 9.1 shows, the A1 securities had hit a high of 90.25 cents on the dollar by March 2013 – more than double the original value over the four-year period. But the market hasn't been without volatility; economic conditions impacting credit affected the credit default spread value between 2009 and 2013 (see Figure 9.1). For example, on 4 August 2011 there was a very large sell-off on Wall Street, followed the next day by an S&P downgrade of US government debt. In June 2012, Moody's cut the credit rating on the

Figure 9.1. Historical MAV note pricing and CDX spreads: 19 November 2009 to 19 March 2013

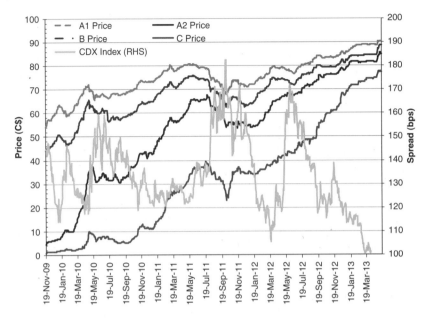

Source: Sterne Agee, Bloomberg

major banks, and later in the month, real GDP growth estimates were revised downward from the poor growth estimates noted earlier at the end of April.

The CDX9 Index[3] spread in November 2009 was about 145 bps (see the right-hand vertical axis); the index fluctuated towards a high value in June and July 2010 of about 160 bps. Spreads then decreased, but increased markedly late in 2011 to about 160 bps. Spreads were volatile in 2012, and by mid-March 2013, they had fallen to about 100 bps. But MAV securities' prices have risen steadily, despite the ups and downs.

The market is also rational, meaning that MAV II note prices at any given time reflect their relative risk in the waterfall, with A1s at the highest price and Cs at the low end. During the same period, the A1s had a higher credit rating than the A2s, and their prices reflect this difference. So, while all prices increased over the period (dipping in late 2011 and then recovering), the largest percentage increases occurred for the C notes, which rose from a level of one or two cents per dollar of face value to a value of about 77 cents in March 2013. These C notes were originally considered to be a giveaway due to their perceived risk as a result of their position in the waterfall and the concern about default in the reference companies in the credit default swaps. But as of March 2013, the C notes have performed strongly, reflecting, among other factors, their reduced default risk and the reduced maturity of the notes. The strip price as of this date is at its highest level, $88.94.

Why are prices only shown up to March 2013 when the market has continued to operate? The reason is very simple: liquidity over the period to the end of 2012 improved, but it was not until 2013 that this market was disrupted by a novel idea – an idea that would and did improve liquidity dramatically for the original and subsequent investors in the MAV notes. The improved liquidity and the reduced risk of the underlying LSSs in the MAV notes led to significant increases in prices. As of March 2015 the prices were $97.50 for A1s, $94.50 for A2s, $94.00 for Bs, and $85.00 for Cs.

The idea was simple but had many complexities in its implementation. Essentially, it involved taking a strip of the MAV notes and unwinding (selling) the underlying transactions for a value greater than the market price of the MAV notes – the constituent parts were greater than the whole – thereby generating a profit. The actual transaction is described in more detail later in the chapter.

This approach to generating liquidity had not been anticipated by the PCIC when it issued the substitute notes, but it has been very successful. Given the negative view of hedge funds during the restructuring negotiations, it is ironic that the salvation of the secondary market was the idea of and implemented by hedge funds that preferred to purchase the MAV securities if they could establish a short-term horizon for their investments.

The Players

Liquidity was the Achilles heel of the ABCP market in Canada, so how is the new market holding up in this regard? It's an over-the-counter market, so the amounts traded and the transaction prices have to be obtained from either brokers or market makers, which don't like to disclose that information. But at a rough estimate, $4 to $5 billion of the paper was traded up to the end of October 2012.

The Sellers

We know that the primary sellers in the market have been the original note holders: pension funds, governments, and corporate treasurers that survived the ABCP crisis and wanted to remove the paper from their balance sheets and move on from the embarrassment. Until 2012, the average transaction size was $5 million to $10 million. The largest trade is rumoured to have been in the $300 million to $500 million range. In 2012, trades in excess of $100 million occurred but didn't significantly impact the prevailing prices. All of these amounts are estimates, since the trades are have not been made public.

The Buyers

On the buy side, there are three main groups. The first is market makers, which buy the paper for their own account, thereby providing liquidity. These buyers include J.P. Morgan, Goldman Sachs, Bank of America, Citibank, Morgan Stanley, Deutsche Bank, and Credit Suisse First Boston, with the first two being the most active. In Canada, Fiera Quantum trades in the paper as a principal for the ABCP fund.

The second group is made up of brokers that cross buyers and sellers but do not buy for their own account. Investors who want to buy (sell) are matched with sellers (buyers). Included in this group are Casgrain, Sterne Agee (now called Stifel), and Seaport. This group was getting a lot of interest in the paper: for example, Sterne Agee confirmed it had discussed the risks and benefits of purchasing MAV II notes with nearly one hundred potential investors.

The final group of buyers is the hedge funds. Large US hedge funds that were large purchasers of the paper include King Street Capital, Anchorage Capital LLC, Third Point, Owl Creek, Cerberus, Golden Tree, and probably at least twenty other funds. These funds were active in the ABCP market, entering into large dollar-value transactions when pricing was acceptable. They tended to approach original note holders directly by presenting them with an exit strategy. They have also purchased the paper through dealers. The problem for hedge funds, however, is the holding period – most want to buy and sell quickly in an effort to turn a profit. But since the notes don't mature until June 2017, acquiring paper presents a duration problem.

The Unexpected Source of Liquidity: The Unwind

The unwind approach initiated by hedge funds is relatively simple but, like everything to do with ABCP, complex when it comes to implementation. It involves taking a strip of MAV notes and selling the underlying transactions for a value greater than the market price – a profit after considering transactions costs. As a simple example, consider the perspective of a buyer who paid $100 for a portfolio of securities; but if the securities underlying the portfolio could be sold separately, their value would be $120. This transaction would generate a $20 gain before transactions costs. In the context of the MAV market, a strip of the MAV notes, which can be bought in the secondary market, is a claim on the underlying transactions. Once owned, those underlying transactions can be sold – the LSS transactions can be unwound (i.e., sold in the CDS market) – thereby generating a profit if the strip price has a value that is less than the assessed market value of the underlying securities – referred to as net asset value (NAV). In the unwind situation, some of the assets are easy to sell (i.e., the traditional assets that are in the structures) and others are more difficult (i.e., LSSs).

Figure 9.2 below shows the relationship between strip prices and estimated NAV values. These estimates include estimates of the costs of undertaking the transaction. Except for the period July 2011 to about December 2011, the NAV was in excess of the strip price, suggesting that this strategy could be profitable.

But there can be costly wrinkles in the process. Hedge funds buying the MAV paper can push up the strip prices with their purchases of the MAV II notes and thus reduce the profitability of the transaction. At the same time, selling the underlying notes can reduce their price (and profits in the strategy). And finally, there are significant transaction costs in this strategy, including payments to parties with contractual claims to cash flows from the underlying assets. These claimants include members of the two funding facilities associated with the MAV II securities, DBRS and BlackRock. All such claimants are parties whose cash flows are based on the dollar amount of the outstanding MAV paper. In addition, investment bankers and legal teams – all essential to the process – do not work for free. These substantial fees reduce the profitability of the transaction.

The major beneficiaries of this strategy are hedge funds, particularly those that have already acquired positions in strips, purchasing them at various prices, typically below current strip prices. This is a compelling

Figure 9.2. MAV II - Historical Strip Pricing vs NAV

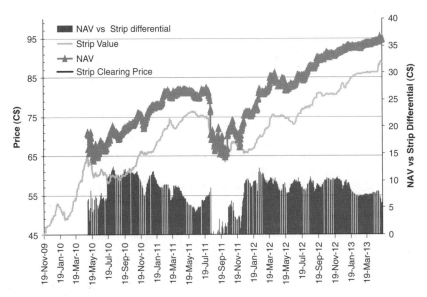

Source: Sterne Agee, Bloomberg

way for them to unwind their current positions and unlock value – an exit strategy. An unwind mechanism could also be helpful to original owners of MAV II notes; since hedge funds were constructing strips with the underlying MAV II notes, original owners could sell the notes to the hedge funds and thereby exit the market.

The unwind strategy moved slowly after 2010, when BlackRock announced in November that it had met with a group of note holders seeking a tender process to effect a partial redemption of notes they currently owned or might acquire. Four hedge funds recognizing the benefits of an optional early unwind of the MAV II notes approached a number of sell-side advisers. In early 2011, they retained Moelis & Company LLC to move the project forward. In mid-2011, Moelis and the legal firm Cadwalader, Wickersham & Taft LLP prepared a structure to implement a transaction that would result in a partial unwind of the MAV II notes. Under this structure, note holders could choose whether or not to liquidate their position. In August 2012, a proposed agreement to amend the original MAV agreement to permit this type of transaction was approved by MAV investors. A four-person committee was established to negotiate and implement definitive legal documents relating to this redemption process. The approved resolution provided a method for calculating payments to the contractual parties, thus eliminating one source of uncertainty in the valuation of the profitability of the unwind. But there remained uncertainty in the value that would be obtained upon the unwind of the LSS transactions. The specifics of the auction procedure to execute the unwind took six months to complete.

Under the amendment, there are two ways to achieve an unwind with a resulting redemption of ABCP. The first is based on a periodic unwind notice issued by BlackRock; the dates of the notices are predetermined, but a notice does not necessarily lead to an auction. The second way occurs when holder(s) of at least $100 million of original MAV II strips call for an optional (ad hoc) redemption. Regardless of the source of the redemption, the procedure remains the same.

BlackRock issues a notice of an unwind including a record date and a deadline date for investors interested in participating in the auction to complete a form certifying they are owners of the strip. Furthermore, there is a date for submitting a reserve tender price for the strip and the amount to be tendered. The tender amounts are in aggregates of $1 million.

Throughout this notice period, BlackRock talks with eligible bidders in the auction. Eligible bidders can be any investor that wants to purchase strips, but with the requirement that the investor be able to clear and face counter-parties, the set of eligible bidders is reduced to the banks. In order to provide some information on what the strip values could be, BlackRock publishes three indicative value prices, one each week until the final auction date, when the final swap prices are determined.

For each indicative price calculation, BlackRock obtains quotes for each of the 30 swaps in the MAV structure from the eligible bidders. The prices provided to BlackRock are live, firm quotes. It takes about one day for each eligible bidder to calculate the required swap prices. BlackRock then takes the highest bid value for each swap and aggregates this in the indicative price, which is the sum of all termination values for the LSSs. The indicative values are used by the potential tendering investors to prepare a strip price.

The unwind strategy requires that holders of a strip submit a price at which they are prepared to tender their strips and the amount they will tender. These prices are reserve prices, and if the actual unwind price – referred to as the strip clearing price – does not reach this level, the holders will not have a successful tender and will have to wait for a subsequent action to try again. Typically, investors will submit a low tender price to increase the probability that they are successful in the auction. Once the tender process is closed, the administrator, Black-Rock, fills the tendered amounts starting at the lowest reserve price and continues to higher prices until the tender maximum is met. The investors receive the strip clearing price and not the tender price they submitted.

The tendering entities have to estimate a reserve price. While most of the values of the variables needed to calculate the reserve price are observable only at the time of the auction, estimates are available before the tender date. For example, estimates are available for the collateral recovery, the aggregate fees, and finally the swap price from the indicative value calculations prepared by BlackRock. At the auction date, the gain or loss on the swap is crystallized and the allocation of the funds under the tender is based on a strip price resulting from the realization of all variables. As an example of the calculation of a tender price, consider the following: The collateral value is, say, 99 cents on the dollar; the total fees are 3% or three cents; the estimated value of the swaps from the third indicative pricing is a negative value of 2% or two cents. The tender price of 94 cents is equal to the collateral value less the fees and the swap unwind value (99 cents – 3 cents – 2 cents). The tenderer may then reduce the price somewhat to increase the probability of a successful tender. Based on the competition among bidders in the calculation of the swap unwind price, tendering investors receive the best possible execution price for their swaps.

The first periodic auction was held on 13 December 2013 and had $1.5 billion of MAV II notes unwound; this amount was equal to 15% of the outstanding value of $10 billion MAV II notes. On 14 February 2014, a second periodic auction was held with $1.87 billion of MAV II notes unwound. This auction was followed by an ad hoc third auction on 13 March 2014, for $1.5 billion. In May 2014 there was a successful auction for $999 million, and on 14 September 2014, another for $480 million. As at the end of 2014, of the $9.9 billion of MAV II notes issued, only $3.3 billion remain outstanding – a reduction of approximately 66%. On 15 March 2015 another successful auction was held for $540 million. The auctions clearly have provided needed access to liquidity over the unwind period.[4]

Table 9.1. Results of unwind auctions

	First auction, Dec. 2013	Second auction, Feb. 2014	Third auction, Mar. 2014	Fourth auction, May 2014	Fifth auction, Sept. 2014	Sixth auction, Mar. 2015
Collateral %	99.74	99.81	99.91	99.91	100.02	99.73
Swap unwind %	(1.66)	(1.96)	(1.69)	(1.40)	(0.78)	(0.32)
Aggregate Fee amount %	(3.80)	(3.45)	(3.45)	(3.20)	(2.99)	(2.36)
Strip clearing price (per $100 of face value)	94.28	94.40	94.77	95.31	96.26	97.05

To provide some specifics to this process we present the results of the six auctions in Table 9.1.[5]

The collateral value in the table is measured as percentage of the face value. The collateral – typically composed of low-risk, short-term financial instruments – has a value close to 100%. This value is the easiest to estimate before the auction. From the collateral amount, two elements are deducted. The first is the swap unwind price. The negative value shows that the swaps were sold at a loss. The second is the aggregate fee. It is large and reflects the direct costs of undertaking the unwind, as well as the indirect costs, which are the present value of losses to contractual parties, including the funding facility lenders. The final entry, the strip clearing price, is used to buy the strips from successful tenderers. That price increased over the six auctions to its value in March of 2015 of $97.05.

The auctions have introduced needed liquidity into the market and improved prices of the notes. Large investors in the MAV II paper, which in the past could sell only in small quantities if at all, can now sell their holdings at prices they view as favourable.

As Greg Foss, senior portfolio manager at Fiera Quantum, noted in correspondence with the authors about the unwind, "Thank god for the U.S. hedge funds ... Canada would never have been able to solve this by ourselves since most Canadians were buyers at par but sellers at all prices below par. It's a shame, really."

Regarding the March 2015 and any subsequent auctions, there was some concern that "the number of holders who want to tender might be too small to meet minimum requirements"[6] This is why Fierra Quantum decided to tender to the March 2015 auction. They noted that the maturity of the MAV notes was June 2017 and that they were expected to yield in the range of 3% per year if held to maturity.[7] The concern over the March auction turned out to be unwarranted, but future auctions may not be as successful. In fact, the scheduled 17 June auction did not occur; participation in the tender from holders of the securities was not sufficient. Bil Fedyna of Stifel stated in that firm's Structured Products Commentary that it is "unlikely that any future quarterly tenders will happen."[8]

Finally, the pricing of the underlying MAV II securities also provides answers to questions concerning the restructuring – specifically, the quality of the underlying assets and the success of the restructuring triggers. From the beginning of the crisis, the common perception – mirroring the problems in US and global markets – was that the LSS assets underlying the ABCP were toxic. In fact, the same term continued to be used by commentators with regard to the restructured ABCP notes. To establish the toxicity of these assets, let's look at the default performance of the assets underlying the new securities. There are certainly toxic assets present, but those assets primarily reflect exposure from the subprime market – these are the "ineligible" assets and have been isolated from the pooled assets underlying the MAV II notes. None of the traditional asset tracking notes, which have no subprime exposure, appear to be in distress. Some have already matured and been paid out.

What about the LSS CDS trades, the major assets in the MAV II paper? Are they truly toxic, or are they "money good," as many institutional investors and conduit sponsors suggest? At first blush, the price performance of all of the MAV II notes suggests they are "money good." There have been no defaults in the underlying corporate debt in sufficient amounts to affect the A1 and A2 notes. Most participants in the structured finance business say that only an end-of-the-world financial scenario would have had any impact on the A1 and A2 notes. Information on the quality of the underlying assets is observed in the ratings on the A1 and A2 paper. On 22 June 2010, DBRS confirmed the ratings for the MAV II A1 and A2 paper, with positive implications for the A1s. The ratings were A (high) for the A1s and BBB (low) for the A2s. On June 27, 2012, DBRS upgraded the rating for the A1 notes to AA (low) and for A2 at BBB (high). On 6 June 2013, the ratings for A1 notes remained the same, and A2 were upgraded to A (low). Most recently (30 May 2014), these ratings were confirmed.

As a final look at the quality of the underlying trades that are now still active, we present the bid/ask prices for the MAV notes by class for the week of 23 March 2015.[9]

Class	Bid	Ask
A1	97.79	98.79
A2	94.79	95.79
B	94.29	95.29
C	85.29	86.26

Clearly, it was not the *quality* of the transactions underlying the LSS that caused the market freeze, but the *structure* of the transactions. That structure included high levels of leverage, liquidity arrangements that did not work, and mark-to-market triggers. In fact, the restructuring of the triggers to a spread-loss mechanism turned out to have a positive influence on the risk of the securities in the MAV II market and hence on valuations in the riskier notes.

Did the secondary market in MAV II notes achieve the goals noted by Crawford – a well-functioning and liquid market? The secondary market for the MAV II notes improved over time. With BlackRock's (administrator) movement to greater transparency following the signing of the Montreal Accord, valuation has become easier (albeit not easy). Unfortunately, transactions in the resulting market have not been large and frequent. Prices of the four note classes have increased in line with the improvement in credit conditions in the CDS market, the lack of many significant credit events, and the successful unwinds.

The role of hedge funds in this market points to another of the many ironies found in the restructuring process. During the Montreal Accord negotiations, hedge funds were demonized – they took the blame for the PCIC's enforced lack of transparency in the underlying LSS trades and the resulting lack of transactions in the frozen paper during the restructuring process. Now, either on their own or indirectly through trading with dealers, they are providing an important element of liquidity and price discovery. The hedge fund influence culminated in the unwind transactions.

Consistent with the idea that the restructuring is about "the art of the possible," liquidity does not mean getting the full value of the investment immediately; rather, it refers to the ability to sell in a market based on fair transaction prices. With the success of the auction process, investors can either sell their holdings to entities that will decide on tendering in an auction or, if their holdings are large enough, enter directly into the auction process. Overall, the structure works, and the investors have a market in which they can exit if they so desire or hold the paper until maturity.

CHAPTER TEN

Regulatory Fallout

The landmark restructuring was, at last, in place, and the new MAV II notes were trading, although the market was far from ideal. For regulators, however, the work was just beginning. The scale of the crisis and the governance failures that led to it meant that their appearance was inevitable.

The Enforcers

Canada's major securities regulators – the OSC, AMF, and IIROC – had all been investigating the ABCP market's key players since the August 2007 meltdown. While the OSC defended its "backstage" role in the crisis on the basis of its decision not to interfere with a private sector solution, some – including the Ontario legislature's Standing Committee on Government Agencies – have criticized it for taking a too-narrow view of its public interest jurisdiction.

The Securities Regulators

The role played by securities regulators before, during, and after the crisis has been the subject of considerable attention, speculation, and occasionally derision. To assess whether all criticism of the regulators is reasonable or unjustified, we need to examine a little more closely the rules surrounding the sale of ABCP and the actions of regulators during the crisis. Criticism of Canadian securities commissions appears to focus on four issues:

1. *Prospectus exemption for sale of ABCP.* According to IIROC's compliance sweep, IIROC dealer members selling third-party ABCP to retail

investors confused the product with bank-sponsored ABCP and did
not consider investor suitability issues citing, among other things,
the high credit ratings, the apparent similarity to bank-sponsored
commercial paper, the similar yield spreads over the Bankers
Acceptance (BA) rate, and also, perhaps, the fact that securities
laws permitted the paper to be sold to investors under a prospectus
exemption. Under securities laws in each of Canada's provinces
and territories, there are basically two ways in which newly issued
securities may lawfully be sold to investors: through a public offering,
or by way of an exempt distribution (or private placement). In a public
offering, the seller must prepare a detailed disclosure document
– a prospectus – which must be filed in advance and cleared with
securities regulators in the province where the securities are to be sold
and distributed to the buyers. A prospectus offering is time-consuming
and expensive, and securities regulators and legislators have
recognized that it is not always necessary or appropriate to require a
prospectus when selling securities. Securities laws and regulations,
therefore, include a number of exemptions from the prospectus rules.
If the seller satisfies one of these exemptions, it may sell securities
without incurring the time and expense of preparing and filing a
prospectus.[1]

The sale of non-bank ABCP raises a broader issue regarding the
role of securities regulators in regulating markets for instruments
that *in form* are appropriate for retail investors but *in substance* are
highly sophisticated, complex instruments that pose valuation and
risk assessment challenges even for financial industry experts. Non-
bank ABCP was not the first example of this sort of form-versus-
substance issue faced by Canadian securities regulators. In the
1990s, the OSC confronted the challenge of "debt-like derivatives" –
debt instruments with returns linked to equity indices or other more
complex financial products. These instruments were being sold
to retail investors in reliance on prospectus exemptions originally
designed to permit the sale of traditional, straightforward, low-risk
debt securities. The OSC struck a task force in 1999 to examine the
regulatory regime surrounding the sale of these new instruments.
The task force recommended that an alternative disclosure regime
apply to the sale of debt-like derivatives. This regime was a
halfway house between full prospectus disclosure and the largely
unregulated private placement market. The proposed regime was
never implemented, however. Provincial securities regulators ran

into a jurisdictional hurdle because many debt-like derivatives were being sold by federally regulated financial institutions, principally chartered banks. Accordingly, federal authorities considered the regulation of these instruments to be properly within the mandate of the federal government and so promulgated regulations of their own under the Bank Act.

Over time, the scope and sophistication of these hybrid products increased. Banks began selling retail investors principal protected notes (PPNs), offering a guarantee of a return of principal but with interest linked to the returns of hedge funds. Hedge funds, of course, are sophisticated investments that normally are unavailable to unsophisticated investors of limited financial means. A Canadian Securities Administrators (CSA) Staff Notice in January 2007 expressed concern that some sellers of PPNs might not be complying with their "know your client" (KYC) and investment suitability rules in connection with their sales of PPNs to retail investors. Once again, jurisdictional issues hobbled regulatory reform. Just as provincial securities regulators seemed poised to tighten the reins on the sale of PPNs, the federal government weighed in with its own new regulations, which took effect on 1 July 2008.

In August 2012, the CSA issued a notice indicating, among other things, its expectation that banks and other federally regulated financial institutions would sell PPNs only through registered dealers that were subject to the usual securities law KYC and suitability rules. The CSA, in other words, was sensitive to the issue of unsophisticated clients participating in a market for instruments that *in form* were low-risk fixed income products but *in substance* actually represented exposure to very complex financial products.

The primary protection for retail investors in such a case must come through the diligence of registered dealers and the proper implementation of KYC and suitability rules. In the case of ABCP, as noted earlier, the IIROC compliance sweep indicated that many dealers had dropped the ball on that score. To justify lack of due diligence and failure to abide by the KYC rules partly on the basis that the securities regulators had permitted such instruments to be sold on a prospectus-exempt basis[2] appears to be a disappointing abdication by the dealers of their responsibilities. For this, the securities regulators are hardly to blame.

2. *Ontario Securities Commission actions during the ABCP meltdown.* But what about the regulatory response to the crisis as it unfolded?

In December 2008, senior members of the OSC, including then-chair
David Wilson and vice-chairs James Turner and Lawrence Ritchie,
appeared before the Ontario government's Standing Committee on
Government Agencies as part of a regular agency review. During that
session, they were asked why the OSC did not launch an investigation
into sellers and manufacturers of ABCP. Turner, in particular, was
asked to address a statement he had made to a *National Post* reporter
in May 2008 (the questioner mistakenly attributed the quotation to the
Globe and Mail), in which he indicated that, once the ABCP market had
frozen, the OSC "didn't feel we had to jump in to protect investors."
This comment was seized upon during the questioning of Turner by
the Standing Committee as suggesting that the OSC deliberately chose
to refrain from taking prompt action to intervene during the heat of
the crisis. In fact, however, as the original context of the quotation
and Turner's explanation before the Standing Committee made clear,
the point was that, once the ABCP market froze in August 2007, no
additional paper was being sold. In other words, there simply were
no more potential investors in need of protection. Accordingly, at that
moment, the OSC could safely allow the then-nascent restructuring
plan to be developed by those best positioned, and best incentivized,
to carry this out.

3. *Is Canadian securities enforcement generally too lax?* It has often been
   suggested that Canadian securities enforcement is "lax" – either in
   absolute terms or at the very least in comparison with the robust
   enforcement efforts of the US Securities and Exchange Commission
   (SEC). In his December 2008 testimony before the Standing
   Committee, then-OSC chair Wilson acknowledged that "there's a
   perception that enforcement in Canada is not as rigorous as it is
   in the U.S." Certainly, few securities regulators worldwide are as
   aggressive at enforcement as the US SEC. However, the perception
   that Canadian securities regulation is lax in absolute terms (rather
   than solely in comparison with the world's leading securities
   regulator) may be distorted, at least in part by a misunderstanding
   of the respective roles of securities regulators and law enforcement
   agencies. For example, critics of Canadian securities regulators
   sometimes point out that a number of high-profile US securities
   cases have resulted in prison sentences for the offenders, while
   incarceration for Canadian securities law violators seems very rare.
   There are at least two fundamental flaws with this comparison. First,
   as has often been noted, incarceration is far more frequent in the

United States for crimes of all kinds, yet it is not usually suggested that this is proof that the United States is generally a safer place to live than Canada.

More importantly, in the United States it is not the SEC that is responsible for sending violators to prison. The SEC has no authority to do so. Such high-profile enforcement actions in that country are undertaken by criminal law enforcement agencies. Similarly, in Canada, although securities regulators play a critical gatekeeping role in the "quasi-criminal"[1] enforcement of provincial securities statutes, no securities regulator has the authority to send anyone to jail for violating securities laws. Indeed, although regulators do have some authority to impose fines (technically dubbed "administrative penalties"), even this authority is limited. So to criticize securities regulators for failing to take steps that are wholly beyond their powers is somewhat wide of the mark.

There is also the perennial problem of determining what the enforcement record of a highly successful regulatory body should look like. If relatively few enforcement actions are taken within a jurisdiction, the regulator may be criticized for being too lax. If, however, a large number of enforcement actions are taken, this may be seen as proof that law-breaking is widespread, so the regulator may be criticized for failing to have prevented wrongdoing in the first place. Indeed, during the Standing Committee's questioning of OSC personnel in December 2008, these seemingly contradictory observations were made by questioners within minutes of one another.[4] To be sure, investors have a right to expect provincial securities regulators to be vigilant in their protection of investors, aggressive in their pursuit of wrongdoing, and diligent in enforcement of securities laws and policies. And the collapse of the non-bank ABCP market was clearly harmful to affected investors and markets more generally. A careful dissection of regulatory actions before, during, and after the crisis is, accordingly, entirely appropriate, necessary, and desirable. It is important, however, that such a review be fully informed so that it may lead to significant practical improvements rather than unproductive polemic.

4. *National (or common) securities regulator and challenges of market regulation.* No consideration of the role of Canadian securities regulators would be complete without some discussion of the perennial question of whether Canada ought to have a single, national (or common) securities regulator. To be clear, generally speaking, the

case for a national Canadian securities regulator is – in the authors' view – compelling, perhaps even overwhelming. It is well beyond the scope of this book to chronicle the decades-long pursuit of a national Canadian securities regulator, culminating in the Supreme Court of Canada's 2011 ruling that the federal government's proposed Canadian Securities Act was unconstitutional,[2] and subsequent developments aimed at creating a cooperative, multi-provincial common securities regulator. For the purposes of this book, however, the relevant question is much narrower: the issue is not whether, in general, a national securities regulator is preferable to Canada's fragmented provincial securities regulatory system. The key question, for our purposes, is this: Would a national securities regulator have made a material difference in this specific case? Framed this way, the question is much more challenging and the answer far less certain.

How might a national securities regulator have prevented the ABCP crisis or lessened its impact? Critics of the provincial securities regulators have argued that a national regulator would have been better equipped (and better resourced) to deal with a major systemic shock such as the ABCP meltdown. For example, in 2015 former Bank of Canada governor David Dodge commented to us on the ABCP meltdown, noting that "the real lesson to be learned from this experience is that our securities commissions were totally incapable of regulating these products. This inability to provide adequate oversight created systemic risk for the financial system as a whole. And we are still in 2015 in the process of trying to create a single securities regulator in Canada capable of overseeing the market for derivatives and structured products. We are apparently very slow learners in this country." Similarly, the 2009 Expert Panel on Securities Regulation (Thomas Hockin, chair) suggested that the Canadian regulatory response to the ABCP crisis was slower and somehow less decisive than the response of a national regulator might have been. Specifically, the panel asserted that the Canadian response to short-selling restrictions imposed by US and UK securities regulators "lagged behind the co-ordinated efforts" of these two major jurisdictions and "was not uniform across the provinces." Needless to say, this criticism assumes that imposing restrictions on short-selling represents a wise and useful policy measure – a conclusion on which expert opinion is, at best, mixed. In any event, it is at least debatable whether the Canadian response can be described as having materially "lagged" US efforts. The OSC, in its capacity as lead regulator of the Toronto Stock Exchange, issued a temporary order under Section 127(5) of the Securities Act prohibiting short-selling of certain financial sector issuers' stocks on 19 September 2008. That was just one day after the SEC's short-selling ban. On the same day, the CSA issued a release supporting the OSC's restriction and indicating that "other jurisdictions in the CSA will be taking similar action today, or in the coming days."

The Expert Panel specifically referred to the regulators' response to the ABCP meltdown as proof of the inefficacy of provincial securities regulation. The panel was especially critical of the "delay between the freezing of the [ABCP] market in August 2007 and the release of a consultation paper by the CSA to seek input on a number of proposals that aim to prevent similar capital market failures in the future." Of course, reasonable people may differ over what constitutes a timely regulatory response. But it is hardly self-evident that a national regulator could have been counted on to have responded more rapidly to unforeseen (and wholly unprecedented) market developments. The financial crisis, after all, was even more severe in jurisdictions such as the United States and the United Kingdom, where national regulators exist. Equally important, perhaps, is the concern that regulatory and legislative haste often leads to knee-jerk overreactions – what Professor Roberta Romano of the Yale Law School has derided as "quack" reforms – rather than measured, reflective, and well-informed regulatory enhancements.

In short, although there are many arguments that strongly support the establishment of a national securities regulator in Canada, it is not entirely clear that the regulatory response to the ABCP meltdown is among them.

Notwithstanding this, the OSC and other regulators wasted little time in preparing cases against the main participants. In so doing, they made two sets of allegations. First, that ABCP dealers had bought or sold the instruments without conducting proper due diligence. Second, that the dealers had failed to properly explain ABCP's risks to purchasers.

The banks were in no mood to fight. On 21 December 2009, the three regulators announced a total of $139 million in settlements. In particular, the OSC agreed to a $22 million settlement with CIBC and CIBC World Markets and a $6 million settlement with HSBC Bank Canada. IIROC, for its part, settled with Scotia Capital, Canaccord Financial, and Credential Securities for $29 million, $3 million, and $200,000, respectively. Finally, the AMF reached a $75 million settlement with

National Bank Financial and a $3 million settlement with Laurentian Bank Securities.

In an unprecedented move, both IIROC and the OSC announced on 21 March 2013 that these ABCP settlement funds of approximately $60 million would be refunded to investors on a pro rata basis. Their cheques, then, provided aggrieved investors with some justice outside of the restructuring process – albeit a small slice of it. For instance, TSX Venture software company Acceleware acquired $1.4 million in ABCP in 2007. It received a $50,000 share of the settlement funds – an amount far less than the $650,000 it lost upon selling its investment in 2009.

One company, however, had no appetite to settle and pushed back. Over a forty-five-day hearing at the OSC from May to December 2010, Coventree vigorously contested the regulator's allegations against it and two of its founders. What made it so different?

Coventree's "Gloves Off" Approach

When Coventree was founded by Geoffrey Cornish and Dean Tai in 1998, the words "mortgage-backed security" had not entered the global vernacular. The firm's investment pool – a mix of credit card receivables, leases, equipment loans, trade receivables, and residential mortgages – grew to $12 billion in its nine years of operation, and its shareholders' equity rose from $3.55 million in 1999 to $46.22 million at the time of its 2006 initial public offering (IPO).

Around July 2008, the OSC made several public statements that it was investigating the Canadian ABCP market. The OSC included in this investigation Coventree's participation in the market and several timely disclosure issues. Coventree formed a special committee composed of Peter Dey and Wes Voorheis, who had become Coventree directors in April 2008, to prepare a response to the OSC. The committee engaged various experts to investigate the issues raised by the OSC at that time. Dey and Voorheis concluded that Coventree had met its obligations under Ontario's securities legislation and that it should defend itself against OSC staff allegations. This report was forwarded to OSC staff well before the formal proceedings were initiated in December 2009 against Coventree, Cornish, and Tai. Following the issuance of the Notice of Hearing, the special committee confirmed that it believed the allegations were unwarranted and unfair given the circumstances. This confirmation formed the basis of Coventree, Cornish, and Tai's decision to defend themselves against the allegations at the formal hearing.

Staff of the OSC levelled four main allegations against Coventree. Three of them were related to Coventree's obligations under securities law to provide public disclosure of information to Coventree's own investors and prospective investors in the run-up to the ABCP crisis. The fourth was an allegation that Coventree had made a misleading statement to the market that would reasonably be expected to have a significant effect on the market price or value of "a security." Note that only the fourth allegation related to the possible impact of Coventree's actions on purchasers of ABCP. The other three were concerned not with the impact of the firm's behaviour on ABCP investors but only with potential harm to Coventree's *own* investors (as it was a public company). The OSC's jurisdiction to pursue a case against Coventree relating directly to the losses experienced by Coventree-sponsored ABCP note holders was highly constrained because Coventree itself was not the issuer or seller of those notes. Also, the notes were, in any event, sold in private transactions that were exempt from the securities law prospectus requirements.

The administrative hearing before an adjudicative panel of the OSC was unusually protracted. The forty-five days of hearings were spread out over a seven-month period, from May to December 2010. And the panel's decision was not released until September 2011, nine months after the conclusion of the hearing. That decision was followed by a second hearing, one month later, on the issue of appropriate sanctions to be imposed.

Of course, the issues were complex, and the factual and legal context was challenging. Two of the OSC's staff allegations concerned Coventree's failure to disclose to its investors important credit rating changes announced by DBRS affecting Coventree's ABCP business: first, at the time of Coventree's IPO in November 2006, then following a further clarifying announcement by DBRS in January 2007. Credit ratings and ABCP sales went hand in hand. Crucial to Coventree's success with ABCP was the ability of the conduits it sponsored to issue the paper to investors on a prospectus-exempt basis. This exemption required the paper to receive an acceptable rating from a credit rating agency – in Coventree's case, DBRS. The DBRS approach to rating ABCP, therefore, was of considerable interest to Coventree.

In November 2006, just three days before Coventree filed its final prospectus in connection with the IPO of its shares, DBRS issued a letter by e-mail to "various market participants." The letter warned that the rapid growth in certain types of ABCP transactions had prompted

DBRS to advise a more "measured approach" to managing the growth of structured financial asset-backed (SFA) transactions in Canada. To that end, DBRS intended to adopt a "new approach" to the rating of future deals "effective immediately." Though the letter was short on specifics, it was clear that DBRS was firing an important shot across the bow. Market participants had been warned: DBRS would be taking a more restrictive approach before approving SFA transactions in the future.

Days later, Coventree filed its final prospectus with securities regulators, qualifying the sale of its shares to the public. The prospectus made no explicit reference to the November DBRS letter. The legal issue for the OSC was clear: if the DBRS letter constituted a "material fact," then the Coventree prospectus should have disclosed it. But was it a material fact? The definition of "material fact" in Ontario's Securities Act is broad and linked to the potential "market impact" of information. Thus, a fact is material if, and only if, it "would reasonably be expected to have a significant effect on the market price or value of the securities." In its September 2011 decision, the OSC panel concluded that the DBRS letter did not constitute a material fact as the act defined it and, therefore, did not need to be mentioned in Coventree's prospectus. To be sure, the panel was "surprised" that the prospectus made no specific reference to the letter. But a surprising omission is not necessarily an unlawful omission. And in this case, the panel concluded that the letter would not have had a significant effect on the market price or value of Coventree's shares. Since the November 2006 DBRS warning was not a material fact, Coventree had committed no breach of the Securities Act in failing to disclose it.

A second OSC staff allegation related to Coventree's failure to disclose the effect of a subsequent January 2007 DBRS press release. In that press release, DBRS announced specific changes to its method for rating credit arbitrage-type transactions. Among other things, DBRS indicated that it would no longer rate credit arbitrage transactions unless they were supported by global-style liquidity, rather than the more limited Canadian-style "market disruption" liquidity facilities discussed in chapter 1. Since global-style liquidity arrangements were unavailable to Coventree, the change precluded Coventree's conduits from entering into any further credit-arbitrage transactions.

By January 2007, Coventree had become a public company. The ongoing or "timely" securities law disclosure obligations faced by a public company are slightly different from the prospectus information disclosure requirements that apply when a company first offers its securities to the public. The timely disclosure rules require information to be disclosed only if it constitutes a "material change" – a term that is slightly narrower than the broad prospectus concept of "material fact." A "material change" is a "change in the business, operations or capital of an issuer that would reasonably be expected to have a significant effect on the market price or value of any securities of the issuer."

Was the January 2007 DBRS release such a "material change"? In the panel's view, it was. First, since Coventree did not have access to global-style liquidity arrangements, it would no longer be able to carry out CDO-related structured financial asset transactions through its conduits – transactions that represented a significant portion of Coventree's business. Such transactions accounted for some 60% of Coventree-sponsored conduit assets and about 80% of Coventree's revenues for the first three fiscal quarters of 2007.

Accordingly, the panel had no doubt that the January 2007 DBRS release represented a direct change to Coventree's business. But was this "change" "material" within the meaning of the Securities Act? That is, would information about the DBRS release reasonably be expected to affect the market price or value of Coventree's shares? On this point, the panel needed to confront a curious fact. Coventree did, eventually, disclose the adverse impact the new DBRS rating method would have on its profitability. This disclosure was included in Coventree's 2007 second-quarter "Management's Discussion and Analysis" (MD&A), which was publicly filed on 14 May 2007. Yet despite this disclosure, there was no subsequent change in the market price of Coventree's shares. The market did not seem to react at all to this bad news. Because a "material change" must have, or reasonably be expected to have, "a significant effect on the market price or value" of an issuer's securities, Coventree argued before the OSC panel that the DBRS January press release could not have constituted a material change. After all, when details of the release were actually disclosed by Coventree, the market price of its shares was unaffected.

The panel rejected this argument, suggesting several reasons that might account for the failure of the market price of Coventree's shares to reflect what was, for the panel, clearly an adverse material change when that change was ultimately disclosed in May. The panel noted that the statutory definition of "material change" referred to a change reasonably expected to have a significant effect on the price *or value* of an issuer's securities. Even if the DBRS release, for whatever reason, might be said not to have affected the market price of Coventree's shares, surely, argued the panel, the *value* of those shares had been affected by this change, so the change should have been disclosed promptly in January.

The suggestion that shares traded in public markets can have a meaningful intrinsic value that departs for any material length of time from the price at which willing buyers and sellers actually trade those shares is a controversial proposition, at least in the absence of specific factors that would cast doubt on the efficiency of the market. The panel alluded in its decision to a few such possible factors in Coventree's case, including the low volume of trading resulting from the control position in the stock held by Cornish, Tai, and related entities. Though this explanation is certainly plausible, some critics, such as Bradley Heys of NERA Consulting, have argued that support for such a conclusion may, nevertheless, call for "a deeper set of economic analysis, and likely expert evidence."

OSC staff had further alleged that Coventree had failed to disclose what it referred to as "liquidity and liquidity-related events and the risk of a market disruption in the days leading up to the disruption in the ABCP market that occurred on Aug. 13, 2007." These events related primarily to the difficulty Coventree-sponsored conduits had encountered by early August in issuing new ABCP and rolling outstanding ABCP as well as to other indications of market disruptions, including widening credit spreads and sales of conduit assets to generate cash.

The OSC panel found that all of these difficulties – separately and collectively – had become a "material change" for Coventree by the close of business on 1 August 2007. Because Coventree had not disclosed these events, the company was in breach of its disclosure obligations for this as well.

The sole staff allegation relating to actions affecting the value of the ABCP, as opposed to the value of Coventree's own shares, concerned statements that Coventree had made in presentations to ABCP investors in April 2007. In those presentations, Coventree had stated that the total exposure of Coventree-sponsored conduits to US subprime mortgages represented just 7.4% of its total assets. Although that overall average exposure figure was technically accurate, staff maintained that it was misleading because the subprime exposure was actually highly concentrated in four of the Coventree conduits. Of those four, three had exposure of more than 15% to US subprime, and one had exposure of more than 40%. Under Ontario securities laws, it is unlawful for a person or company to make a statement that that person or company knows or reasonably ought to know is misleading in a material respect and that would reasonably be expected to have a significant effect on the market price or value of a security – *any* security, not simply a security issued by the person making the misleading statement. Indeed, the OSC panel set aside the possibility that these statements would have had any effect on Coventree's own shares, and considered only whether they might be expected to have had a significant effect on the market price or value of Coventree-sponsored ABCP. Though the panel did regard Coventree's use of an average subprime exposure figure in these circumstances to be misleading, it nevertheless concluded that the statements did not constitute a violation of securities law. The reason? Even if accurate disclosure had been made of the extent of subprime exposure faced by each series of notes, the panel said, "it is unlikely that disclosure would have had a significant effect on the market price or value of the ABCP with the highest subprime exposure." Timing is everything. As of April 2007, the panel suggested, the fact that ABCP was backed by US subprime mortgage assets had not yet become a significant issue for Canadian ABCP holders.

Coventree was found to have breached the Securities Act and to have acted contrary to the public interest in failing to properly disclose the material change that had occurred when DBRS issued its January 2007 release, and again at the time of the so-called liquidity events that had occurred by 1 August 2007. But the panel's findings of liability were not limited to the corporation. In addition to finding that Coventree itself had breached Ontario securities law, the panel also found Cornish and Tai responsible for permitting or acquiescing in Coventree's disclosure breaches. Cornish – a former securities lawyer – and Tai headed Coventree's disclosure committee. In the circumstances, however, it might have been wiser to have obtained an opinion from outside counsel.

Following the subsequent sanctions hearing, the panel ordered Cornish and Tai each to pay $500,000 to the OSC (although the order explicitly said they were not to be prevented from seeking indemnity for these amounts from Coventree itself). In addition, the panel ordered Coventree to be cease-traded and imposed a $1 million administrative penalty against Coventree as well as an order to pay $250,000 in costs incurred during the OSC investigation. The paradox of imposing an administrative penalty on a corporation in the name of shareholder protection is that it is the shareholders themselves whose financial interests are harmed by such a penalty. Securities regulators have long been cognizant of this inescapable problem. In the case of a company that is a going concern, it is generally hoped that such penalties will indirectly discipline managers. In the case of a company that is being wound up, however, it is less clear how aggrieved shareholders are assisted by penalties that simply decrease the value they will be able to receive from the dissolved firm. Of course, in Coventree's case, Cornish and Tai remained Coventree's largest shareholders.

Nevertheless, despite the penalty's sting – and that of the inevitable legal fees – Cornish and Tai would go on to net $17.6 million and $15.4 million, respectively, as Coventree shareholders in September 2012 from Coventree's wind-up: the company still had $71 million in cash. Moreover, the penalties imposed against Cornish and Tai were one-tenth of the $5 million initially sought by the OSC staff. Staff had also sought to recover costs in the amount of $1.5 million jointly from Coventree, Cornish, and Tai, but received only $250,000 from Coventree and nothing from Cornish or Tai.

Still, Why Go Through the Trouble of Fighting at All?

A key point here was that, except for the ultimately unsuccessful allegation relating to Coventree's April 2007 presentations on their conduits' exposure to US subprime assets, Coventree was not being pursued primarily for how its actions (or lack thereof) affected ABCP investors, but for how they affected the firm's *own* investors. It may have been that Coventree, Cornish and Tai's legal advisers – a team of twelve lawyers from leading Bay Street firms Lenczner Slaght, Davies Ward Phillips & Vineberg; Bennett Jones; and Stockwoods – saw the company and the directors' alleged missteps as falling well below any threshold that could reasonably justify the $5 million in sanctions originally sought by OSC staff.

Indeed, the OSC's ultimate findings hint at a few reasons why Coventree, Cornish and Tai's counsel may have seen limited risk from a "gloves-off" approach. Neither of the disclosure shortfalls was found by the panel to be intentional. Moreover, the pair did not personally profit from the breaches. There were, according to the panel, "difficult and relatively complex issues" faced by Cornish and Tai "in the face of the unprecedented market impact of the crisis that occurred in August 2007." And the panel stressed that the directors' conduct, in fact, was less egregious than that seen in other recent cases (such as in the YBM Magnex and Biovail debacles).

Beyond this, Coventree was being wound down as the OSC pursued it. The firm had already attracted media scrutiny after the ABCP crisis, with some ABCP investors in Coventree-sponsored conduits having lost money, access to their funds, and confidence in the firm. Cornish said that any Coventree shareholders who contacted the company expressed continued confidence even after the market disruption and the start of the OSC proceedings.

Cornish and Tai were upset with the suggestion that they had done something wrong, and for reputational reasons, they decided to challenge the OSC sanction order with an appeal to the Ontario Divisional Court in March 2013. This challenge was undertaken despite the fact that the actual financial cost of the order, if unchallenged, would not have been that significant.

The Divisional Court dismissed the appeal and upheld the reasonableness of the OSC panel's decision. Motions for leave to appeal to the Ontario Court of Appeal brought by Cornish and Tai were refused in September 2013. Along with other directors and officers, Cornish and Tai had an indemnity agreement with Coventree – a relatively standard agreement used by public companies. As required by the agreement, Coventree paid the costs of Cornish's appeal. The independent directors of the Coventree board were involved in the decision relating to the indemnities.

One other entity seemed poised to fight the regulators – that is, until recently. In January 2013, Deutsche Bank settled its long-standing dispute with IIROC. Admitting that it had failed to engage its compliance department with emerging issues in the ABCP market contrary to IIROC rules, the bank agreed to a fine of $1 million.

That left Coventree as the only entity to have fought the regulators' ABCP allegations – and the only one to have folded as a result of the crisis. Had Coventree been an unfortunate scapegoat or an example of an observation made in Shakespeare's *Measure for Measure*: "What's open made to justice / That justice seizes"?

Devonshire and Barclays: The Odd Ones Out

Although Coventree was the only ABCP party to take on the regulators, its battle with the OSC wasn't the crisis's only skirmish. However much the restructuring aimed to quash litigation, two players, Devonshire Trust and Barclays, could not turn away from the option to opt out of the restructuring. However, both were part of the Montreal Accord group for a period of time. As the only third-party ABCP conduit to opt out of the restructuring, Devonshire did not benefit from the CCAA stay order and so was exposed to liability for its role in distributing the paper.

In the transaction, in addition to its buyer–seller relationship in the paper's underlying assets, Barclays bought credit protection from Devonshire for LSS assets it did not own. The agreement stipulated that if those assets depreciated past a certain point, Devonshire would pay Barclays an agreed amount, up to $3 billion. In the meantime, to secure the obligation, Devonshire had to provide Barclays with $600 million in collateral, to be held in trust. Making matters more complicated, Barclays was also a liquidity provider to Devonshire and so could be called upon to provide liquidity if there were an MDE. As we note later, the first trial of issues in the lawsuit between Barclays and Devonshire did not consider whether Barclays was justified in declining to meet the Devonshire liquidity call.

When ABCP matters went awry in August 2007, Devonshire issued a "market disruption" notice and asked Barclays to fund. Barclays refused, arguing that an MDE had not occurred. When Barclays refused to provide liquidity, Devonshire issued a default notice. At this point, Devonshire was still part of the Montreal Accord. Due to a standstill agreement reached under the Montreal Accord, however, Devonshire agreed on 16 August 2007 to suspend its default notice against Barclays without prejudice. Devonshire also agreed not to attempt to enforce its rights arising from Barclays's alleged default until the expiration of the standstill agreement. Both parties soon left the Montreal Accord but continued to negotiate between themselves. Most discussions to restructure Devonshire, however, were held without Devonshire's direct participation. Indeed, Barclays negotiated directly with the major note holders of Devonshire, in particular the Caisse, which held Devonshire notes with a face value of $385 million.

The back and forth continued until 8 January 2009. On that day, Barclays sent Devonshire a term sheet resembling the PCIC framework agreement. The proposal embodied in this term sheet, in effect, disregarded eight months of bilateral negotiations between the two parties. The proposal came with a deadline: Devonshire had until 12 January to accept. When no acceptance arrived, a war of letters ensued on 13 January. Barclays launched the first salvo in the form of two notices to Devonshire: the first noting its intention to pay its liquidity support by a wire transfer of funds, and the second – delivered just four minutes later – alleging that Devonshire had terminated the agreement early by going insolvent (due to the trust's inability to roll over the paper). What was Barclays trying to accomplish? By "curing" its liquidity requirement (Notice 1) and claiming default by Devonshire (Notice 2), it would gain creditor status and trump any claims of Devonshire's investors.

Devonshire repaid the favour by sending the bank a notice of its own: that it was terminating the contract due to Barclays's failure to provide liquidity as requested in August 2007.

Ultimately, the matter reached the Ontario Superior Court. The lawsuit between Barclays and Devonshire was "bifurcated" – that is, split into two separate trials, each of which was to involve separate legal issues. The decision to bifurcate the action in this way was reached following a negotiation process between the parties that led to a Consent Order, granted by the judge, Colin Campbell. The parties agreed to bifurcate the issues in this way because, depending on how issues were determined in the first trial, the second trial might become unnecessary, thus saving both parties (and the court) time and money. The four specific issues that were not to be dealt with in the first trial were: (a) whether a market disruption event had occurred in August 2007, (b) whether the market disruption notice and default notice issued by Devonshire were valid, (c) whether Barclays was in default under the various notices sent by Devonshire to Barclays, and (d) whether Devonshire was precluded from claiming that a market disruption event had occurred. For the purposes of the first trial (the only trial that has ever taken place), all four of these issues were to be assumed to be decided in favour of Devonshire.

Unusual for a commercial matter, the first trial was closed to the public. Frank Newbould, the trial's presiding judge, found the agreement "byzantine in its complexity" and rejected Barclays's case. First, he found that Barclays was not entitled to rely on the Notice of Early Termination that it had delivered to Devonshire on 13 January 2009. Why not? The notice of termination could only be validly delivered if Barclays was not itself in default under the agreement. Having failed to honour its liquidity obligation (assuming, for the purposes of this first trial, that an MDE had occurred), Barclays was in default. The judge also noted that Barclays had not technically cured its default by wire-transferring funds to Devonshire four minutes prior to sending its termination notice. Such haste, the judge found, was unreasonable. In fact, Devonshire's account was credited with the transferred funds only *after* it had received Barclays's Notice of Early Termination. Barclays, in the judge's view, should have waited for a reasonable time to ensure, at least, that the funds had reached Devonshire's bank account. Four minutes didn't cut it.

Second, the judge interpreted Barclays' three-day payment grace period as having lapsed on 10 January 2009 – in other words, days before Barclays delivered its termination notice. His reasoning? Barclays's 8 January ultimatum, in his view, reflected an intention to terminate the contract.

Newbould found that Devonshire had agreed to the extension of the standstill agreement following fraudulent (not merely negligent) misrepresentation by Barclays: Barclays had misrepresented to Devonshire the state of its negotiations with the note holders when it requested extension of that standstill agreement. In fact, the court found that Barclays had decided to terminate the swaps and that it knew an ultimatum it had delivered to the Caisse, one of the principal note holders, would be refused. Accordingly, the court decided that the extensions should be set aside and that resolution of the dispute should turn on each party's respective rights under the contract. The judge ruled that Devonshire was entitled to the return of its $600 million in collateral, minus the liquidity call payment and interest it had received, for a total of $532.7 million.

The Devonshire–Barclays dispute had at last brought aspects of the ABCP crisis to court, but it disappointed those seeking light regarding whether a "market disruption" had in fact occurred on 13 August 2007. The parties agreed to a separate trial on that issue, a trial that never took place. Interestingly, the judge noted that evidence indicated that "Barclays had no intention of meeting the liquidity demands from Devonshire on Aug. 13 to 15 of 2007." That is, according to Newbould, it was clear from internal Barclays documents that Barclays had always intended to take the position that no MDE within the meaning of the contract would occur as long as the notes of bank-sponsored conduits were rolling on days when the notes of non-bank conduits such as Devonshire failed to roll. Indeed, Barclays determined from 13 to 15 August 2007 (when liquidity calls were being made by Devonshire) that the notes of bank-sponsored conduits in Canada were continuing to roll. Accordingly, Barclays's position was that no MDE had occurred, despite disruptions in the non-bank ABCP market. The practical implication of Barclays's position was that there never would be an MDE. This is because bank-sponsored ABCP was by far the bulk of the outstanding ABCP so that there was a minuscule possibility of bank paper failing to continue rolling.[3] Still, this question, important as it was that August, became moot for those that signed on to the Crawford-led restructuring. The comprehensive releases to be delivered as part of the CCAA arrangement made those legal linguistics "water under the (liquidity) bridge."

Barclay's appealed Justice Newbold's judgment to the Ontario Court of Appeal. The Court of Appeal dismissed the appeal on 26 July 2013, although it varied one finding relating to Barclay's loss amount. Barclay's sought leave to appeal the Court of Appeal's judgment to the Supreme Court of Canada, but application for leave was dismissed on 16 January 2014. Barclay's and Devonshire subsequently settled, with the settlement to be implemented by a plan of compromise and arrangement under the CCAA. That plan was dated 6 August 2014, was approved at a meeting of noteholders on 7 August 2014, and was sanctioned by the court on 20 August 2014. Because that settlement resolved the dispute between the parties, the second part of the "bifurcated trial" (in which the issue of whether an MDE actually occurred was to have been litigated) will never take place.

DBRS: Off the Hook

Certainly, any mention of the ABCP crisis's root causes cannot exclude DBRS, the one agency willing to provide the LSS with an AAA rating. Without that, the market wouldn't have existed. DBRS continued to grant its stamp to new ABCP trusts until January 2007 and to existing non-bank trusts until May 2008 (when, at the trusts' own request and in the wake of the crisis, DBRS revoked its ratings). Why, then, was no one going after the rating agency?

Rating agencies were essentially self-regulated prior to the crisis based on the theory that agencies trade on their reputation – "internalizing" the costs if they give opinions that are inaccurate or lacking in diligence. In the United States, rating agencies had been required to register as Nationally Recognized Statistical Rating Organizations pursuant to SEC guidelines under the 2006 Credit Rating Agency Reform Act. But that was the extent of their regulation, and there was no similar registration requirement in Canada. American agencies were sued from time to time, but they met their claims with the defence, accepted by courts, that absent a malice finding, their opinions were protected by the First Amendment's free-speech guarantee.

The International Organization of Securities Commissions (IOSCO) has argued that agencies have been made unfair targets in the financial crisis. Their role, it says, is simply to determine credit risk, not predict overall market volatility or liquidity crises. But is this valid in the Canadian context? The liquidity problems at the core of the ABCP crisis arose from the issuers' inability to fund their maturing obligations or pay their notes on schedule – the essence of the credit risk that it was DBRS's business to evaluate.

With only two, or at most three, credit rating agencies dominant in Canada's market, the "reputational capital" model appears wrongly to assume the existence of viable alternatives. Given the significant economies of scale in the ratings market, this appears unlikely to change. In the ABCP crisis, of course, the only player was DBRS: competitive discipline was non-existent.

What can be done to make the ratings market more contestable and more accountable? In the United States, the Dodd-Frank Act has introduced a slew of new rules for agencies. These relate to such items as annual reports on internal controls, disclosure of credit rating methodologies, analyst training, and consistency guidelines for rating symbols and definitions. For its part, the European Union has made agencies subject to a registration procedure as well as to new rules that, among other things, prohibit their provision of advisory services, restrict them from giving ratings without sufficient quality information, mandate internal ratings reviews, and stipulate that they maintain at least three independent directors on their boards. Also, regulators in both the United States and Europe have taken steps to inject more competition into the agencies' field. For instance, the SEC has stripped numerous credit rating requirements embedded in statutory provisions on the theory that an alternative measure can protect investors without giving preference to the established agencies.

Canadian regulators have implemented a regulatory framework whereby agencies must now apply to become "designated rating organizations" and adopt and comply with a code of conduct, which must include specifically mandated provisions relating to conflicts of interest, governance, and various conduct issues, among other things.

While limited competition in the industry was a key factor in the ABCP crisis, Canadian regulators, despite noting their monitoring of SEC changes, have thus far been silent on improving competition in the delivery of ratings.

An increase in competition requires a number of elements. First, there have to be potential competitors with the ability and resources to undertake thorough analysis and review. Of course, for sophisticated investors, that expertise exists, but for others, there have to be credible external agencies or individuals available that can produce a rating. A regulatory standard that requires a rating by an agency that has been in the business for a minimum number of years will dramatically reduce potential competitors. However, the crucial element in increasing competition is transparency in the elements of the security/assets being rated – for instance, in the structure of complex underlying assets and in the specific liquidity contracts supporting payment obligations. With this transparency, agencies can review and provide a rating for the ABCP structure. It was this lack of transparency, resulting from the confidentiality agreements between DBRS and the ABCP conduit sponsors, that would not allow divulgence of the underlying assets to investors even after a market disruption or default.

But it may be asking too much to have a significant number of competing rating agencies. All that might be needed is for high net worth investors, lacking the necessary sophistication to undertake the rating themselves, to be able to hire outside independent companies or individuals to scrutinize and confirm the rating provided by a rating agency. To introduce this approach, however, would still require transparency.

Transparency does introduce problems, since there may be legitimate reasons to keep the underlying assets and structures confidential. But in that case, it is up to the investors to behave appropriately: if the specifics of the contract are not available, do not invest.

One approach overlooked by these reforms would be to legislatively introduce liability for gross negligence of credit rating agencies. This would create a market-based feedback mechanism to reduce or eliminate the incentive for agencies to venture into areas they don't understand – a particular problem in the subprime crisis as agencies applied historic mortgage industry metrics to rate subprime mortgages issued without proof of income or assets.

The US Department of Justice has seen no need to wait on such changes. In early April 2013, it brought a fraud suit against S&P, alleging that it falsely represented its ratings as being "independent" and "objective." S&P denied the allegations in a motion filed later that month to throw the case out. While defending its ratings' quality, S&P pointed to a prior court decision describing such assurances as mere commercial "puffery" rather than statements investors would rely on. On 3 February 2015, the US Department of Justice and 19 US states plus the District of Columbia announced that they had entered into a $1.375 billion settlement agreement with S&P along with its parent company, McGraw Hill Financial Inc. The settlement resolved the lawsuit launched in 2013.[4]

No parallel case has been brought against DBRS north of the border. Moreover, the broadly worded releases granted to DBRS in the restructuring process immunize the Canadian agency from claims brought by the crisis's main players.

Soft Solutions

Beyond the "hard" remedies of litigation or enforcement, a rudimentary look at the ABCP crisis presents another preventative solution: disclosure. Regulators could make more asset-backed vehicles subject to prospectus requirements, reducing the market's dependency on ratings. In a 2011 consultation paper, the OSC discussed removing ABCP's eligibility for sale under the prospectus exemptions for short-term debt, for sales to "accredited investors" with more than a threshold level of income or assets, and for purchases of at least $150,000 – each of which would allow it to fall into the hands of retail investors more easily. The regulatory response evolved, as discussed in chapter 12.

IIROC, for its part, has focused on registrants' poor understanding of KYC and "know your product" rules in the context of the crisis. These rules require that brokers understand, respectively, their clients' investment needs and objectives as well as the attributes and risks of products they recommend. According to a 2008 review by IIROC, none of the twenty-one Canadian brokerage firms selling non-bank ABCP reviewed the products in question to determine whether they were suitable for their clients. This lack of due diligence it found also reflected the reliance brokers placed on DBRS's rating – some brokers simply assumed the paper was a typical low-risk money market instrument. In 2012, IIROC published additional guidance on these obligations as part of its ongoing project to develop a new "Client Relationship Model" for registrants.

These duties could be buttressed, of course, by the judicial or statutory recognition of a fiduciary duty owed by brokers to clients. Investor advocates, such as Canada's Foundation for Advancement of Investor Rights (FAIR), have long supported this idea. In 2009, the US Department of Justice endorsed it when it suggested that a duty to act in the best interests of one's clients be extended to *all* financial professionals. The significance of such a duty was recognized in Section 13(g)(1) of the Dodd-Frank Act, which empowered (though did not mandate) the SEC to establish fiduciary duties for brokers. There are, however, nuances to considering introducing such a fiduciary duty, as discussed in chapter 12, and for a number of reasons the brokerage industry has generally opposed such a duty. Courts, too, have hesitated to recognize it. For instance, the Supreme Court of Canada in its 1994 decision in *Hodgkinson v. Simms* endorsed the view that the imposition of a fiduciary duty will depend on the facts, which can range from the client's "total reliance" on the broker's advice to his or her "total independence" from it.

Whatever the solution to the issues raised by the ABCP crisis, it is clear that incentives must be realigned. Investors, who often have short memories, must become less reliant on ratings and "do their homework." If they do not have the expertise to do their own ratings or the resources to purchase a confirmation of a rating, they should not purchase the investment. Rating agencies, for their part, must be made more cautious in issuing ratings – a change that would force investors, in turn, to seek information more proactively. And regulators must make greater efforts to keep up with the ever-accelerating pace of developments in the industry, rather than merely "plugging the gaps" after the fact.

Broadly speaking, there are three types of prospectus exemptions: those based on the presumed low-risk nature of the type of security being sold; those based on the presumed wealth or sophistication (or ability to withstand loss) of the investor; and those intended to facilitate the raising of capital by smaller issuers under certain specified circumstances.

For many years, conventional commercial paper could be sold under a prospectus exemption that had both "nature of security" and "nature of investor" elements. Specifically, as long as the paper being sold was short term (and, therefore, at lower risk of default) and was being sold in denominations of at least $50,000 (and therefore, presumably, out of the reach of the smallest retail investors), no prospectus was required. That exemption was amended in 2005. The minimum $50,000 purchase requirement was removed, and in its place, a requirement was added that commercial paper sold without a prospectus must have received a minimum credit rating from an approved credit rating agency. In the wake of the ABCP meltdown, Canadian securities regulators were often criticized for making this change by those who suggested that it improperly opened up the commercial paper market to small, unsophisticated retail investors. However, it would appear that this particular criticism may not be entirely well founded. The retail investors most seriously affected by the ABCP debacle were those that had invested considerably more than $50,000 in the paper, and so would have been eligible to purchase it on an exempt basis even under the old regime. Furthermore, it is only in hindsight that the requirement of an approved credit rating can fairly be viewed as *less likely* to afford protection to retail investors than a rather arbitrary (and non–inflation-adjusted) $50,000 minimum purchase amount.

PART FOUR

Conclusions

CHAPTER ELEVEN

Winners and Losers in the ABCP Debacle

Whether through a sense of competition – or, more generously, our sense of compassion – people want to identify winners and losers in Canada's ABCP restructuring. For the parties involved in the ABCP restructuring, the outcome was a zero-sum game. No third party funded the losses, there was no bailout, and, with an estimated total cost of approximately $200 million,[1] the solution was not cheap. Nor will we ever know if a litigation route would have been fairer or less costly.

Only two sets of investors were unambiguous winners, in the limited sense that they lost nothing and received their money back in full after the market froze. The first was National Bank's retail investor group, holding paper with a face value of under $2 million (others were stuck with their paper). The second was made up of Desjardins's clients.

Drawing conclusions about ultimate winners and losers among the ABCP restructuring's original participants is more challenging. The process was a negotiation, after all – driven by a need to recognize the art of the possible.

Parties to a negotiation can lose on some issues and win on others. Furthermore, the participants would only agree to terms if they felt the agreement made them better off than they would be had there been no agreement and had a decision been left up to the courts. In cases like this, there are no conclusive winners or losers.

As an example, consider the SFF. The SFF represented the response of governments to the task of providing a margin fund of last resort to be called upon only if collateral calls had exhausted the capacity of the junior MFF. The members of the SFF receive payments under the funding facility contract until the MAV notes mature, even after their risk exposure is eliminated. At first blush, this looks like a gain for the SFF participants and a loss to the investors who paid the insurance fee. However, the governments did accept risk, albeit small, and if their compensation reflects this risk, it cannot be said that there were clear winners or losers, *ex ante*. The extension of their payments beyond their risk exposure appears to be a gain, but if the junior funding facility had been unable to meet a collateral call, even after the maturity of the SFF exposure, there was an expectation that the governments would step in. This expectation cannot be quantified, so the net effect on the investors is difficult to assess.

The Winners

We begin with the participants that were not parties to the original ABCP, including the monitor, the administrator, and the legal and financial advisers. We also include a set of investors that were not part of the negotiations but became very important in the resulting market: the hedge funds. Together, these players are the unambiguous winners in the ABCP crisis, some groups (lawyers) charging big fees to fix the mess and others profiting handsomely from the spoils (hedge funds).

Justice Colin Campbell granted approval on 15 October 2013 for the fees and disbursements to the monitor and its legal counsel in an amount of approximately $25 million, of which $20.4 million was for the monitor. Campbell provided a number of comments justifying the costs incurred, and concluded that "[i]n this case, I have no hesitation in concluding that the public, the court, and all those involved in this complex CCAA process were well served by the monitor and counsel and hereby approve the fees and disbursements as sought, which I have reviewed."

The Legal Teams

The number of lawyers involved in the ABCP restructuring was impressive. A July 2009 issue of the business law magazine *Lexpert* named more than 150 lawyers involved in the transaction. This number was not surprising, given the complexity of the transaction and the number of practice areas that had to be covered: tax, structured finance (traditional and synthetic), corporate and securities, litigation, banking, and bankruptcy/restructuring. This count excludes the many in-house counsel deeply involved in the proceedings.

Nearly all of the major law firms – fourteen of them – were represented. With forty-one lawyers on the file, Goodmans, representing the PCIC, led by numbers and perhaps by billings as well. In second place was Fasken Martineau, with thirty-nine lawyers. Fasken represented a number of different clients, ranging from Desjardins to the original issuer trustees, to the trustees and agents for the new MAV notes. As for the other major players, thirty-two lawyers from Stikeman Elliott represented foreign bank asset providers and their affiliates, and twenty-nine lawyers from Ogilvy Renault represented the Caisse and the Province of Quebec.[2]

The involvement of the Ad Hoc Committees also added to the legal expenses, all of which were covered by the PCIC or by the original conduits and cash flows from the ABCP.

The Financial Adviser: J.P. Morgan

J.P. Morgan was a crucial player in the restructuring – it developed the models for the MAV structures, generated their relative valuations, and negotiated with dealers and margin funding parties. Needless to say, given this extensive involvement, one would expect significant fees, many of which we described in detail earlier in the book. The actual amount paid is difficult to quantify, but based on contractual arrangements and the CCAA ruling, it was likely around US$87 million.

The Hedge Funds

Hedge funds, contrary to what their names might imply, do not necessarily reduce risk using hedging strategies. Many pursue high-risk investment strategies and expect to earn high rates of return over a short time period. Take, for example, so-called "vulture funds," which purchase corporate distressed debt. Once such a fund acquires its position, it may generate returns using strategies that may not be consistent with the wishes of the investee company's management.

During the negotiations, the PCIC was wary of hedge funds buying the frozen ABCP and becoming involved in the negotiations or trading in the paper. To counter this possibility, no information about the underlying ABCP transactions was released, leaving any hedge fund to make its purchases "in the dark." That did not stop – but likely reduced – their buying activity.

However, once the restructuring was complete and the MAV notes were tradable in an over-the-counter market, American, Canadian, and

European hedge funds snapped up the notes from investors. In addition, a Canadian fund established a MAV fund sold to retail investors. As we saw in the case of Fiera Quantum, the returns have been surprisingly good as prices of the MAV II notes increased substantially from their initial value. The key success factor for hedge funds was their understanding of the product, including the tracking notes, and their calculated decision to take the risk. They understood that, under the new structure, the probability of loss was small, thanks to the quality and diversification of the LSS notes and the revised triggers.

The unwinding of ABCP swaps now under way and described in chapter 9 has provided original investors in ABCP and hedge funds with liquidity, allowing them to exit the market at prices approaching the face value of the notes.

The Canadian Banks

As liquidity problems in the ABCP market were occurring, Canadian banks continued their ABCP operations. On 21 August 2007, the six largest Canadian banks presented a joint statement of their intention to work together to ensure that the bank-sponsored ABCP market would "continue[] to perform satisfactorily." No comment was made about the non-bank ABCP market, which had frozen, with some liquidity and collateral calls unmet. The banks had little exposure to third-party ABCP; however, they *were* exposed to the financial crisis. First, they had a number of clients that had purchased third-party ABCP. This retail function was ultimately addressed by regulatory agencies (IIROC and OSC) through fines or administrative penalties. These proceedings were not directly relevant to the restructuring process. More important were banks' own ABCP holdings, as they continued to maintain markets in ABCP. Some of this paper was of dubious quality, impacting the banks' balance sheets and potentially their regulatory requirements. With a reduction in bank capital, the banks would face a reduction in lending capacity.[3] Over the period starting with the market freeze, the government, not the Bank of Canada, had to make a decision as to how much risk the Government of Canada would take. Early statements by the finance minister, Jim Flaherty, suggested that taking risk with respect to the third-party non-bank ABCP was not in the cards. However, the decision with respect to the banks was different. In early 2008, banks began to take their ABCP back onto their balance sheets. The Bank of Canada allowed sponsoring banks to use some forms of their own ABCP as collateral in the Standing Liquidity Facility.[4] The cost of using this facility was higher than the charge on other commercial paper. With the Bank of Canada as their liquidity provider, the banks were able to resolve their liquidity problems without great difficulty. Later in 2008, during the restructuring and the worst of the financial crisis, the Government of Canada announced that it would buy up to $25 billion worth of National Housing Act (NHA) insured mortgages from the banks through the Canada Mortgage and Housing Corporation (CMHC). The purpose of this purchase was to permit the banks to obtain long-term funding.

The banks reluctantly became engaged in the restructuring on two fronts. First, they accepted the legal releases, which were, on the whole, a positive development for them. Second, and more importantly, they were part of the crucial MFF for the MAV II notes. As part of the MFF, they provided insurance against the risk of collateral calls for a fee – 120 bps. The specifics of the restructuring agreement – notably the spread-loss triggers – actually reduced the risk facing the MFF. Also, the agreement reduced their risk over time in two ways: first, as the underlying transactions came closer to maturity, they became less risky; and second, when they matured, or if they were unwound before maturity, the funds released did not go to the investors but remained locked in the collateral pool, to be released upon the MAV notes' maturity. Risk was reduced as the time to maturity decreased and the collateral pool grew.

Were the banks winners or losers in the restructuring process? The usual response is that the banks always win. But is it true here? Since the legal releases were a positive development, the net effect depends upon whether, given the risk assumed by the banks, the MFF fee was sufficiently below market to offset the positive impact of the releases. Unfortunately, we have no way to measure what the financial damage would have been had releases not been in place. Thus, we can only refer to the impact of the MFF transaction itself.

Calculating the MFF's net impact on the banks' wealth is not possible, given the data required. However, we provide some observations that may be helpful. First, in its 14 March 2008, report, J.P. Morgan provides an estimate of 160 bps for the MFF fee, or 222 bps when adjusted for maturity differences. It estimated that a market-based fee would be 473 bps greater than this maturity-adjusted MFF fee. This differential was intended to demonstrate that the banks were not gaining in the transaction but were being good corporate citizens.

Unfortunately, there are a number of problems in the market rate's estimation. First, with information on the underlying transactions unavailable, no dealer would be prepared to quote a rate to provide the funding facility. Second, the triggers were spread-loss, not mark-to-market, which made a collateral call less likely. Finally, a number of rough assumptions had to be made to arrive at the insurance premium estimate. In the final deal, the MFF fee was reduced to 120 bps even in the face of higher spreads as the global economy faced added financial risk in late 2008. This reduction could reflect the fact that the original fee was too rich or that the investors had added bargaining power.

The Losers

The Investors

The investors were not a homogeneous group. They ranged from the unsophisticated, both retail and commercial/corporate, through the corporate investors to the institutional group, including pension and mutual funds.

Although the retail and corporate investors were represented on the PCIC, by and large the PCIC was composed of large institutional investors, including National Bank and Desjardins, which became investors as a result of their purchase of some clients' positions in ABCP. Each of these investor groups was affected by the restructuring in a different way.

Probably the saddest outcome was for the small retail investors, followed by the commercial and small corporate investors. When the market froze, all investors were faced with the inability to access funds they had invested for the short term while waiting to invest or use them for other purposes. For the retail investors, other planned uses for the money included funds for retirement and money to purchase new houses, for example.

Finally, on 9 April 2008, approximately eight months after the market froze, Canaccord announced a "relief plan" for a subset of the investors who had bought ABCP through it. Investors would receive their cash on the successful completion of the CCAA procedure and the *close* of the restructuring. While this plan appeared to end the retail holders' travails, at the time of Canaccord's announcement, the restructuring still had ten months to go until completion. Also, some retail investors were still left with funds in ABCP when these were converted to the new MAV notes, and their liquidity depended on the establishment of a liquid market in the notes.

For the corporate and commercial investors, National Bank announced its "Support Program" on 8 April 2008, once again conditional on approval of the CCAA arrangement and the successful completion of the restructuring. The program had about $2.1 billion allocated to it and was intended to provide credit facilities for liquidity needs until the maturity of the MAV notes. Approximately 100 clients would be affected by this program.

This facility offered standard credit terms for matching the funding to customers. Like the Canaccord relief program, National Bank's program was intended to address investors' hostility to the plan and obtain a positive vote. While the program appears to have had some positive elements, customers would only have access to the funds after the close of the deal. Also, the interest paid on their new replacement notes would be a banker's acceptance (BA) rate minus 50 bps. This would not go very far towards paying the interest on the new credit facilities.

Corporate investors holding large amounts of ABCP were likely able to negotiate access to their funds on favourable credit terms directly with the banks that had sold them the paper. Many of these investors had sufficient resources to credibly threaten to sue, change banks, and harness political pressure. Furthermore, for corporations with ongoing business operations generating cash flows, the fact that their ABCP funds were frozen did not pose as big a liquidity issue as it did for the smaller corporate/commercial and retail investors.

The final group of holders was comprised of the large, presumably sophisticated institutions. Unfortunately, managing large amounts of money does not necessarily guarantee investment sophistication or even a high standard of care. Regarding the large institutions, there was often a lack of due diligence on ABCP, in terms of assuming too much based on the limited information that was readily available and not undertaking sufficient independent analysis. Some examination of the structure underlying the third-party ABCP, for example, would surely have led to careful questioning and perhaps different decisions.

One of the most discouraging aspects of the behaviour of sophisticated investors was how they handled credit risk: they didn't. All non-government, short-term investments require a credit risk analysis when funds are advanced. This analysis, however, involved a lot of effort,

effort that seemed out of proportion to the short time period for which the funds would be outstanding. Even investors with large exposures to ABCP appeared to justify a lack of due diligence, reasoning, *what can go wrong in three months?* or *we can always sell if we don't like the results.* They also deferred to the judgment of the credit rating agency, which had assigned a rating of R-1 (high) to the paper, as a further justification for not undertaking a full credit risk analysis. Many heads rolled in the institutional market as a result of the ABCP crisis.

Finally, all investors lost under the restructuring agreement because any proceeds of a wind-up of any underlying transactions in the ABCP went to the collateral pool to reduce the risk of the MFF participants and were not paid out to investors. These funds were locked in the facility until the maturity of the MAV notes.

Overall, the large institutions lost, but the severity of the loss to these organizations paled in comparison to the impact on the smaller commercial/corporate investors – and especially the retail investors.

Coventree Inc. Shareholders

Coventree Inc. was not the only non-bank ABCP sponsor to be affected by the freeze, but given that its sponsored conduits had issued approximately $16 billion of affected ABCP, it was the largest. As a listed company on the Toronto Stock Exchange, Coventree reported information to shareholders on a timely basis through various public reports. The reporting and its timeliness became the subject of an OSC hearing subsequent to the restructuring, as discussed in the previous chapter.

With the benefit of hindsight, including information about meetings held before the market freeze, it is now apparent that even before the freeze, Coventree's future was not bright. According to Coventree's David Allan, the beginning of the end was obvious on 13 August 2007, the date when ABCP froze and when Coventree released the first of a series of press releases it would issue over the next three days. Reviewing the press releases was like watching a train wreck in slow motion or, as former Coventree employee Ching describes it, a "horror show."

The end game for Coventree was painfully evident in its continuing and expanding inability to roll the outstanding ABCP, the mixed responses of liquidity providers to liquidity calls, and the 16 August 2007 notice by DBRS that it had placed the ratings of ABCP issuers affected by the market disruption under review with "developing implications."

On 6 September 2007, Coventree established a special committee to investigate strategic options for the firm that would maximize shareholder value in light of the market disruption. The special committee concluded that independent of the success of the restructuring that was under way, there were no viable business opportunities for Coventree, and an orderly wind-down of operations was required. This wind-down would begin upon the completion of the restructuring activities under negotiation. During the restructuring period, Coventree was paying a portion of the restructuring committee expenses.

On 2 November 2009, Coventree shares were delisted from the TSX and began trading on NEX, a special trading venue of the TSX Venture Exchange.

The impact on the Coventree shareholders is seen in the share price activity over the period of the crisis and the restructuring. The share price closed at the end of July 2007, prior to the market freeze, at $14.53, with a high for that month of $16.30. In August, the month-end closing stock price was $2.25; its low for the month was $1.64. Following this severe reduction, the share price slowly increased to slightly above $4.00 in mid-2009; as of 27 July 2011, it was about $2.40. By then, the shareholders had passed a resolution (on 30 June 2010) approving a voluntary wind-up of Coventree at a date to be determined by the directors. That voluntary wind-up commenced on 15 February 2012.

Looking at the share price movement from prior to the crisis, in July 2007, to the resolution of the restructuring at the end of January 2009, it is clear that shareholders at the start of this period who held the stock suffered severe losses. The shareholders included the principals of the company – Cornish and Tai. Investors who bought in subsequent to the market freeze would have earned a significant rate of return. Trading patterns are also revealing. Trading activity was concentrated in the period just after the market freeze, late 2007, and then not again until early in 2009.

The litigation was protracted and resulted in a delay in paying dividends to shareholders and a substantial reduction in the amount of cash available for distribution. If the purpose of the OSC action was to help Coventree shareholders, permitting the company to unwind would have met this goal.

The Caisse

Like all other investors, the Caisse was a loser in the ABCP crisis. With the largest amount invested in ABCP of any investor, the Caisse had the most to lose and, of course, the most to gain from an orderly and timely restructuring. The major gain to the Caisse was the avoidance of a fire sale of the underlying assets in the ABCP trusts, which would have led to significant crystallized losses, not just the book losses that already had been taken. The Caisse decided to participate in the MAV I vehicle. Because there was no external funding facility in MAV I, investors had flexibility to deal with the underlying trades that were not available to the MAV II investors.

The Caisse ended up with extensive exposure to ABCP because the pension fund needed substantial amounts of short-term liquid investments as part of a broader investment initiative. The Caisse became very heavily exposed because of a gap in risk management. According to the Caisse's investment policy, no more than 5% of the invested funds could be placed in a single financial issue. The decision facing the money manager was whether to invest the funds in banker's acceptance notes, T-bills, ABCP, or some combination of these instruments. Given the Caisse's investment policy, each ABCP trust could be considered a separate financial issue even if the underlying assets were similar. This pointed to an important and fatal gap in the system. If the Caisse wanted to invest the cash in ABCP, it simply needed to ensure that enough conduits were available. And, of course, there were.

This investment policy left the Caisse with unexpected large and ex-post risky exposure in ABCP. ABCP was considered to be low-risk since the underlying assets had good diversification and the attachment points on LSSs were, on average, sufficiently high to ensure that most risk would be absorbed by holders of lower-ranking tranches, effectively eliminating LSS risk. As for liquidity risk, it was either never considered or, if it was, the investors believed that third-party liquidity arrangements removed that risk.

This was a vast miscalculation. The Caisse's decision to invest an aggregate of $13 billion in non-bank ABCP was made on an individual trust basis. With the large number of trusts, it is possible that the Caisse risk systems were unable to detect the total amount invested in ABCP. The names of the issuing trusts were identified, but whether they were bank- or third-party-sponsored was not. Although the money managers would have known this information, the risk management committee members were likely not aware of the specific details of the trusts unless they asked.

In addition, the diversification the Caisse thought it had achieved from the number of different trusts it held and constraints around investment size proved to be illusory. The trusts' similar exposure to LSS and the fact that a financial crisis has a negative effect on all investments meant that the overall ABCP portfolio turned out to be highly risky. Finally, in most cases, the liquidity calls issued by the ABCP conduits were not met by the liquidity providers.

Why did the money managers choose ABCP rather than other, more conventional short-term investments? One possible factor was the bonus target for money market managers. This target was set at the three-month T-bill rate plus 25 bps. Even if ABCP generated only three-month T-bills plus one bp per month, after one year, almost half of the manager's target would be achieved with little expected risk.

The Caisse took away a number of lessons from this experience. First and most importantly, it now recognized a need to implement a risk management system that would provide information on the risk exposure of the overall portfolio. In addition, risk management was to be pushed down to the investment decision-making process. Thus, since the debacle, risk exposure management has been enhanced at both a micro and macro portfolio level. The concern with this approach is that it may stress the mere avoidance of risk rather than its accurate pricing. Risk in an investment vehicle is not necessarily bad per se, but it has to be compensated *ex ante* by appropriate expected returns. In the end, it is not in the best interests of any pension fund to eliminate risky or innovative investment products simply because they have risk. The pendulum may be swinging too far.

The Surprise: DBRS

To the shock and confusion of many investors and financial market participants, DBRS, far from being left bloody in the wake of the crisis, has arisen Phoenix-like to continue its ratings business in North America and Europe. Just recently, it was bought out by a private equity company.

Regardless of the sophistication of ABCP investors, they all agree that it was DBRS's R-1 High rating on the paper that cemented their decision to purchase it. While reliance on ratings is understandable for most retail and many commercial and corporate investors, sympathy is harder to muster for sophisticated investors. They surely ought to have done a better job of due diligence; at the very least, they should have worried when transparency about some of the aspects of the products was non-existent.

The DBRS ratings were prepared on the underlying assets and on the ABCP trusts that included those assets. The US agencies' ratings on the subprime assets included in third-party ABCP were accepted by DBRS in its ABCP rating. This reliance was understandable: the cost of DBRS undertaking its own analysis on a small component of the ABCP issues was not reasonable, so it relied on respected rating agencies that had the resources to undertake the needed analysis.

Unfortunately, the ratings turned out to have problems.

However, the story is different for the remainder of the assets. DBRS was well aware of the mark-to-market triggers, the leverage undertaken on the LSS assets, and, most important, the terms of the liquidity arrangements. The liquidity arrangements, which were originally based on the OSFI Guideline B-5 for use in bank-sponsored ABCP, changed over time. It is not known whether DBRS recognized this but decided the market was so buoyant that the new liquidity arrangements would never be problematic. Suffice it to say that the amount of business being done by DBRS was significant, perhaps to help fund opening operations in Europe.

Given the problems that arose due to the liquidity agreements, it is no surprise that DBRS was interested in the legal releases. The exposure of rating agencies to legal liability for inappropriate ratings is an open question. Prior to the crisis, at any rate, it was widely thought that such exposure was minimal. In the United States, ratings have been insulated from civil actions as a form of protected free speech. In Canada, restrictive common law rules surrounding the tort of negligent misrepresentation and an express exemption from securities law statutory civil liability for rating agencies make it very difficult to successfully sue rating agencies. But no doubt, rating agencies would prefer the certainty of an explicit legal release.

What losses existed that would offset the gain from the granting of the release? It is hard to see what those might be.

Certainly, there were changes in personnel in the company along with a hit to its reputation. On the other hand, DBRS provided advice to the PCIC on the new MAV notes after US-based rating agencies expressed reluctance to get involved. DBRS also rated the new notes, and it continues to earn a small fee for this rating responsibility.

In addition, DBRS has been recognized as a legitimate rating agency for European debt and has provided some interesting ratings on sovereign European debt.

To put the icing on the cake, in November 2014 there was an announcement that three private equity firms were looking at buying DBRS. On 22 December 2014, alternative asset manager Carlyle Group LP and private equity firm Warburg Pincus LLC announced an agreement to acquire DBRS for a reported US$500 million. The rationale for the acquisition was to provide a credible alternative to the three largest US rating firms. This competition would not be in the US market but in Europe, where DBRS has been active, and in emerging markets. Regarding the former, European regulators in 2013 introduced guidance to companies to use rating firms with less than a 10% market share. This guidance is intended to introduce competition in the ratings market. The acquisition closed on 4 March 2015, and Walter Schroeder, the founder of the firm, took an equity interest in the new firm.

Obviously, DBRS appears to have weathered the crisis quite successfully.

Deutsche Bank

Deutsche Bank is a global financial institution with the bulk of its activities in Germany and elsewhere in Europe. The bank has been expanding into North America, Asia, and selected emerging markets. Deutsche Bank has three divisions: corporate and investment banking; private clients and asset management; and corporate investments. It is the first of these divisions that was significantly affected by the market turbulence in 2007 and 2008, specifically in the structured credit and subprime areas.

The financial crisis hit Deutsche Bank very hard. As noted in Table 11.1, net revenues fell from 2007 to 2008, largely because of the reduction in corporate and investment banking revenues. The book value of equity also fell.

In addition, the fair value of LSS exposure fell dramatically from 2007 to 2008. In 2007, its value was €34.9 billion; in 2008, €0.9 billion. In 2007, the bulk of the exposure was in North America – €25.8 billion versus €9.2 billion in Europe and Asia. In 2008, the value for North America was €0.8 billion. With the design of Canadian-style liquidity arrangements, the bulk of the LSS transactions were with Canadian clients.

In Canada, Deutsche Bank had many fingers in the ABCP pie. Like most of the banks in this area, it was both an asset provider and a

Table 11.1. Selected financial information as of 31 December: Deutsche Bank

Year	Net revenues (€ billion)		Some balance sheet values (€ billion)	
	Total operations	Corp and I.B.	Assets	Equity
2008	13.5	3.1	2,202	3.2
2007	30.7	19.1	1,925	3.9

Source: Annual reports, 2007 and 2008

liquidity provider for LSS transactions. This situation is particularly problematic. When the decision to make a collateral call is the responsibility of the same party that must respond to a liquidity call, there is a clear conflict of interest that will operate to the detriment of the investor. Deutsche Bank was also a distributor agent for seven third-party ABCP conduits. Of these conduits, two were composed of 100% LSS transactions (Silverstone and Skeena). Deutsche Bank was by far the largest asset and liquidity provider in the Canadian third-party ABCP market; regarding the latter, it was the liquidity provider behind thirty-seven LSS transactions.

As a liquidity provider that was able to avoid the negative impact of taking LSSs back onto its balance sheet, Deutsche Bank was on the winner side of the ledger, unless it were to be exposed to legal liability for refusing to provide liquidity in response to liquidity calls – now an unlikely outcome. If Deutsche Bank had to take back the LSSs, it would have to unwind them in a turbulent market at the same time that it was in trouble in other global markets. However, Deutsche Bank, along with the other large global banks, did have write-downs for their ABCP, which in turn had impacts on regulatory requirements and lending capacity. Although near the bottom of the list in write-downs during the 2007 and beginning of 2008 period, the amount of US$3.2 billion was still significant.[5] As a member of the MFF, Deutsche Bank could have received a benefit, given the size of the insurance fee. Also, by negotiating for and achieving an SFF, Deutsche Bank and the other asset providers were able to obtain a backstop and an expectation that the federal government would step in to deal with any serious problems that might arise after the agreement was completed.

But on the negative side, once the restructuring talks began, Deutsche Bank, along with the other asset providers, agreed to standstill arrangements, which eliminated their ability to make collateral calls even as credit default spreads and the volatility in the spreads increased.

In addition, even if they had been able to make successful collateral calls, liquidating the positions would have impacted the market and reduced the amount they would obtain. Deutsche Bank faced a serious financial problem over this period.

On 26 May 2015, the SEC issued an order against Deutsche Bank (DB) for financial misstatements related to its Canadian ABCP LSS positions during 2008 and the first quarter of 2009.[6] Deutsche Bank agreed to pay a US$55 million civil penalty to settle the SEC proceedings. The proceedings stemmed from misstatements in DB's financial statements related to its position as credit protection buyer and the impact of limited collateral posted by the credit protection sellers. The trades in question were leveraged 11 times, and the collateral was 9% of the $98 billion notional value or approximately $8.5 billion. Because the trades were leveraged, DB was exposed to the risk that the collateral value supporting the transactions could be less than the market value of DB's position – so-called "gap risk." As spreads increased during the financial crisis, DB's position as a credit protection buyer increased in value, and this increase was reflected in its financial statements. However, the very events that led to the increase in market value simultaneously increased the gap risk. The increase in gap risk resulted from an unchanged amount of collateral as the value of DB's instruments increased. DB's position was really only protected to the extent of the asset collateral because in the event of default, the credit protection seller could simply refuse to post additional collateral, leading to an unwind of the trade by DB. During 2008, DB used a variety of methods to measure the gap risk of the LSS trades. Each new method generally resulted in a lower value being assigned to DB's gap risk for the purposes of DB's 2008 financial statements. In fact, beginning in October 2008, DB was valuing its gap risk for financial statement purposes at zero. Furthermore, under the restructuring agreement the collateral call triggers were changed from mark-to-market to spread-loss. One effect of this change was that DB would not be able to call for collateral as early as it could under the original mark-to-market triggers. The result would be an increase in DB gap risk and in the likelihood of losses in an unwind (sale) situation following an unsuccessful collateral call. These impacts of the new trigger approach on asset providers were recognized by all parties during the restructuring negotiations.

Overall, we cannot slot Deutsche Bank exclusively in either the winner or the loser column.

Conclusions

Not every party to the restructuring was a winner. In a negotiation, not everyone gets what they want. While there was a range of winners and losers, on the whole the parties together were able to construct a deal that was better in aggregate than what would have resulted had the process been left to market forces and private litigation. Unfortunately, we cannot be definitive in this conclusion.

CHAPTER TWELVE

Lessons Learned

One question remains: Was the ABCP restructuring a "uniquely Canadian solution to a uniquely Canadian problem"? The answer this book comes to is yes. There are clearly Canada-specific elements in both the crisis and the ultimate solution. Canada's ABCP crisis – unlike the crisis in other countries – was not about institutions holding too many toxic subprime assets. Rather, it was about a crisis of confidence in the market and liquidity problems. Unique to Canada, only a "general market disruption" would contractually force ABCP liquidity providers to come to the table. The definition of a "general market disruption" varied from contract to contract, and not all liquidity providers were equally magnanimous in their interpretation of their obligations.

Another made-in-Canada part of the ABCP story involved the LSSs, for which Canada had become the niche market. By issuing these instruments with (ex post) questionable liquidity arrangements, the mainly foreign asset providers – which were also the liquidity providers – could shed risk from their balance sheets. The restrictive liquidity covenants meant that the banks acting as asset providers were permitted by bank capital rules to keep bad assets off their balance sheets during a stress period. In US deals, broader global liquidity provisions closed off such risk shifting by the liquidity providers.

Moreover, the LSS instruments used mark-to-market triggers for collateral calls. These triggers were not unique to Canada; however, they were not widely used globally and gave asset providers a distinct advantage. Because these arrangements were typically non-recourse, the asset providers would only enjoy the benefit of these triggers if the liquidation value of the assets plus the collateral could make the asset providers whole. Otherwise, the conduits issuing the ABCP could simply refuse to contribute collateral in response to a collateral call, leaving the liquidity provider in the unenviable position of holding assets worth less than the outstanding obligations and with no further recourse against the conduits for the balance.

Furthermore, only one credit rating agency rated Canadian non-bank ABCP: DBRS. The major US agencies took one look at the Canadian-style liquidity arrangements and walked away. Since the paper was sold to investors on a prospectus-exempt basis, there was limited disclosure available to investors, which meant that the single DBRS rating became particularly important.

The solution to the ABCP debacle was equally unique to Canada. Globally, it was the only private sector restructuring completed during the financial crisis. In one sense, it exemplified the stereotype of Canadians as non-confrontational, less litigious, and more willing to engage in discussion and compromise. But other, more tangible and practical factors played a clear role in directing the process to a negotiated restructuring.

First, saving the assets was an overriding goal of the restructuring. All participants were keenly aware of the threat that a fire sale presented to asset values and the overall market. As the Caisse's Rousseau noted, the interests of the collective dominated those of the individual parties. This shared commitment did not, of course, ensure frictionless negotiations. Every participant naturally sought to obtain a net benefit.

Second, unlike all other countries that faced ABCP problems, the Canadian solution involved no direct government intervention. The feds, in particular, were adamant about this: it was a private sector problem that needed a private sector solution. Non-intervention significantly delayed the resolution process, but it also forced the negotiating parties to be results-driven.

Third, despite the vast number of parties with a stake, two entities dominated the negotiations: the Caisse, which had billions of dollars invested in the paper, and Deutsche Bank, which was by far the market's largest asset and liquidity provider. Both faced serious financial strain during the crisis and so had an even bigger reason to strive for a compromise.

Fourth, the innovative use of the CCAA – to that point, a statutory lifeboat for individual bankrupt companies, not a vehicle for restructuring an entire industry – was unique to Canada. By imposing an industry-wide stay of proceedings and then releasing all parties involved from legal liability, the CCAA procedure avoided the expense and delay of the multiplicity of court cases launched in the United States. Another benefit to the CCAA process was that it was managed by commercial lawyers rather than traditional litigators; this focused the legal work on compromise, not adversarial conflict.

Finally, unlike in the rest of the world, the underlying assets involved in the trusts were mostly sound. The underlying strength of these assets is demonstrated in the performance of the post-restructuring MAV II notes.

The Art of the Possible

A perfect solution rarely presents itself in a negotiation. No party receives exactly what it seeks. Rather, the outcome is the imperfect result of strategizing, bluffing, and even bullying. And all of this occurs in real time, as events, positive and negative, change the dynamics of the deal and the relative bargaining positions of the parties. In fact, the final resolution here was, in effect, a series of deals that had to be renegotiated as external factors – usually CDS spreads – changed and made previously agreed-upon terms unpalatable to some of the parties. It was the shared sense of the collective benefit of an overall agreement that paved the way for a renegotiation and stopped the deal from being killed late in the negotiations. Of course, last-minute efforts to reach an accord were undertaken in the shadow of the knowledge that killing the deal would be harmful to everyone.

Canada's ABCP crisis was the product of a unique set of vulnerabilities, vulnerabilities that both parties and regulators must now take note of, and address, if they are to avoid a future contagion and its attendant losses. But in addition to the forces of luck, the restructuring also benefited from a set of uniquely Canadian advantages. In the end, it was no one's best option. It was, however, in the words of "promoter-in-chief" Crawford, "the art of the possible," and the investors, institutions, and governments involved proved themselves up to the task.

The ABCP crisis is not without its lessons. It was a major embarrassment to many involved. It was a blow to supposedly sophisticated investors, who should have been more alert to the paper's risks. Moreover, the prevalence of ABCP in the portfolios of retail investors revealed some alarming gaps in the process whereby investments are deemed "suitable" for clients at brokerages and financial institutions, as well as some disappointing shortcomings in the knowledge of individual dealers and advisers that service the retail market. Also, the limited oversight of the paper exposed gaps in regulatory oversight.

Below, we identify a number of important lessons that can be drawn from the crisis.

Lesson 1: A more competitive landscape for credit rating agencies –
investors need to check their overreliance on ratings

Credit rating agencies have been lambasted for their role in rating many of the complex securities that were at the centre of the financial crisis, including, for our purposes, third-party ABCP. DBRS's awarding of its highest commercial paper rating to ABCP was the key factor leading many investors to embrace it as a low-risk asset. Those investors didn't look beyond the gold-plated recommendation, and throughout the industry, the high credit rating pushed the paper into portfolios where it should never have been allowed.

At least three regulatory issues relating to credit rating agencies have been debated since the ABCP meltdown. First, questions have been raised about whether it is appropriate for securities regulators to embed the ratings of certain credit rating agencies within securities regulatory instruments, such as the commercial paper prospectus exemption. This sort of legislative or regulatory "incorporation by reference" had been the subject of discussion for many years preceding the financial crisis. It had become a particularly salient issue following the accounting scandals associated with Enron, WorldCom, and a number of other large issuers at the turn of the twenty-first century. Though legislators and regulators have acknowledged the need to decrease the extent of regulatory reliance on private credit rating agencies (see, for example, ss. 939 and 939A of the Dodd-Frank Act), as a practical matter, ratings will continue to play a major role in financial markets until an acceptable substitute emerges.

Second, following the crisis, many market watchers called for increased scrutiny of credit rating agencies in Canada, particularly in light of regulatory developments internationally. Canadian regulators responded by introducing a new regulatory regime for credit rating agencies: National Instrument 25–101, which came into effect in 2012. The rule was originally proposed as a "comply or explain" regime tied to provisions of the Code of Conduct for Credit Rating Agencies produced by the International Organization of Securities Commissions. However, the Canadian rule that was ultimately adopted went beyond "comply or explain" to impose a requirement on every credit rating agency seeking recognition[1] as a designated rating organization to adopt and adhere to a code of conduct, including provisions specifi-cally mandated by the new rules. This change was made so that Cana-dian rules would satisfy EU regulatory requirements for European Commission recognition of ratings issued by firms outside the EU. This European recognition has been particularly helpful for DBRS, which now rates a number of international debt issues, occasionally for firms or sovereign issuers that the larger rating agencies will not rate.

Finally, some critics have questioned the propriety of provisions in Canadian securities legislation that exempt credit rating agencies from the statutory civil liability rules designed to facilitate civil actions by aggrieved investors. In Ontario, for example, the exemption is found in the provisions of Ontario's Securities Act dealing with the liability of experts whose reports or opinions are referenced in a securities issuer's secondary market disclosure documents.[2] It is important to understand that the issues raised by this specific statutory exemption from liability have no bearing on the broader general question of the extent to which credit rating agencies may be held liable under common law to inves-tors that have relied on negligently issued ratings – a question that is beyond the scope of this discussion.

To understand the significance of the statutory exemption for credit rating agencies, it is important first to review the basic elements of the special statutory civil liability regime created under the Securities Act. Under this regime, buyers or sellers of securities are permitted to sue certain experts if a misrepresentation relating to the expert's reports, statements, or opinions has been made on behalf of the issuer of the securities. This statutory civil liability provision is important to poten-tial plaintiffs because it enables them to sue for damages without first having to prove that they actually relied on the misrepresentation that resulted in the damages. It is enough, in other words, simply to prove that the misrepresentation was made, even if, for example, the misrep-resentation was contained in a document that the individual buyer or seller never actually saw or read.

Retail investors, after all, rarely have the time or the expertise to read all of the information published by issuers of the securities in which they invest. Yet the statements in those documents certainly do have an impact on the price of the securities being purchased because they are read carefully by securities analysts and other industry experts, and they form part of the informational matrix that is factored into the market price of the securities. Therefore, a misrepresentation in those documents can seriously harm a retail investor, even though the retail investor may not have relied directly on the misrepresentation. At common law, however, any investor suing for damage would be required to prove actual reliance to succeed in an action based on the torts of fraud or negligent misrepresentation. It is not enough to prove that a misrepresentation was made and that the price of the security in the market was affected by that misrepresentation. The law demands that the individual plaintiff prove that he or she personally relied on the misrepresentation when buying or selling the security. It has long been thought that the need to prove actual reliance poses an almost insurmountable hurdle for most individual purchasers of securities and that it creates a formidable barrier for plaintiffs seeking to have an action certified as a class action as well. That is the hurdle that the "statutory civil liability" provisions in the Securities Act are intended to overcome.

However, designated credit rating organizations are expressly excluded from the definition of "expert" for the purposes of this statutory civil liability provision. In other words, plaintiffs seeking to sue credit rating agencies for misrepresentation cannot take advantage of the statutory civil liability provisions. Their only legal recourse is to sue for fraud or negligent misrepresentation and so face the practical obstacles of bringing such claims, including the daunting task of having to prove actual reliance on the alleged misrepresentations.

Why were credit rating agencies carved out of the statutory definition of "expert" in this way? In the release accompanying the final version of National Instrument 25–101, the CSA explained that credit rating agencies had been excluded from the secondary market civil liability rules because, unlike other experts, credit rating agencies are not required under Canadian securities laws to consent to the inclusion of their ratings in prospectuses. This is important, because only consenting experts can be held liable for misrepresentations under the statutory civil liability rules that apply to prospectus offerings. Accordingly, the CSA explained, it would be anomalous if non-consenting experts were exposed to statutory civil liability on a different basis in the case of secondary market trading. The CSA acknowledged that, in the United States, the Dodd-Frank Act (s. 939G) had the effect of removing the provision in US securities legislation that exempted credit rating agencies from providing a consent to inclusion of their ratings in prospectuses. The practical result, however, had not been expanded liability for credit rating agencies. Rather, agencies had simply refused to grant their consent to the use of their ratings for this purpose. A similar result, evidently, had also occurred in Australia. Accordingly, retail investors in those jurisdictions have, in many cases, simply lost access to credit ratings altogether. In light of these factors, the CSA concluded that it did not believe "the benefits of subjecting designated rating organizations to 'expert' liability in Canada would outweigh the potential costs." To reiterate, however, these statutory exclusions relate to only one specific *statutory* cause of action. Common law claims against credit rating agencies are still possible, at least in theory, and indeed, such claims have been pursued against rating agencies in both the United States and Australia.

The lack of significant changes in the regulatory framework for credit rating agencies in Canadian jurisdictions heightens the importance of a competitive landscape. Yet there has been little focus on increasing competition among these agencies. Barriers to entry remain high – perhaps a result of regulatory constraints as well as a reliance on reputation in the market and the difficulty of building this reputation. The implication is that investors will have to take more responsibility in assessing creditworthiness.

There are also some general commonsense lessons to be learned from the ABCP collapse. The first is that sophisticated investors cannot pass on their due diligence duties to outside parties such as rating agencies. Pension funds, for example, must dedicate the time and resources to examine and understand what is under the hood of the assets they invest in. Credit ratings are no substitute for basic due diligence, no matter how many resources that due diligence demands.

One option could be to encourage fiduciaries to buy investments only when those investments have received consistent and uniform ratings from at least two major credit rating agencies. Certainly, this would open up the playing field for competition in the rating agency space around the world. The fact that DBRS was the only agency willing to rate Canadian third-party ABCP should have been a sign of trouble and should have, at the very least, encouraged investors (sophisticated investors, at a minimum) to ask why other agencies had declined to provide a rating. This simple question would have uncovered important flaws that were ignored because of the high rating.

In the United States, S&P's letter-grade ratings service has come under scrutiny as regulators raise questions about its objectivity and the inherent conflicts in its business model. This led the US government to launch an ambitious $5 billion civil lawsuit against the agency, accusing it of defrauding investors through inflated ratings and understated risks associated with mortgage securities. When this lawsuit was settled in February 2015, S&P admitted, in the agreed statement of facts, that business concerns had affected decisions on its ratings models (see chapter 10).

We do not believe that lawsuits like this are the answer for DBRS. True, the firm has survived and even thrived in the wake of the crisis. In fact, DBRS provided advice to the PCIC on the new MAV notes; when other US-based rating agencies were reluctant to get involved, DBRS rated the new notes and earns a continuing (albeit small) fee for this rating responsibility.

Lawsuits could be counterproductive. They might increase perceived risks for credit rating agencies and so possibly lead them to withdraw from certain lines of business, further reducing the very kind of competition that we feel is needed in the credit rating agency space. It would be far better to encourage investors to seek multiple ratings and opinions from different firms when they are making their investment choices. But facilitating high-quality firms to enter the industry remains a formidable challenge.

Lesson 2: The role of IIROC and the question of broker fiduciary standards

The role brokers play in selling third-party ABCP, especially to retail investors, also highlights some important lessons for the future. In October 2008, IIROC released a regulatory study dealing with the manufacture and distribution of ABCP by IIROC members.[3] That study included details of a "compliance sweep" undertaken by IIROC following the crisis. The compliance sweep revealed that as of April 2007, IIROC dealer members held about $6.6 billion of third-party ABCP at the Canadian Depository for Securities Ltd. (CDS Ltd.). The number of dealers that had distributed ABCP to retail investors was small. In all, 99% of the dollar value of the distribution of IIROC dealer members was to institutional clients and inventory holdings. Only fourteen dealer members held positions for retail clients, and the amount of ABCP held for all such retail clients totalled $372 million. Most of the retail activity involved a mere five dealers. Those dealers accounted for 95% of the roughly 2,500 non-corporate retail accounts; one of those dealers alone accounted for 63%.

One goal of the compliance sweep was to identify the due diligence controls and processes in place at IIROC dealers that were selling ABCP. IIROC's investigation found that, although most dealers that sold third-party ABCP to retail clients had product due diligence processes in place, surprisingly, none of them put third-party ABCP through those processes.[4] The reasons offered for this decision included an assumption that non-bank ABCP was not a new product but rather a product similar to (or perhaps indistinguishable from) bank-sponsored ABCP; a reliance on the paper's high credit rating; and an assumption that due diligence had already been performed by the carrying broker (i.e., the firm providing the principal administrative and back-office functions on behalf of the introducing brokers that dealt directly with investors). Yet according to the IIROC report, several dealer members indicated that even if they had put third-party ABCP through a product review process, it would have been approved in any event.[5]

Furthermore, none of the dealer members contacted by IIROC had provided any training or special material to their representatives selling ABCP[6] – again, presumably, because the product was regarded as sufficiently similar to other money market instruments. Significantly, at least in hindsight, retail representatives and compliance officers reported that they were unaware of the nature of the liquidity guarantees – specifically, of the important difference between the limited Canadian-style "general market disruption" liquidity protection and global-style liquidity guarantees.[7] Furthermore, the fact that the paper was regarded as a "fungible money market instrument with a high credit rating" meant that none of the dealer members interviewed had considered investor suitability issues.[8]

The IIROC report concluded, among other things, that the market drew no distinction between bank-sponsored ABCP programs based on traditional assets and third-party ABCP that used structured finance products. Nor did it seem likely that dealers were aggressively peddling ABCP to unsuspecting clients. In fact, the sale of third-party ABCP to retail investors was not, evidently, highly profitable. According to the IIROC study, traders viewed third-party ABCP trades "as a loss-leader service to clients."[9]

But the ABCP debacle raises a more fundamental point: perhaps KYC and suitability rules are sometimes simply not enough. As noted earlier, the widespread distribution of ABCP to retail investors is a prime example of why there is merit in considering the suggestion that the adviser profession should be governed by fiduciary standards. However there are many important nuances to such a proposed change.

In the United States, Section 913(g) of the Dodd-Frank Act explicitly authorized (though it did not mandate) the SEC to promulgate rules that would place brokers or dealers providing investment advice to clients under the same duties as investment advisers under the Investment Advisers Act of 1940 – namely, a fiduciary duty standard rather than merely an obligation to apply suitability rules. Although the SEC has intimated that it is close to announcing a proposed rule on this subject, it is clear that there are very serious political obstacles to overcome. In a March 2014 speech to the Consumer Federation of America, 2014 Consumer Assembly, SEC chair Mary Jo White indicated that she had directed staff "to evaluate all of the potential options available" to the SEC on this issue, including "a uniform fiduciary standard for broker-dealers and investment advisors when dealing with retail customers." She went on to say that she had directed staff to make their evaluation "an immediate and high priority so that the Commission has the information it needs to come to a decision as to whether, and, if so, how best to exercise the authority provided in Section 913 of the *Dodd-Frank Act*." But in July 2014, the US House of Representatives passed an amendment by voice vote to the House Appropriations bill prohibiting the SEC from expending any funds to promulgate rules related to such a new fiduciary standard for brokers, dealers, and investment advisers.[10]

Though this amendment did not survive the final Appropriations Act, the House vote reveals the extent of the controversy surrounding this issue. In March 2015, SEC chair White, in testimony before the House of Representatives Committee on Financial Services,[11] stated her belief that "broker-dealers and investment advisers should be subject to a uniform fiduciary standard of conduct when providing personalized investment advice about securities to retail customers." But she also acknowledged the challenges posed by introducing such a standard, including defining the standard, providing clear guidance on how such a standard would apply, and providing effective examination and enforcement so that imposition of such a standard would be meaningful.

In the meantime, the US Department of Labor has made separate proposals to amend the definition of "fiduciary" under the Employee Retirement Income Security Act (ERISA). In April 2015, the Department of Labor released for comment its proposed rule. As of the date of writing, the comment period has not expired. The department's initiatives in this area have attracted criticism from various quarters. For example, in a recent comment letter on the department's proposals, the Financial Industry Regulatory Authority,[12] though supportive of the principle of a best interest standard, expressed concern that the Labour Department's standard fell short in several areas. Among other things,

FINRA argued, they did not "sufficiently build upon the existing regulatory system under the federal securities laws" and would lead to a "fractured approach" that "would confuse retirement investors, financial institutions, and advisers" and "impose a best interest standard on broker-dealers that differs significantly from the fiduciary standard applicable to investment advisers registered under the federal and state securities laws, and it would impose the best interest standard only on retirement accounts."

A similar change is being considered in Canada. In October 2012 the CSA released Consultation Paper 33–403 to explore "the appropriateness of introducing a statutory best interest duty" for advisers and dealers providing advice to retail clients. Release of the paper was followed by a series of industry roundtables in 2013 through which the CSA sought input on the ideas raised in the paper. In December 2013 the CSA issued a staff notice summarizing the results of CSA staff consultation work on the issue. The staff notice noted, among other things, that through the consultation process, the CSA had concluded that more work needed to be done on the matter.

The creation of a more robust legal duty may not be enough to push brokers to make changes to adequately protect clients. The cost of seeking legal redress could be daunting to many investors and thus not provide an adequate deterrent. We believe that in addition to considering possible expansion of statutory fiduciary duty, IIROC must play a sustained monitoring role in this area by committing greater resources towards assessing registrants' day-to-day compliance. For instance, if used fairly and judiciously, information-gathering practices such as "mystery shopping" (i.e., posing as a potential client to a registrant) could help the organization make more tailored best practices recommendations. Whatever the approach, IIROC must retain staff with sufficient expertise to understand the extent of the asymmetries at play when complex products such as ABCP come before retail investors. IIROC must do more to ensure that brokers stay attuned to, and be able to explain in plain terms, the circumstances in which a client's profile may warrant diversification or even the avoidance of a particular product altogether.

Lesson 3: The need for a risk management investment framework

One important aspect of the crisis involved the extent to which ABCP was held within some pension funds and corporations. While it is clear that many money managers purchased the paper without undertaking due diligence, relying primarily or perhaps entirely on its high rating, the extent of some pension funds' holdings was surprising. Both the decision to purchase the product and the extent of the holdings were the result of less than ideal risk management.

At the product level, risk management is not the imposition of a risk constraint (or even a veto) limiting the decision-making power of a manager. Rather, it should be a procedure in which the risk elements of the investment being considered are identified and integrated into the decision-making process. Thus, a ban on investments in products that are based on complex derivatives or structured products as a reaction to the ABCP crisis is not what we mean by a risk management policy. Risk management can be accomplished either by a well-defined process implemented by investment managers or by the introduction of a dedicated risk manager to ensure that all of the elements of risk have been identified. In a well-functioning risk management process, the investment manager identifies the product specifics based on available information and, factoring in return expectations, makes an informed investment decision. A well-designed risk management process should not introduce tension between the risk manager and the investment manager.

Risk management also includes monitoring the investments' risks over time. A lack of vigilance here can introduce unintended risk. For example, what was at one time a conventional, low-risk product (commercial paper backed by real assets) evolved into an innovative higher-risk product backed by leveraged CDSs. This risk creep can only be avoided by a periodic review and current assessment of the risk of the portfolio. The problem is partly related to insufficient due diligence on new products and a lack of systems to evaluate the evolving risk of the portfolio. A similar problem was found in the liquidity arrangements. As the products evolved over time, so did the liquidity arrangements. Part of the blame resides with the rating agencies, in that vigilance would have resulted in changes in ABCP ratings as the liquidity arrangements evolved. A passive assumption that there had been no changes either in the products or in the structures associated with those products was a recipe for disaster.

At the overall portfolio level, risk management should evaluate the aggregation of the individual investments into an overall portfolio and the resulting risk relative to the policy level targets established by the pension fund. While this is standard procedure in most pension funds, it should be a best practice adopted by all funds.

The question of how best to compensate dedicated risk managers also raises challenging issues. While the best people must be hired for this function, unlike with investment managers, it is difficult to introduce a bonus based on performance.

Lesson 4: The need for board-level risk engagement

Effective risk management also demands a corporate governance response. One factor linking the ABCP crisis to the broader global financial crisis was the extent to which those at the boardroom table were blind, or were left blind, to major financial and reputation risks affecting their organizations. How many board members of ABCP market participants could describe, in layman's terms, the products their companies were trading in? More to the point, how many could appreciate their potential systemic impact? Our discussions with market participants suggest that much work remains to be done here.

One possible solution, already in place at many financial institutions, is structural: in addition to audit, nominating, and compensation committees, boards should consider striking a "risk committee" and delegating to it the task of evaluating a firm's risk exposures on an ongoing basis. Directors serving on these committees should be sufficiently independent of management and qualified to make the requisite assessments. In the United States, the post–financial crisis Dodd-Frank Act now requires banks holding more than $10 billion in assets to form such committees.[13] Provided directors take these committees seriously, they could do much to fill the risk accountability gap observed in the ABCP collapse. Unfortunately, this suggestion is appropriate for larger corporations and pension funds, which have more resources, but not for the smaller institutions affected by the investment in ABCP. For these entities, we have to fall back on the need for due diligence by the investment decision-maker.

Lesson 5: Securities regulation: Disclosure and transparency

The specific regulatory problem posed by complex financial instruments such as third-party ABCP may actually be related more to shortcomings in our traditional model of securities regulation than to whether that regulation is administered by a federal or provincial body. Securities regulation in Canada depends significantly on mandating full disclosure as the principal means of achieving the twin regulatory goals of investor protection and market efficiency. Some commentators have suggested revisiting the notion of relying exclusively or primarily on disclosure in the case of highly complex derivative products. Professor Henry Hu of the University of Texas, for example, has suggested that "a fundamental rethinking of the SEC disclosure paradigm"[14] is called for today. Some complex securities, he suggests, may simply be "too complex to depict." Professors Eric Posner and Glen Weyl of the University of Chicago have argued even more provocatively that new types of financial contracts ought to be subject to prior government approval, similar to US Food and Drug Administration (FDA) approval in the case of food and drug products.[15] New financial products should be approved, they argue, only if they can be shown to have genuine social utility. This standard, they suggest, should focus mainly on whether the products are likely to be used primarily as insurance and not merely for gambling. To be sure, such a merit-based review system poses serious difficulties, and we would not support its implementation in Canada. The only point made here is that securities regulatory weaknesses revealed by the ABCP meltdown call for creative rethinking that goes well beyond the long-standing question of whether Canada should have a national securities regulator.

Postscript: Canadian Securities Regulators Propose Changes

There were a number of important shortcomings in the ABCP structure. These related, for example, to the type of underlying assets used, the leverage rate employed with synthetic CDOs, liquidity arrangements, and the use of a single rating. A number of these shortcomings would have been corrected by market forces if there had been sufficient transparency, which there was not, and if investors had chosen to undertake the necessary due diligence. But even with full transparency, the ABCP structure and some of the underlying assets would simply not have been appropriate for retail investors.

The financial crisis heightened regulators' concerns about the potential for systemic risk. Not surprisingly, the capital market made its own adjustments with the demise of non-bank ABCP and the use of synthetic CDOs both with and without leverage. However, there continued to be calls from many quarters for enhanced regulation of securitized products. Since securitization and the resulting reduction of credit risk for financial institutions are important, any regulation of these products must walk a fine line aimed at strengthening investor protection without impairing an important market.

Non-bank ABCP had been sold to investors under a short-term debt prospectus exemption, originally designed to permit the sale of traditional commercial paper. The collapse of the ABCP market prompted Canadian securities regulators to revisit that exemption as well as several related issues. In April 2011 the CSA released a series of wide-ranging and dramatic regulatory proposals. If enacted, these proposals would have significantly changed the Canadian securitization regulatory landscape. The public offering of all securitized products – not just ABCP – would have become subject to new prospectus, continuous disclosure, and certification rules. Tight restrictions and burdensome information requirements would have been imposed on the sale of securitized products in the exempt market. These proposals sparked fierce opposition. Commentators derided the proposals as "a disproportionate response to the risk posed by Canadian securitization activity."[16] The CSA had evidently struck a nerve. By 2014, the CSA had retreated. The regulators had concluded, and rightly so, that securitized products did not contribute to systemic risk. They retreated from the comprehensive 2011 original proposals, announcing that they had determined that the original proposals were "unnecessary."[17] In their place, the CSA proposed a more narrowly crafted set of rules for securitized products. The new proposals consisted of two principal elements:

- An amendment to the short-term debt prospectus exemption in NI 45–106, limiting its use to traditional short-term instruments such as commercial paper (CP) (rather than securitized instruments). The new exemption would change the previous "split rating condition" that had, inadvertently, created an incentive for CP issuers not to seek more than one credit rating. (Under the old rule, one rating that met the prescribed threshold was sufficient to satisfy the exemption; yet if an issuer received a second rating that was below the threshold, the exemption was unavailable.)
- A new short-term securitized products exemption available only for the sale of conventional or traditional ABCP (i.e., not for credit arbitrage ABCP backed by synthetic assets). This new exemption would become the only prospectus exemption that would enable issuers to sell ABCP on a basis that would not subject the buyers to restrictions when they tried to resell the paper. (Issuers would still be free to sell ABCP – including credit arbitrage ABCP – relying on other prospectus exemptions that *did* impose resale restrictions on investors, such as the widely used "accredited investor" and

$150,000 minimum purchase exemptions. However, the resale of securities purchased under these exemptions is subject to a hold or restricted period that would be less attractive than the freely tradeable securities that could be obtained if securities were eligible for issue under the new short-term securitized product exemption.) The new exemption would require, among other things, that the seller obtain at least two credit ratings, with a higher prescribed minimum credit rating than under the existing short-term debt exemption. Also, the ABCP would need to be backed by a global-style liquidity facility from a liquidity provider satisfying certain requirements. Issuers would be required to prepare a special information memorandum for investors. They would also be required to provide investors with ongoing disclosure reports. Finally, although Canadian securities regulators would not require ABCP sponsors to retain a portion of the securitized instruments as a kind of fidelity bond, they would mandate specific disclosure about risk retention and the incentives and alignment of interests within the ABCP structure. Some other jurisdictions, including the United States, had introduced mandatory "risk retention" (an approach facetiously described as a rule that required ABCP issuers to "eat their own cooking"). The CSA, however, had concluded that the forms of credit enhancement typically used in Canadian securitization transactions (viz., overcollateralization, excess spread and cash reserve accounts) mitigated the need for mandatory risk retention.[18]

The final version of these amendments came into force on 5 May 2015. The new prospectus exemption rules seem to address the problems found in the original non-bank ABCP, although market forces have already gone a long way towards that end. When the new regime was first proposed, some commentators voiced concerns about the impact of these new rules on financial innovation (or "novel approaches") as well as the inevitable trade-off between the benefits to investors of mandating greater information disclosure and the increased costs of these requirements.

Final Words

This book set out to tell the (largely untold) story of the eighteen months from the day that Montreal stood still to 31 January 2009, when the third-party ABCP restructuring deal was closed and the market opened for the restructured notes. As other markets around the world went into freefall during the 2008 financial crisis, the non-bank ABCP market in Canada narrowly survived through the sheer will of the groups at the negotiating table. This is not to say that the negotiations and ultimate restructuring were not controversial – the legal releases from liability and the gaps and failures on so many levels were hugely controversial.

While the popular press provided coverage of the plight of retail investors who received bad advice or poor disclosure, this book has shared many other important stories and details that would otherwise have remained untold. We have described what went on behind the scenes to bring together the players who eventually negotiated a solution during one of the largest financial crises in history.

This book has also tried to provide context for how and why decisions were made that led us to where we are today. Importantly, the crisis and the resulting restructuring raised many policy questions that to this day have not been adequately resolved – questions we have addressed at length in this book. Many lessons were learned from the made-in-Canada crisis and the made-in-Canada solution, and we have made several key recommendations for improving the market and regulatory oversight, which we hope will be considered.

Notes

Chapter 1

1 "Subprime" refers to loans (mortgages) issued by a bank to borrowers of poor credit.
2 Andrew Willis, "Moody's unimpressed by Desjardins risk-management approach," *Globe and Mail*, 4 March 2009, B11. The article refers to a statement by Peter Routledge, Moody's senior credit officer, which we have cited.
3 Marlene Puffer, "The Big Freeze," *Canadian Investment Review*, Winter 2007.
4 CDOR is calculated as a simple average of the BA values submitted by the banks after removing the high and low values. Prior to 2013, Deutsche Bank Limited and its affiliate were included in the BA calculation. CDOR is a very important variable since many loans and securities are priced off of it. There has been a concern that the rate could be manipulated – a concern also found in the LIBOR setting. In March 2014 a new calculation methodology for CDOR was introduced to address the potential problems.
5 The maturities range from 1 to 10 years.
6 This super senior was based on a bespoke portfolio of corporate bonds. The structure is described in the Ontario Court of Appeal Decision in *Barclays Bank PLC v Metcalfe and Mansfield Alternative Investment VII Corp*, 26 July 2013, paras. 16–30.
7 John Chant, "The ABCP Crisis in Canada: Implications for the Regulation of Financial Markets," a study prepared for the Expert Panel on Securities Regelation, available online at http://www.expertpanel.ca/documents/research-studies/The%20ABCP%20Crisis%20in%20Canada%20-%20Chant. English.pdf.
8 Closing submission, Lenczner Slaght et al., Ontario Superior Court of Justice, *Barclays Bank v Metcalfe & Mansfield Alternative Investment VII Corp*, May 2011, para. 246.

9 Ibid., paras. 261, 262.

10 The mark-to-market trigger value and the 10 times leverage were used in the Barclays transaction.

11 Of course this is equivalent to a 5% decrease in the market value of the swap transaction.

12 An example of gap risk is presented in Chapter 11; it relates to an SEC order regarding Deutsche Bank, which agreed to pay a $55 million penalty for its misstatements related to its LSS positions in Canadian ABCP during the financial crisis.

13 One estimate suggested that about 13% of the total losses were due to credit losses while the remainder were mark-to-market losses. More on this topic later in this chapter.

14 The study compared the yields of Rocket Trust to BMO-sponsored ABCP over the period.

15 Originally part of National Bank Financial (NBF), Quanto was formed as an independent company in 2005 with NBF retaining a minority interest.

16 *Barclays Bank PLC v. Metcalfe & Mansfield Alternative Investment VII Corp.*, Reasons for Decision, Mr Justice Colin Campbell, 19 February 2009, para. 20.

17 It is important to note that this "Attempted Manipulation" theory was not the subject of any court finding.

Chapter 2

1 The Supreme Court of Canada had not yet rendered its important 2014 decision in *Bhasin v. Hrynew* concerning the role of good faith contractual performance in Canadian law. [2–14] 3 SCR 494.

2 In the Nortel bankruptcy proceedings, Justice Newbould (the same judge who presided over the Devonshire and Barclays litigation) observed that "insolvency practitioners, academics, international bodies and others have watched as Nortel's early success in maximizing the value of its global assets through co-operation has disintegrated into value-erosive adversarial and territorial litigation described by many as scorched-earth litigation." The vigorously litigated Nortel bankruptcy was reported to have resulted in professional fees in excess of $1 billion. *Nortel Networks Corp. (Re)* [2015] O.J. No. 2440.

3 Press release, Montreal Accord, 16 August 2007.

4 Ibid.

Chapter 4

1 It is no surprise that DBRS accepted the ratings by the US rating agencies. The exposure in the Canadian conduits was small, and there was no reason to assume that the ratings were not correct. Furthermore, a DBRS analysis would have been costly, as well as not sensible, given the size of the exposure.
2 http://www.thespec.com/news-story/2236414-city-launches-11-million-lawsuit.

Chapter 5

1 J.P. Morgan Report on Restructuring, March 2008, page 29.
2 Another piece of evidence on the benefits of the MFF pricing to its participants arose when it came time to sign the final deal. After the CCAA hearing and related court cases, the CDS spreads widened, which meant that the cost of the MFF should have increased. However, none of the participants in the MFF walked from the deal; instead, they respected the pricing that had been agreed upon in relatively better times – in fact, they ultimately reduced the rate to 120 bps. Was this the result of the "a deal is a deal" perspective of the fund participants? Or was it that the original scheme was already rich and that the bargaining power of the fund participants had diminished with the increased spreads?
3 A substantial amount of information on MAV II and MAV III notes is available on the BlackRock website, http://www.blackrock.com/X/CMAV2/public/index.html.
4 The structure ultimately accepted was similar, with only one change – the MFF block included a second funding facility that was senior in ranking to the original funding facility.
5 Mark-to-market triggers have an additional problem not faced by loss-related triggers. Since there is not a robust market in the swaps, models are used to estimate values. The models rely on unobservable and, hence, calculated inputs. The resulting inputs to the model are inferred from market prices and, in times of stress, can result in unreasonable values. Spread-loss triggers depend on observable loss values and, thus, are not totally model dependent.
6 The spread levels under the maturity entry of 8.67 years are based on the expected closing date of the restructuring, 20 April 2008.
7 However, market value would have been a factor in calculating the "indicative value."
8 The indicative value approach and the relative contribution analysis are presented in the Report on Restructuring, dated 14 March, prepared by J.P. Morgan.

Chapter 6

1 Reported in the *Globe and Mail*, 7 May 2008, B1.
2 Technically, their fee was the greater of that described above and $30,000.

Chapter 7

1 The application was heard by US bankruptcy judge Martin Glenn in late 2009. In January 2010, he decided the Canadian orders should be enforced in the United States in accordance with the principles of comity (the legal doctrine whereby countries recognize one another's judgments). That meant that the broad third-party releases would also be enforced in the United States, even if such third-party releases could not necessarily have been approved in a US Chapter 11 case.

Chapter 8

1 The spread levels reached 263 bps on 27 October 2008; 307 bps on 27 November 2008; and 327 bps on 5 December 2008.
2 See Shawn McCarthy and Konrad Yakabuski, "Quebec, Alberta Spurn ABCP Action," *ReportonBusiness.com*, 15 December 2008, http://www.investorvoice.ca/PI/3676.htm.
3 Since the changes were in favour of the investors who had prevailed at the CCAA hearing, there was no need to bring the changed deal to the court. First, the parties agreed to drop the CDX5 seven-year spread-loss matrix. Second, for a given loss, the spreads necessary to precipitate a collateral call were widened for the longer maturities, which had a higher risk of problems. For example, for the two CDX spread-loss matrices that have 10-year maturity ending 20 December 2016, all of the spreads for dates up to 20 December 2010 have been increased for each loss level. For example, looking at the 10-year CDX7, maturity 20 December 2016, as of 20 December 2010, the spread at 0% loss was 686 bps and is now 736 bps. For a 12% loss, the spread was 344 bps and is now 394 bps. Similar widening in spreads for the other spread-loss matrices was introduced. With this widening and the reduced likelihood of a collateral call, the MFF fee in the original deal was reduced from 160 bps to 120 bps per annum.
4 For the technically interested reader, the SFF was a risk-free bond with a one-month window in which the SFF participants were exposed to an

option that if the financial world came to an end, they would incur very large losses.

5 The letters referred to in this section are available at Ernst & Young document centre, documentcentre.eycan.com, public documents, "eighteenth report of the monitor," 2 January 2009, Appendix DD.

Chapter 9

1 A "strip" is composed of holdings in each of the class of notes in the MAV II structure in proportions outstanding at a particular point in time. The proportions reflect notional values.
2 Fiera Quantum letter to investors, 2 March 2015.
3 The CDX is a credit index that reflects 125 investment grade reference entities. Its spread value is affected by economic conditions that influence credit conditions in general and the loss given default for the reference companies' debt.
4 Sterne Agee Structure Product Commentary, 5 January 2015. The dollar amounts reflect amounts of Canadian Dollar Issuance – US dollar–issued bonds are not included.
5 This information is obtained from the BlackRock website dedicated to MAV II notes. See https://www.blackrock.com/X/CMAV@_OR/public and Sterne Agee Structured Products Commentary.
6 Sterne Agee Structured Products Commentary.
7 Fiera Quantum.
8 STIFEL – Structured Products Commentary, 22 June 2015, page 2.
9 Sterne Agee Structured Products Commentary, 30 June 2015.

Chapter 10

1 Because criminal law in Canada is constitutionally a matter of exclusive federal legislative authority, provisions in provincial statutes that create offences that may subject violators to fines and imprisonment are often referred to as "quasi-criminal" measures.
2 Reference re Securities Act [2011], 3SCR 837.
3 The banks did distribute non-bank ABCP, which included LSS exposure.
4 See "Justice Department and State Partners Secure $1.375 Billion Settlement with S&P for Defrauding Investors in the Lead Up to the Financial Crisis," 3 February 2015, available online at https://www.justice.gov/opa/pr/justice-department-and-state-partners-secure-1375-billion-settlement-sp-defrauding-investors

Chapter 11

1 This amount is based on amounts found in the Eighteenth Monitor Report, page 34, para. 73. This total is composed of $87 million invoiced up to 8 December 2008 and a reserve for all professionals of $112 million, of which $87 million was set aside for J.P. Morgan. The payments were allocated to the PCIC and Conduits. The conduits were responsible solely for the costs associated with the monitor and its counsel and the Ad Hoc Retail Holders Committee advisers.

2 The legal participation can also be seen at http://lexpert.ca/magazine/deals/32b-restructuring-of-canadian-third-party-restructured-abcp-4355.

3 PWC in a report dated 21 February 2008 provide some indication of the impact of the write-downs resulting from the ABCP market. The write-downs ranged from a low of $190 million for the Bank of Nova Scotia to a high of $525 million for the National Bank of Canada. Of course, Toronto Dominion comes in at zero.

4 Lori Zorn and Alejandro Garcia, "Central Bank Collateral Policy: Insights from Recent Experience," *Bank of Canada Review*, Spring 2011. The authors also note that the first time ABCP was eligible temporarily as collateral was to support potential liquidity issues associated with the year 2000 scare.

5 See PWC presentation, page 15. At the top of the list was Citigroup, with an amount of US$18 billion.

6 Securities Exchange Act of 1934, Release No. 7540, 26 May 2015. Administrative Proceeding File No. 3–16557.

Chapter 12

1 See, for example, Securities Act (Ontario), RSO 1990, c.S.5, ss. 22–24.

2 Ibid., Part XXIII.1, s. 138.1, definition of "expert."

3 IIROC, "Regulatory Study, Review and Recommendations Concerning the Manufacture and Distribution by IIROC Member Firms of Third-Party Asset Backed Commercial Paper in Canada" (October 2008), http://docs.iiroc.ca/DisplayDocument.aspx?DocumentID=3CAB660DB44E41C2875D D3DBD27FADEA&Language=en.

4 Ibid., 55.

5 Ibid., 56.

6 Ibid., 57.

7 Ibid., 57.

8 Ibid., 57.

9 Ibid., 59.

10 House Amendment 1102 to H.R. 5016, sponsored by Representative Lankford (R-OK). See online at http://appropriations.house.gov/uploadedfiles/07.16.14_fy_2015_financial_services_bill_-_floor_adopted_amendments.pdf.

11 http://www.sec.gov/news/testimony/2015-ts032415mjw.html.

12 Letter from FINRA to Department of Labor et al. (17 July 2015), Available online at: http://www.finra.org/sites/default/files/FINRACommentLetter_DOL_07-17-15.pdf.

13 OSFI also requires a risk committee comprised of non-executive directors as well as a senior officer responsible for risk. http://www.canadiansecuritieslaw.com/2013/01/articles/corporate-governance/osfi-releases-final-revised-corporate-governance-guideline.

14 Henry T.C. Hu, "Too Complex to Depict? Innovation, 'Pure Information,' and the SEC Disclosure Paradigm" *Texas Law Review* 90 (2012), 1601.

15 Eric Posner and E. Glen Weyl, "An FDA for Financial Innovation: Applying the Insurable Interest Doctrine to 21st Century Financial Markets," *Northwestern University Law Review* 107 (2013), 1307.

16 See CSA, Notice of Publication and Request for Comment, Proposed Amendments to National Instrument 45–106, *Ontario Securities Commission Bulletin* 37 (2014), 1043 at 1052.

17 Ibid., 1053.

18 Ibid., 1055–6.

Index

smaller corporate/institutional investors

Countrywide, 37, 38, 62

Coventree: at 10 August 2007 meeting, 41–2; and "acquire to distribute" business, 17–18; as administrator, 120; allegations against, 167; as biggest issuer of Canadian non-bank ABCP, 78; Caisse and, 18, 34–5; and CIBC, 38; conduits, 34; Cornish's and Tai's indemnity agreements with, 173; and credit-arbitrage transactions, 168; DBRS and, 167–8, 169–70, 192–3; decision to defend self at hearing, 166; delisting from TSX, 193; disclosure of information, 167, 168–9, 170, 171; as first issuer of third-party ABCP, 17–18; founding of, 166; and global-style vs. Canadian liquidity, 168, 169; and institutional investors, 34; investment pool, 166; IPO, 35, 36; and liquidity/liquidity-related events, 170, 171, 192; and LSS, 17, 18–20; and material change, 169–70, 171; and material fact, 168; and misleading statement, 167; National Bank and, 34, 38, 40; and onset of ABCP crisis, 43; OSC and, 166–72, 173, 192, 193; and Planet Trust, 78; press releases, 192; as public vs. private company, 34–5, 167, 168–9, 192–3; and retail investors, 78; rise of, 17–22; sanctions against, 167, 171–2; Scotiabank and, 38; and Securities Act, 168, 171; selling of ABCP, 33–4; share price movement, 193; shareholders, 171–2, 173, 192–3;

special committee to investigate strategic options, 193; subprime mortgage exposure, 4, 38–9, 170–1; synthetic CDOs and, 17; and TAO Admin Corp, 121; on Toronto Stock Exchange, 192; wind-down of, 172, 173, 193

CP Rail, 5

Crawford, Purdy: about, 71; on Allan's idea, 83–4; announcement of restructuring deal, xi; and "art of the possible," 87, 92, 203; and Caisse's problems, 132; and Canaccord, 79–80; as chair of Montreal Accord investors' group, 71–2; Clark and, 100; and collateral calls, 98; connections, 72; cross-Canada "road show," 111, 114–16; and Flaherty, 138; and Hunter, 113, 116; and IMASCO, 100; on J.P. Morgan and MFF, 99; on market for new/restructured notes, 81, 108–9; and MFF, 96–8, 97; on Perimeter's trading in ABCP notes, 81; reputation, 72; and restructuring plan, 95–6; and retail investors, 79–80, 112, 114–15; on secondary market, 147; task of, 87; unwillingness to renegotiate deal, 132

Credential: buyback of retail ABCP, 116; IIROC settlement with, 165; and retail investors, 64, 78, 84

credit arbitrage-type transactions, 168, 215

credit default swaps (CDSs). See CDSs (credit default swaps)

credit enhancements, 22–3

credit rating agencies: caution in issuing ratings, 181; CDOs and, 11;

and Washington Mutual, 130; as "winner," 187
Juroviesky, Henry, 90, 115

King Street Capital, 151
know your client (KYC), 161, 180, 209
Kresse, Andrew, 74, 105, xi

Laporte, Pierre, 67, 72
Laurentian Bank, 33, 166
lawsuits: Ad Hoc Committee members and, 75; assumption of risk vs., 128; bankruptcy, 51–2; Barrick/Sun Media and, 118–19; in Canada vs. US, 74; CCAA and, 90–2; chain reaction, 125; City of Hamilton v. Deutsche Bank Securities, 90; class action, 115; corporate ABCP holders and, 76; counterproductivity of, 208; and DBRS, 208; dissenting groups and, 111; fear of, 87; liquidity calls and, 60; misrepresentations and, 206; as omnipresent threat, 56; PCIC and, 90, 91; against rating agencies, 196; restructuring plan and, 51–2, 96; retail investors and, 115; retention of right to, 127–8; and signing of Montreal Accord, 73; against S&P, 207–8; spread-loss vs. mark-to-market triggers and, 108; subprime exposure and, 119; US Department of Justice v. S&P, 179. See also Barclays; Devonshire Trust
lawyers: numbers involved, 186–7; as "winners," 186–7
legal liability: CCAA and, 202–3; and credit rating agencies, 179, 205–8;

and Deutsche Bank, 198; expert status in, 206–7; rating agencies and, 196; restructuring plan and, 96; under Securities Act, 205–6
legal releases: Ad Hoc Committee and, 117–18, 119, 123–8; Ad Hoc Retail Investor Group and, 118; banks and, 189; carve-outs from, 124; CCAA and, 91–2, 99; claims process and, 124; DBRS and, 179, 196; effectiveness of, 127; fraud carve-out from, 117–18, 119, 124–7; and negligence claims, 124, 125; PCIC and, 92; rating agencies and, 196; restructuring plan and, 92, 96; for third parties, 124–5, 126, 127; in US, 222n1
Lehman Brothers: bankruptcy, 62, 73, 119, 130, 132; consideration by PCIC as financial adviser, 73
leverage: of CDSs, 16; and collateral, 30, 52; conduits' credit protection provision and, 16; in LSS structures, 101; in MAV structures, 101; and risk, 30, 31. See also LSSs (leveraged super seniors)
LIBOR, 8, 142
liquidity: about, 22–4, 158; arrangements akin to insurance policies, 23; and auction process, 158; Bank of Canada role in preservation of, 66; banks and, 102, 189; and Barclays vs. Devonshire Trust, 26–9, 176; Caisse and, 132; Canadian- vs. global style guarantees, 209; Canadian-style (see under general market disruptions (GMDs)); changing contracts and, 40–1; commercial paper and, 6; in